FAIR GAME

CHARLIE PARKES & JOHN THORNLEY

FAIR GAME

THE LAW OF COUNTRY SPORTS AND THE PROTECTION OF WILDLIFE

PELHAM

First published in Great Britain by
Pelham Books Ltd
27 Wrights Lane, London W8 5TZ
1987

British Library Cataloguing in Publication Data
Parkes, Charlie
Fair game: the law of country sports
and the protection of wildlife.
1. Wildlife conservation—Law and
legislation—Great Britain
I. Title   II. Thornley, John
344.1064'695   KD1035
ISBN 0 7207 1734 5

Line drawings by John Paley
Photographs by the authors unless otherwise acknowledged.

Typeset by Cambrian Typesetters, Frimley, Surrey.
Printed and bound by Butler and Tanner Ltd, Frome

CONTENTS

ACKNOWLEDGEMENTS

We are grateful to the following for their generous help during the writing of this book:

Gerald Barry, Scottish Landowners Federation; Stevan Beale; British Association for Shooting and Conservation; British Field Sports Society; Neil Brunt, Derbyshire Constabulary Library; Paul Copestake; Country Landowners Association; Department of Agriculture and Fisheries for Scotland; Phil Drabble; John Eley, Department of Environment, Bristol; Major P. A. Gouldsbury, M.B.E., British Shooting Sports Council; John Goldsmith; Roger Greenlay, Yorkshire Water; Bob Hannabal; Kevan Horsfield; John Hotchkis, Vice President of the British Deer Society; Brian Hughes; Bertel Hutchinson; League Against Cruel Sports; Norman McCullock, Red Deer Commission; Roy Merrifield, H.M. Explosives Inspectorate; Ministry of Agriculture, Fisheries and Food; National Association of Game Dealers; National Federation of Badger Groups; Henry Naylor; John Paley; Major Neil Ramsay; Royal Pigeon Racing Association; Royal Society for Prevention of Cruelty to Animals; Royal Society for the Protection of Birds; Scottish Rights of Way Society; Gerald Springthorpe, Forestry Commission; The Game Conservancy; Barry Thornley; Austin Thomas; Dave Bardon of Walkers of Trowell (tackle supplies); Brian Wall; Welsh Office Agriculture Department; Fred Westmorland; R. B. Williamson, Inspector of Salmon and Freshwater Fisheries for Scotland; Joan and Mike Woodhouse.

We are particularly grateful to John Hotchkis for permission to reproduce his deer chart on page 160; John Paley for the line drawings; David Price for the photographs on pages 52, 82, 89, 96, 145, 156, 180 and 245; to Alan Fern for processing our own photographs and to The League Against Cruel Sports for the photographs on pages 252 and 257.

Charlie Parkes and John Thornley

TO

Mary, Pip, Elizabeth, Kathryn
and Christopher Parkes

AND

Julie and Lewis Thornley

Pollution, industrial activity, modern methods of agriculture and land management, leisure activities in the countryside, poaching and egg-collecting, and the behaviour of some irresponsible sportsmen, keepers and farmers are all piling pressure on what is left of the wild populations of plants and animals in this country.

Much of the damage can be contained by self-restraint and consideration for the natural environment, but in the end sensible and responsible behaviour must be backed up by the law.

It has always been a principle of our judicial system that ignorance is no excuse for breaking the law, but the complexity of the firearms, wildlife and game laws is often too great for the layman to comprehend. The British Association for Shooting and Conservation has always been concerned to promote responsible behaviour, safety, the conservation of nature and compliance with the law, and I think it was a splendid idea of the Association to encourage the authors to write this practical guide to countryside law. *Fair Game* answers all those questions which are bound to crop up sometime or other for all users of the countryside.

King George VI said 'The wildlife of today is not ours to dispose of as we please. We have it in trust. We must account for it to those who come after.' Those words are even more relevant today, and there is no doubt that compliance with the law is the first line in the defence of wildlife. I am sure that this excellent book will make an important contribution to the conservation of our natural heritage for the continuing enjoyment of our children and grandchildren.

1987

PREFACE
by
The Director, The British Association for Shooting and Conservation

John Thornley and Charlie Parkes have done us a major service in writing *Fair Game*. We are more than pleased to recommend it to all who shoot and who have the good of the British countryside at heart.

Game, firearms and wildlife law has never been a simple matter. The Wildlife and Countryside Act 1981 added new and byzantine requirements. For years The British Association for Shooting and Conservation has been striving to foster the highest possible standards of safe and knowledgeable behaviour in the field and respect for the law, as well as the lores of the countryside. In this endeavour we have produced, over the years, numerous booklets, codes of practice, information sheets and run instructional courses with the purpose of trying to ensure that all who shoot are taught those standards and a knowledge of the law, if not provided by family or friend. This information is also available to gamekeepers and others whose job it is to use and enforce the law so that they have a clear understanding of it.

At a time of popular disrespect for authority, the shooting public has an enviable record as being law-abiding – indeed, it might well be said that the shooting community is by definition the most law abiding – but we continue our efforts as a group to ensure that youngsters and newcomers to the various disciplines involved have a clear and practical understanding of what is expected of them, not only by their peers but also by the courts. *Fair Game* will prove to be a major contribution towards this objective which we share with many others.

This excellent book sets out the law impartially on both established and legitimate country sports, as well as in respect of illegal and unacceptable activities. We have strongly supported the authors in this approach to the subject since we believe that it will render the book more valuable as a weapon in the fight against rural crime and for the promotion of lawful country sports which we work to foster and promote with all our might.

JOHN ANDERTON

LIST OF ACTS AND ORDERS

INTRODUCTION

Among those whose life, employment or recreation is dependent on the countryside, its fauna and flora, there is increasing concern about the activities of poachers, trespassers, anti-field-sports campaigners, errant sportsmen, egg thieves, bird trappers, etc.

In a democracy, the freedom of the individual is maintained by the rule of law; any unlawful action by the hunt saboteur or huntsman threatens that freedom. In writing this book we have not entered into the debate on the morality of field sports: our objective has been to present the law relating to field sports and conservation as it is and how it affects those of widely differing views.

As Wildlife Liaison Officers specializing in countryside law for the Derbyshire Constabulary, we receive enquiries from all parts of the country, all sections of society, and from those for and against field sports. At talks to police officers, keepers, rangers and conservation bodies on poaching or wildlife law, we have become aware of the demand for a greater knowledge of the law and its enforcement. In this book we have tried to explain as clearly and concisely as possible a complex (even rag-bag) body of law so that it is intelligible to the layman. We hope to have provided sufficient detail for it to act as a reference work not only for the landowner, the keeper, bailiff, shoot manager, field-sports enthusiast but also for others interested in the conservation and preservation of plant and wildlife generally.

Within the space available, we have tried to include all legislation that affects England, Wales and Scotland. Since 1707 Scotland has shared a common Parliament with England and Wales and many Acts of Parliament are law on both sides of the border. Nevertheless, the Scots possess their own legal system which contains many laws markedly different from those found in England. Legislation applicable to Scotland, therefore, has been included in three forms:

1 Some Acts, e.g. Wildlife and Countryside Act 1981, apply to England, Wales and Scotland. The reader can assume that unless otherwise indicated, the law as stated applies to Scotland as well as England and Wales.

2 Some English Acts, e.g. Protection of Animals Act 1911, have an equivalent in Scottish law, e.g. Protection of Animals (Scotland) Act 1912. In these cases, reference to the title of the Scottish Act is made in the text and minor variations in wording or meaning are also included.

3 Where Scottish law is totally different from English law, as in respect of deer and fish for example, the legislation is dealt with as two separate sections within the chapter.

The game laws, in particular, are a patchwork of inter-related Acts of Parliament that are either updated versions of previous Acts, intended to close loopholes, or new Acts created to meet modern situations. This overlapping of legislation leads to confusion: for example, game has different meanings in different Acts; one Act specifies the requirements for a game licence but many others provide exceptions; some Acts define what is night – others do not; is sunset G.M.T., B.S.T. or local time?

It is impossible to include all the information on one subject in a single chapter as a multitude of Acts have a bearing on the many individual facets of a subject. The main topics have been put into chapters and cross references to other legislation relating to the subject have been included in the text. Marginal references also help the reader to locate items required. Measurements are stated as given in the relevant Act, and therefore include a mixture of imperial and metric units. For simplification and brevity, the wording of legislation has been reduced to the minimum necessary for explanation; where the reader requires the exact words, he should obtain the Acts from his local library service or seek the advice of a solicitor.

The Law is rarely black and white but more frequently a grey area and it must be appreciated that the courts may interpret a person's actions in a specific case in different ways. Such interpretations may also be based on precedent (previous cases decided in a certain way) and many of our arguments are based on such cases, which will stand until a new case decides otherwise. Cases of particular importance are named within the text, e.g. Harrison v Duke of Rutland.

CHAPTER 1

Trespass

MANY OF THE principles of trespass apply equally to Scotland as to England and Wales. However, there are some differences in law in respect of trespass to land and, in particular, trespass by taking up residence on the land; these are dealt with below on pages 10–11.

To understand the law in relation to trespass, it is necessary to appreciate the distinction between civil and criminal law. An unlawful act under civil law is a *tort* (civil wrong) in England and Wales and a *delict* in Scotland; under criminal law it is a *crime*. The civil law is dealt with by the county courts and is basically concerned with *compensation* for injury. Offences of a criminal nature are tried in the magistrates' or crown courts, depending on their seriousness; the object of criminal proceedings is primarily punishment and the police are the principal agents for enforcing the criminal law.[1] The majority of law contained in this book is of a criminal nature, but trespass is a tort and therefore comes within the civil law.

In some cases, the same facts may disclose both a crime and a tort. As a general rule, however, proceedings are only

---

[1] Although a private individual may institute proceedings for some offences.

taken through one particular court and this would usually be the criminal court. In certain circumstances, there may be a legal bar to proceedings in both courts for the same offence, as in assault cases and trespass in pursuit of game (see page 37).

Trespass may take many forms: it is not confined to merely setting foot upon another's land without permission. But for convenience, we can divide it into three categories: trespass to land, trespass to the person and trespass to goods.

TRESPASS TO LAND

Trespass to land is the entry upon the land of another without permission and includes any interference with the land. In order to establish whether such a trespass has been committed, it is essential to understand the rights that exist to enter land without specific permission.

ACCESS TO LAND

Two main rights to enter land exist:

1 Private Rights of Way
Private rights of way are granted for the benefit of the owner of one property in respect of another's land, e.g. to allow one person to have a right of way over another's land to have access to his own.

2 Public Rights of Way
There are several types of *way* over which the public may travel across land: e.g. footpaths, bridleways and metal-surfaced roads. They are all collectively known as *highways* over which the public have a right to pass and re-pass. If the highway may only be used for walking along, it is known as a footpath; whereas a bridleway, as its name implies, may be used amongst other things as a right of way on horseback.

The responsibility for all rights of way, including mainten-ance and signing, rests with the Highway Authority in whose area they are situated. Problems encountered, such as obstruction or nuisance, whilst negotiating a right of way should in the first instance be reported to the Highway Authority.

Anyone using a right of way may have any item generally

regarded as a *usual accompaniment*,[1] such as a walking stick, camera or haversack. It would also include a dog which should be kept under control, ideally on a lead; on certain rights of way, the Highway Authority may make an order requiring dogs to be kept on a lead. It is largely a matter of commonsense; but whatever the item, it should not cause a nuisance or damage.

Rights of way in themselves do not allow entry into the surrounding countryside, unless access agreements exist as in some National Parks. These agreements have the effect of protecting those entering the land from being treated as trespassers and are occasionally restricted for certain periods of the year to facilitate farming or conservation work. In some areas where access agreements have been obtained over private moorland, restrictions may be imposed to facilitate grouse shooting.

A landowner or occupier must not molest, nor obstruct the path of, a user of a right of way. Should the person have diverted from such a right of way onto land where he has no authority to be, he can be asked to leave and should do so. If he refuses, he can be physically moved, but only by using no more force than is necessary and reasonable in the circumstances.

The protection against trespassing afforded by footpaths or other rights of way, including highways, is conditional, inasmuch as the path or right of way must be used for the purpose for which it is intended, i.e. to pass and repass as a means of communication. The courts have held that a person crossing the land of another by the use of a right of way may be a trespasser if he exceeds or abuses his right to pass and repass. For example, in Harrison v The Duke of Rutland (1893), Harrison had attempted, whilst on a highway, to disrupt the Duke of Rutland's shoot by disturbing driven game. The Duke was shooting on moors owned by him, although the sporting rights were disputed by Harrison. During one particular drive, Harrison stood on a highway near to the butts, the land being owned on both sides by the Duke. As grouse were driven towards the butts, Harrison attempted to divert their course out of range of the guns. He had been known to disrupt previous shoots on the moor and on this occasion his efforts consisted of waving his

---

[1] R v Mathias (1861). In this case a pram was referred to as a 'usual accompaniment'.

Harrison disrupting
the Duke of Rutland's
grouse shoot.

handkerchief and opening and closing his umbrella. The
Duke's gamekeepers, obviously annoyed at Harrison's attempt to spoil the drive, took hold of him and physically held
him to the ground until the drive was over. During the court
case that followed, in which Harrison pursued a claim for
civil damages against the Duke and others, it was held that
Harrison was a trespasser on the highway at the time because
of his actions in attempting to disrupt the shoot.[1]

THE EXTENT OF TRESPASS TO LAND

Trespass to land is of three kinds: actual entry on the land of
another; remaining on the land of another; placing or
throwing any material object upon the land of another.

Land in this context includes not only the surface, but
everything fixed to it, such as buildings, everything beneath
it and the air space above it. Aircraft passing over are exempt
from trespass provided their height is reasonable in the
circumstances; they are not exempt from any damage which
they may cause.[2]

The term *land* also includes water. A fisherman may
trespass merely by casting his bait into the wrong swim, if he

---

[1] Note also R v Pratt (1855) where it was decided that someone using the highway
for purposes other than for reasonable use, whether they be lawful or unlawful,
becomes a trespasser. This case is dealt with in greater detail on pages 32–3.
[2] This is also an offence under the Civil Aviation Act 1982 where unnecessary
danger is caused to persons or property. However, low flying is permitted in certain
circumstances.

has no authority to fish that particular stretch of water. A person swimming, sailing a boat or paddling a canoe on water where he has no authority to be commits a trespass.

Depositing anything on the land without permission, e.g. domestic refuse, is a trespass even if there is a right to be on the land for other purposes.[1]

Contrary to the much-used *Trespassers will be prosecuted* sign, simple trespass on land, in the majority of cases, will only amount to the committing of a civil tort (or wrong): there is no provision for prosecution in the criminal courts. However, certain statutory authorities, such as the National Coal Board and the British Railways Board, are entitled to prosecute trespassers on their land.

Carrying a firearm onto land can turn simple trespass into a crime.

The tort of trespass also remains an essential part of some criminal offences, such as certain poaching offences and trespass with a firearm (see pages 32 and 101). It is an act of civil trespass to fire a gun into the land of another without permission, irrespective of the possible poaching offences that may be committed. This type of constructive trespass is discussed in greater detail on page 33.

[1] Under Section 1 (1) Litter Act 1983 a criminal offence may also be committed of depositing litter without consent or authority into or from any place in the open air to which the public are entitled or permitted to have access without payment.

REMEDIES AND ACTION

Landowners, occupiers or anyone with their authority have certain rights which they may enforce personally without the need to resort to costly court proceedings.

Trespassers found on land may be requested to leave and should be allowed to do so in a peaceful manner. On refusal, they may be physically removed by using as much force as is reasonable and necessary in the circumstances. The old saying *don't bite off more than you can chew* is not a bad maxim: it is not always the best policy to be over zealous, as arguments often end in violence and this may lead to the landowner himself being sued or prosecuted for assault.

Although there are no legal provisions to prosecute for simple trespass in the criminal courts, civil action may be taken by the landowner or occupier against anyone setting foot on the land without permission. It is not necessary to prove actual damage to the land:[1] the tort is actionable in itself.

To go on land without permission to pick up dead game, even though legitimately shot on the shooter's land, is a trespass for which there is a civil remedy. However, although the *scope* of trespass is wide, its effectiveness in practical terms is slight. Civil proceedings do not provide a strong deterrent; all that can be hoped for is nominal damages and/or an injunction against the trespasser to prevent further trespass.

The landowner may apply to the court for both damages and an injunction. The effect of such an injunction is that the trespasser becomes liable for contempt of court should he trespass again. The court will need to be satisfied that there is a risk of further trespass before granting such an injunction.

Trespassers are not legally obliged to give *anyone* (and this includes a police officer) their names or addresses. There remain therefore obvious practical difficulties in pursuing civil action for simple civil trespass when identities are not known. Not until a criminal offence is committed by a trespasser do the police have a power to arrest.[2] The police may then arrest anyone who refuses to give his identity or when that given is suspected of being false.

[1] Except in Scotland.
[2] Police and Criminal Evidence Act 1984.

INTENTIONAL OR RECKLESS DAMAGE

If the trespasser intentionally or, in certain circumstances, recklessly causes damage to the land or property, it would be a criminal act and a citizen's arrest[1] could be made, e.g. where a person deliberately breaks down a fence (Criminal Damage Act 1971). In Scotland, a citizen's arrest can be made under common law only if one sees the offence being committed (Criminal Justice (Scotland) Act 1980).

POWERS OF POLICE TO DIRECT TRESPASSERS TO
LEAVE LAND: ENGLAND AND WALES

The police do not have a specific power to remove trespassers *Public Order* unless certain circumstances exist in which the trespass *Act 1986* becomes aggravated in some way either by the commission of a criminal offence or by actions which contravene the Public Order Act 1986. The police may, of course, be present when trespassers are removed by owners of land to ensure that there is no breach of the peace for which, if committed, they would be able to take more positive action.

Practical difficulties also arise where trespass is committed en masse by groups of demonstrators or hippy-type peace convoys making camp. Until recently, the police in England and Wales were relatively powerless to deal with such trespass unless a serious breach of the peace or criminal offences were committed. However, under the provisions of the Public Order Act 1986, powers have now been given to the police to deal with such situations.

Occupation of private land
Under Section 39 of the Public Order Act, if the most senior *Public Order* police officer present reasonably believes that two or more *Act 1986* persons have entered land as trespassers with a common *Section 39* purpose of residing there for any period and that reasonable steps have been taken by or on behalf of the occupier to ask them to leave and if

1 any of them has caused damage to property on the land or used threatening, abusive or insulting words or behaviour

---

[1] Citizen's arrest, in England, Wales and Scotland, is discussed in more detail on page 75.

towards the occupier, a member of his family or an employee or agent of his, or

2 they have between them brought twelve or more vehicles onto the land,

he may direct them to leave the land. If they fail to leave the land as soon as reasonably practicable or, having left again, enter the land within three months, they commit an offence for which they can be arrested by the police.

Disorderly behaviour on private land

Sections 4 & 5 Anyone whose conduct is disorderly or threatening either in behaviour or by words used or by the displaying[1] of any writing, sign or other visible representation commits an offence even in a private place.[2] Section 4 covers behaviour intended to cause another person to believe that immediate unlawful violence will be used; Section 5 covers behaviour within the presence of another that is likely to cause harassment, alarm or distress.

The police have power under the Act to arrest without warrant anyone they reasonably suspect is committing these offences. A power of arrest also exists under the Police and Criminal Evidence Act 1984 if the police suspect an offence *has* been committed, provided that the general power of arrest conditions are met.

The provisions of the Act mean that groups of demonstrators such as hunt saboteurs on private land can be arrested by the police; equally, huntsmen and hunt followers overreacting would be liable to arrest.

TRESPASS ON LAND BY ANIMALS

Animals, whether pets or livestock, can trespass on land and their owners may become liable for such trespass depending on the circumstances.[3] Wild animals – *ferae naturae* – cannot trespass since they are not owned or possessed by anyone and

[1] Distributing to another person any such material is sufficient for an offence under Section 4.
[2] *Private place* does not include a dwelling (i.e. any structure occupied as a person's home or other living accommodation, including tent, caravan, vehicle, vessel or other temporary or movable structure).
[3] Cat owners are in a unique position in that they are not liable for the consequences of their cats' trespasses.

are free to roam where they please. When wild animals pass back and forth from one person's land to another, neither landowner is subject to liability should damage be caused. For example, failure to keep a natural increase in the rabbit population down resulting in a neighbour suffering crop damage would not constitute an act of trespass and no liability would be incurred.[1]

Owners of trespassing livestock, whether it be on private land or on the public highway, are liable to civil action under the provisions of the Animals Act 1971. Livestock is defined as cattle, horses, mules, hinnies (offspring of she ass by stallion), sheep, pigs, goats and poultry. Deer are included when not in the wild state.

A trespass on land is committed by sending or allowing dogs onto another's land without permission. If a dog of its own accord enters land where it has no right to be, its owner is not liable under civil law for trespass. In some circumstances – e.g. the disturbance of game by dogs roaming free whilst their owners continue along a footpath or the chasing of deer in some areas where dogs are released for exercise – owners may be liable for civil trespass particularly if a dog is known to be addicted to disturbing or destroying game or causing damage in some other way. But the practicalities of bringing such an action to court are often prohibitive and as a deterrent against further trespass not very effective.

Sportsmen hunting or coursing upon lands with hounds or greyhounds and being in fresh pursuit of any deer, hare or fox previously found upon land where permission had been granted are exempt from the offence of *trespassing for game* under the Game Act 1831 (see page 35). They are not, however, exempt from civil trespass in these circumstances: the case of Read v Edwards (1864) decided that sending or allowing hounds onto another's land without permission is a trespass, even if no person enters the land. This decision still stands: in 1983 a county court ordered the Master of the West Somerset Vale of Foxhounds to pay nominal damages to the League Against Cruel Sports for allowing a number of hounds to run through a League sanctuary near Bridgewater.

Since hunting and coursing take place in open countryside many unwilled acts of trespass occur, whether by hounds,

---

[1] However, in cases of serious damage, the Minister of Agriculture is empowered under the Agriculture Act 1947 to take steps to clear the land of such pests.

Masters of hounds have a responsibility to prevent dogs and followers from trespassing.

members of the hunt or their followers. All commit acts of trespass if they pursue the hunted animal into an area they do not have permission to enter. Masters of Hounds or other appropriate hunt officials may in fact find themselves held liable for the trespass of others concerned with the hunt, even if they do not enter the land themselves.

TRESPASS ON LAND IN SCOTLAND

The common law of Scotland is similar to that of England and Wales in that owners are given the exclusive right to the surface of their land and trespassers may be dealt with as described above. However, there is one fundamental difference: in Scotland, simple or common trespass, where a person simply passes over the land of another without permission, is not in itself an offence[1] and there lies no grounds for civil action against that person unless actual damage is caused.

INTERDICT

Although civil action is not generally possible in these circumstances against the ordinary trespasser, a civil action could be considered against a *persistent* trespasser by way of *interdict*. The effects of an interdict are limited in that it only

[1] But although not an *offence*, there is no legal *right* to walk on land without the landowner's permission.

prevents future trespass by the same trespasser. It will only be granted at the discretion of the court if there is a likelihood of further trespass. The interdict may be obtained by the owner or tenant of land and is enforced in just the same manner as an injunction is in England and Wales.

Scotland has a great heritage of rights of way and an excellent booklet giving a guide to the law concerning these rights is available from the Scottish Rights of Way Society in Edinburgh.

CRIMINAL TRESPASS

The Trespass (Scotland) Act 1865 creates a criminal offence of trespass in Scotland, but is restricted in its scope. Under Section 3, every person who lodges in any premises,[1] or occupies or encamps on any land, being private property, without the consent of the owner or legal occupier of such premises or land and every person who encamps or lights a fire on or near any private road or enclosed cultivated land or in or near any plantation without the consent and permission of the owner or occupier or on or near any turnpike road, statute labour road or other highway shall be guilty of an offence. *Trespass (Scotland) Act 1865 Section 3*

Section 4 of the Act provides a power of arrest without warrant to a police officer in respect of any person committing such an offence. *Trespass (Scotland) Act 1865 Section 4*

The current application of the Act is restricted by the terms of instructions of the Lord Advocate to Procurators Fiscal for a policy of toleration to traditional travelling people in areas where the provision of sites is inadequate. However, the toleration policy does not apply to large groups of people who are not part of established traveller movement in Scotland; hippy peace convoys, for example, would undoubtedly come within the scope of the provisions of the Act.

TRESPASS TO THE PERSON

The civil law creates three forms of trespass to the person: assault, battery and false imprisonment.

---

[1] *Premises* are defined as any house, barn, stable, shed, loft, granary, outhouse, garden, stockyard, court, close or enclosed space.

ASSAULT

Assault may be defined as an attempt, threat or offer to apply unlawful force sufficient to create the fear that actual violence or harm may ensue.

Verbal threats of violence would not generally constitute an assault unless those threats were accompanied by threatening behaviour such as an attempt to throw an object. A gun pointed in such a manner as to cause fear of being shot would constitute an assault irrespective of whether the weapon was loaded. A similar situation would exist if the firearm used was an imitation.

BATTERY

Battery is actual physical assault. It may consist of just a push in the back or the holding of an arm. Where a person receives injury or any physical discomfort (including shock) as a direct result of battery, then a criminal offence would also be committed and the police would be obliged to investigate, if a complaint was made.

FALSE IMPRISONMENT

The term *false imprisonment* suggests some form of actual imprisonment or holding of a person behind locked doors or in a vehicle. This is not so. Such a trespass may extend to the mere detaining of a person by the holding of an arm. The trespass is actionable where it can be proved that actual bodily restraint of another person without lawful justification has taken place. It is not even necessary to use actual force. A threat of force would be sufficient, for example where a person is detained under the verbal threat of being shot should he try to move.

Actual restraint on a person must be total, complete and unconditional. For example, to restrain someone from entering land where he has no right to go but at the same time giving him the opportunity to leave by a nearby footpath would not constitute a false imprisonment.

COUNTER CLAIMS

Landowners, gamekeepers and others with an interest in land or property may themselves be vulnerable to counter claims for false imprisonment should their actions against trespassers or poachers be considered to be unlawful by the use of more force than was necessary in the circumstances.

DEFENCES

Common defences put forward to actions of trespass against the person are those of self-defence and defence of property; where these are proffered, it must always be shown that no more force was used other than was necessary and reasonable in the circumstances. It will be for the court to decide whether in fact such actions were necessary in the light of all the circumstances of that particular case.

TRESPASS TO GOODS

Trespass to goods is the intentional or negligent interference with another's possessions. The meaning of goods is very wide and would include any article in the possession or constructive possession of another. Animals (other than in the wild state), preserved game or fish, garden produce or harvested crops are all examples of goods subject to trespass.

Moving livestock from one pasture to another without authority, interfering with shooting pegs or moving bale hides would all be acts which may constitute trespass to goods. It is not essential for the person to know his actions are wrong provided they are intentional or negligent. Accidental touching of goods is not actionable.

The interference with goods may also amount to a crime in circumstances where actual damage is caused to the goods either intentionally or recklessly (Criminal Damage Act 1971 and Criminal Justice (Scotland) Act 1980) or where someone treats the goods as his own to dispose of regardless of another's rights. Borrowing or lending may amount to so treating, if it is for a period and in circumstances making it equivalent to an outright taking or disposal (Theft Act 1968; in Scotland, the common law).

Defences to trespass to goods include defence of self or property or where someone believes he has a legal right to the goods.

CHAPTER 2
Liabilities of Landowners and Occupiers of Land

THE LANDOWNER OR occupier has a legal duty not to cause injury by negligence to anyone entering land for legitimate purposes. He must also exercise a certain duty of care towards other people on or near his land as must everyone pursuing a potentially dangerous activity, e.g. shooting rabbits in an area adjacent to a highway or other public place. There are of course many situations where a duty of care is owed to another, particularly in relation to field sports. The more potentially dangerous the activity the greater is the degree of care required.

OCCUPIER'S LIABILITY

The Occupier's Liability Act 1957 imposes on the occupier of premises[1] a *common duty of care* to all visitors: that is to take such care as is reasonable in the circumstances to ensure the visitor's safety in using the premises for the purpose for which he is invited or permitted by the occupier to be there. This does not mean the occupier has to go to elaborate

---

[1] *Premises* should be taken in its broadest context as meaning the property of the occupier.

lengths of protection; but if there are obvious dangers on the property where persons have legal sporting access, then he must take reasonable steps to safeguard them from the danger unless he has exonerated himself of the liability under the conditions of a sporting lease.

The common duty of care does not apply to trespassers. Poachers, for example, trespass at their own risk and have no claim against the occupier of the land if they suffer injury as the result of mere neglect of property by the occupier. However, the owner may not place trespassers in deliberate danger by some form of trap in which they may suffer injury. Man traps, for example, were made illegal many years ago. The test would be whether a humane person with the knowledge, ability and resources of the occupier could and would take steps to protect trespassers from any danger on the land.

Liability for injury or damage caused by animals
Where livestock or other domestic animals come into contact with people crossing the land, owners cannot generally be held liable for any damage or injury caused by the animals even to those who have legitimate access to the land.

All domestic animals, which includes livestock, are presumed harmless. The only redress one may have if injured would be to prove that the owner or person in charge of the animal knew of its unnaturally harmful tendencies. Those injured by over boisterous cattle, horses or a ram protecting his territorial rights have generally no claim against their owners.

Man traps were once used to protect game but were made illegal many years ago.

Where a right of way exists, restrictions are placed on the owners of certain breeds of bulls (see below); but no such restrictions are placed on the owners of other domestic animals not regarded as dangerous species.

Animals Act 1971   The Animals Act 1971 which makes provisions for civil liability concerning animals defines a dangerous species as *being one which is not commonly domesticated in the British Isles and when fully grown is likely, unless restricted, to cause damage, which includes injury.* Most animals falling into this class, including those not normally domesticated in Great Britain, are kept in zoos and in safari parks, which must be licensed by the local authority under the provisions of the Zoo Act 1981. Their keepers are liable for any damage or injury they may do unless caused by the fault of the aggrieved person (for example, someone alighting from a car against advice in a safari park and being mauled by a tiger).

The keepers of certain dangerous wild animals also need to be licensed by the local authority under the Dangerous Wild Animals Act 1976. The provisions of the Act would include the keeping of such animals privately and the local authority would need to be satisfied that the applicant was not only suitable but that appropriate accommodation was available and that it was not contrary to public safety nor would create a nuisance.

Bulls

No liability is incurred by the owner of an untethered bull roaming free in an area not crossed by a footpath or other right of way. The situation is different where bulls are allowed their liberty in areas where confrontation is likely between the bull and anyone legitimately negotiating foot-paths or other rights of way. The potential danger here should not be underestimated as bulls can be extremely dangerous beasts.

Obviously, farmers have to pasture their bulls somewhere, but in choosing a field crossed by a public footpath they are effectively closing it to the more prudent walker or endanger-ing the lives of the less prudent. In 1968 a Government-appointed committee spent a great deal of time deliberating on footpath matters, particularly in relation to the problem of untethered bulls. It recommended a legal ban on the pasturing of any bull more than one-year-old in a field crossed by a public path and, if this created difficulties for

The potential danger of untethered bulls should not be under-estimated.

the farmer, provision would be made for him to apply for the Highway Authority to have such a path diverted or closed for up to three months at a time. Whilst the recommendation gained the support of both the National Farmers Union and the Ramblers Association, it was not included in the legislation introduced in the Wildlife and Countryside Act 1981.

Under Section 59 of the Wildlife and Countryside Act 1981 a farmer who allows an untethered bull to roam free in a field or enclosure crossed by a footpath or other right of way, commits an offence subject to the following exceptions:

1 The bull does not exceed 10 months of age.
2 The bull is not a recognised dairy breed[1] *and* is at large in a field with cows or heifers.

This part of the Act does not apply to Scotland, but similar provisions are to be found in Section 44 of the Countryside (Scotland) Act 1967.

Local byelaws in some areas also provide additional legislation creating similar offences.

---

[1] *Recognised dairy breeds*: Ayrshire, British Friesian, British Holstein, Dairy Shorthorn, Guernsey, Jersey and Kerry.

CHAPTER 3

The Rights to Game

IT HAS ALWAYS been accepted that man has the right to take birds and animals of all kinds on his own land, although for centuries landowners and occupiers have been restricted by laws as to the methods used or the species to be hunted. The principle of *ferae naturae* has also long been accepted: that where wild animals and birds are free to roam from one person's land to another they are ownerless and not capable of being stolen. The poaching laws of today still reflect these attitudes.

POACHING OR THEFT

Poaching is not theft, nor even a particular kind of theft. Poaching is the *unlawful taking or killing of game*, whereas theft is the *dishonest taking of property belonging to another*. Wild animals at liberty are ownerless and cannot be deemed *property*: they can be poached, but not stolen.

It is often argued that the landowner who releases previously captive stock owns those birds, if not legally then morally. But morality has no place in deciding cases at court and it will be seen that game released in this way cannot generally be stolen. Once game is released into the wild, there is no restriction where it may roam; it becomes *ferae naturae* and no longer capable of being stolen. It can, of course, be poached.

THEFT OF GAME

Game and other wild creatures can only be stolen if, tamed or untamed, they have been reduced into possession by or on behalf of another person. The Theft Act 1968 states:

Wild creatures, tamed or untamed, shall be regarded as property; but a person cannot steal a wild creature not tamed nor kept in captivity, or the carcase of any such creature, unless either it has been reduced into possession by or on behalf of another person and possession of it has not since been lost or abandoned, or another person is in the course of reducing it into possession.[1]

Theft Act 1968 Section 4 (4)

As a general rule, it will only be theft if the game is stolen after it has passed into someone's possession or constructive possession. For instance, where live birds are penned up with no means of escape or the birds are in the course of being reduced into possession, e.g. where they are caught in traps but not yet removed.

If game is shot but falls dead some distance away from the shooter and he sends his dog to retrieve the game or goes to pick it up himself, he is said to be *in the course of reducing it into possession*. If in the course of reducing it into possession another person removes the game without authority, this would be theft. However, if the shooter gives the bird up as a lost cause, he abandons his rights to it and anyone picking it up later would not commit theft.

Game in pens, no matter how wild, once caught up and prevented from escaping, perhaps by the use of brails (a device attached to the wing to prevent the bird from flying), can be stolen. When birds are in release pens in more remote areas of woodland and are allowed to come and go from the pen, as at feeding times, they are wild, no longer captive, and not capable of being stolen even if they were in the release pen at the time of being taken. A gamekeeper who drives game into certain coverts and feeds them on a regular basis in

---

[1] The Theft Act 1968 does not apply in Scotland, although the common law offence of theft in Scotland does impose similar criteria.

Wild pheasants fitted with brails under the wing so that they cannot escape become private property.

an effort to *hold* the game would not be deemed to be in the process of reducing the game into his possession so long as the birds remain free.

The Theft Act clearly indicates that birds or animals that are tame or normally kept in captivity can be stolen, unless of course they have been lost or abandoned in some way. Tame peacocks kept in the grounds of a house could therefore be stolen, but what of the guinea fowl allowed to roam free in pheasant coverts in a semi-wild state? It is doubtful whether anyone taking such birds would commit theft, since rights of ownership may be deemed to have been lost or abandoned in just the same way as for the once captive and semi-tame pheasants.

A pheasant released into a wood with no restriction on its liberty technically becomes a wild bird, even though it may remain reasonably tame. This is so even if the bird is wing-tagged or marked in some other way to enable eventual identification for shoot management purposes. To argue that the tag itself may remain as *property belonging to another* is worth consideration, but since it is fixed with the knowledge that the bird is free and capable of flying anywhere and becoming legitimate quarry for anyone on whose land it is found, it cannot, legally speaking, be seriously considered that the rights of ownership in the tag are retained.

RIGHTS OF OWNERS OR OCCUPIERS
TO TAKE GAME

ENGLAND AND WALES

In England and Wales, the owner of land normally has the right to kill or take game on that land and he may give such authority to other persons without restriction, provided of course they observe the law in terms of close seasons and the requirement of game licences (see pages 56–63). If he lets the land to a tenant, the right to take the game automatically passes to the tenant unless the owner has previously reserved the right under some form of agreement. The terms of the tenancy may therefore take one of three forms:

1 The tenancy agreement grants full game rights to the tenant.
2 The owner expressly reserves the game rights for himself, or shooting tenant.
3 The tenancy agreement does not include any direction regarding the game rights; in which case the rights pass to the tenant.

Game rights, as they may loosely be referred to, should always be in writing. The term *game* can lead to some misunderstanding unless a specific definition of what constitutes game is included; for there is no standard definition of game within poaching legislation, as it varies between different Acts of Parliament. The use of the words *shooting rights* or *sporting rights* are far more suitable, since they have been interpreted to mean the right to kill all things which are usually the object of sport.

Where a person holds the game rights to the exclusion of the occupier or tenant, then, unless given authority by the holder of such rights, the occupier has no right to take or pursue game other than ground game.[1] Should he do so, he would commit an offence under the Game Act 1831 (Section 12) and would also commit this offence if he permitted someone else to do so.

A non-occupying owner who infringes a shooting tenant's rights by pursuing or killing game, *including* hares and rabbits, may be held liable for a breach of contract; civil

[1] Ground game: hares and rabbits, subject to the limitations of the Ground Game Act 1880. See page 23.

action may also be taken by a person with exclusive game rights against anyone who interferes with the enjoyment of such rights. This would not include any act done in the ordinary course of estate management or farming. Should this situation arise the advice of a solicitor should be sought at an early stage.

OWNERSHIP OF GAME

The ownership of illegally taken game, if in dispute, is for the court to decide upon, but usually it will be found to be the property of the person on whose land the game was taken.[1] However, there are situations where rightful ownership may not be so straightforward:

1 Where a poacher finds game on the land of Smith and kills it there, the game is the property of Smith; but if having found game on Smith's land, he then pursues it and kills it on the land of Jones, the game may be held to be the property of neither Smith nor Jones, but the property of the poacher!

Ownership of game shot over boundaries may be in dispute.

2 If Smith legitimately shoots a pheasant over his own land and it falls *alive* on Jones's land, although he has some claim on the bird and may feel morally obliged to pursue it, he commits a poaching offence if he retrieves the bird without Jones's permission.

[1] In Scotland the poacher owns his unlawful haul, and even if caught and convicted, the court does not have the power of forfeiture as in England.

3 If Smith retrieves from Jones's land *dead game* which was in the first instance legitimately shot over his own land, then he commits an act of civil trespass if permission is not sought to retrieve the game, even though Smith has a legal right to ownership of the game.

RIGHTS OF OCCUPIERS TO TAKE GROUND GAME

Ground game: a rabbit, hare and leveret.

During the eighteenth and nineteenth centuries considerable resentment was felt by tenant farmers over the damage caused to crops by hares and rabbits, which they were not allowed to shoot. The Ground Game Act 1880[1] sought to rectify the situation and improve the tenant farmer's lot. It gives a statutory right to every occupier of land to take and kill ground game. The tenant farmer has no legal right to claim compensation from his landlord for damage done by ground game, but the passing of the Act has ensured that occupiers of land without shooting rights will always have the right to take hares and rabbits and so protect their crops, irrespective of any agreements to the contrary.

[1] The provisions of the Act extend to Scotland with exception of Section 6 (night shooting); but similar provisions to Section 6 are to be found in the Agriculture (Scotland) Act 1948.

Under the Ground Game Act the occupier can never divest himself of the right which is inseparable from his occupation of the land. Should any other person be entitled to kill and take ground game on the same land, e.g. the landowner or person with sporting rights, then the occupier would have a *concurrent right* with such persons to take and kill ground game. Any agreement, condition or arrangement which purports to divest or alienate this statutory right or which gives any advantage in return for not exercising the right, or which imposes any disadvantage in consequence of him taking ground game, would be void and not legally binding.[1]

The occupier exercises his statutory right to take ground game under the Ground Game Act 1880 subject to the following restrictions; if the shooting rights are not reserved and are vested in the occupier, then the restrictions on the exercise of the statutory right do not apply.

GROUND GAME ACT 1880

Ground Game Act 1880 Section 1 1 The occupier himself and one other person authorised by him, in writing, shall be the only persons entitled to kill ground game with firearms.

2 No person shall be authorised by the occupier to kill or take ground game, except:
(*a*) members of his household resident on the land in his occupation
(*b*) persons in his ordinary service on such land (employees), and
(*c*) any one other person, bona fide employed by him for reward in the taking and destruction of ground game.

3 Every person so authorised by the occupier, on demand by any other person having a concurrent right or any person so authorised by him in writing, must produce their written authority. In default, a person would not be deemed to be an 'authorised person'.

Game Act 1831 Section 30 Non-compliance with any of the above restrictions may make the person taking ground game a trespasser within the scope

---

[1] *Scotland*: an agricultural tenant is also entitled under Scottish common law to kill rabbits and he may give permission to anyone else to do so, which need not be in writing. Where the lease expressly reserves rabbits to the landowner, the tenant's rights must be exercised within the terms of the Ground Game Act.

of poaching legislation, e.g. trespass in pursuit of game. A defence that the person had permission from the occupier would not apply.

The occupier ferreting with two authorised persons. Only the occupier and one other may use a firearm.

Occupier

The 'occupier' includes a person who is the owner of the land he occupies. For, although in the majority of cases the occupier will be a tenant farmer, there may be situations where other persons not resident on the land may be deemed occupiers. For example, where a farm is carried on by trustees or executors by means of a bailiff residing at the farmhouse, it may be that each of the trustees or executors could be deemed 'occupiers'. In other words, occupying does not necessarily mean living on the land in question. Where there is more than one legal occupier, it would appear each has equal authority to exercise his right to take ground game (*see* Morrison v Anderson (1913)). However, they may be jointly restricted in authorising other persons to do so, and the limitations imposed by virtue of the Ground Game Act would apply.

A person is not deemed to be an occupier under this act by virtue of having a right of common over the land. Nor would he be treated as such, if he merely had the grazing rights for sheep, cattle or horses for nine months or less in each year.

The Act treats persons with long-standing grazing rights (of more than nine months) as occupiers of land and not merely as licensees entitled to the grass. The word *grazing* is not intended to include the grazing on arable land of crops *in situ* (e.g. strip grazing of kale or root crops). It is doubtful whether the grazing of sheep on stubble would come within this exception.

In Scotland, landholders with an interest in a common grazing approved under the Small Landowners and Agricultural Holdings (Scotland) Act 1911 may appoint not more than two of their number and authorise in writing one person bona fide employed by them for reward to kill and take ground game on common grazing land. This does not apply to the former counties of Argyll, Caithness, Inverness, Orkney, Ross and Cromarty, Sutherland and Shetland, but similar provisions in respect of these areas are contained in Section 27 Crofters (Scotland) Act 1955.

Firearms
The use of firearms is restricted to two people: the occupier and one other person who must also fall within the criteria to be legally authorised as given at (2) above.

Authorised persons
There is no restriction on the number of authorised persons provided they are residents or employees; if they are neither, the occupier can only authorise *one* other person who must be employed by him for reward specifically to take ground game.

Reward
The keeping of rabbits caught has been held in a Scottish case (Bruce v Prosser 1898) to satisfy the requirement of a reward in the absence of payment of monies; but the arrangements of employment of a person must be genuine and not merely a friendly concession to allow a person a day's sport whether they keep the rabbits or not.

Resident
A member of the household resident on the land could quite clearly cover family and relations living with the occupier. It would also extend to servants, provided they were resident in the occupier's house or cottage. In the case of Stuart v Murray (1884) in Scotland a person who was invited by the occupier to stay with him for a week was held to be a member of the household resident on the land. It is very much a question of fact in each case for the magistrates to decide, but

a friend invited for a weekend's sport would not be so resident.

Ordinary service
'Ordinary service' means a person employed by the occupier and who actually works on the land. It is doubtful whether casual labour would satisfy this particular restriction. Persons connected with other work elsewhere than on the land would therefore be excluded.

MOORLANDS AND UNENCLOSED LANDS

In England and Wales, under the Ground Game Act 1880 as amended by Ground Game (Amendment) Act 1906 occupiers or authorised persons may only take and kill ground game on moorland or unenclosed land between 1 September and 31 March inclusive.[1] An additional restriction exists in respect of the use of firearms which must not be used for such purposes between 1 September and 10 December (Ground Game (Amendment) Act 1906). The prohibition on such lands can be waived provided all persons having a statutory right to take and kill game enter into an agreement for their joint benefit to kill ground game by the use of firearms between 1 September and 10 December inclusive. *Ground Game Act 1880 (Amendment) Act 1906 Section 1 (3)*

In Scotland, Section 1 (3) of the Ground Game Act 1880 has been modified by the Agriculture (Scotland) Act as follows: *Ground Game Act 1880 Section 1 (3) Agriculture (Scotland) Act 1948*

The occupier of land or persons authorised by him may kill ground game on moorlands and unenclosed lands (not being arable) in the occupier's occupation by all legal means other than by shooting over the whole year and by means of firearms over the period from 1 July to 31 March.

EXEMPTION OF LICENCE TO KILL GAME

Under the Ground Game Act 1880, the occupier and any person authorised by him, subject to the above restrictions, are exempt from the need to obtain a licence to kill ground game on land in occupation of the occupier. The occupier is also exempt from such a licence if he wishes to sell the game. *Ground Game Act 1880 Section 4*

---

[1] Land *which is arable* or detached portions of less than 25 acres adjoining arable lands are not included; therefore there is no close season.

Occupants and authorised persons are not exempt from the need to observe days or seasons in which the taking or killing of ground game is prohibited by law. Since there is no close season for hares or rabbits, other than as stated above in respect of moorlands or unenclosed land, this effectively refers to the taking of hares on Sundays and Christmas Day which is prohibited by virtue of the Game Act 1831 in England and Wales (see page 56). There is no restriction on the taking of rabbits. In Scotland the killing of ground game on any particular day is not prohibited by statute.

NIGHT SHOOTING OF GROUND GAME
England and Wales
Until 1981 Section 6 of the Ground Game Act prohibited occupiers or other persons with their authority from exercising their statutory right by using firearms for shooting ground game during the night. This restriction was lifted by the Wildlife and Countryside Act so as to deem it lawful for the occupier of any land himself, or one other person authorised by him, to use firearms for the purpose of killing ground game at night if the occupier has the written authority of a person entitled to kill or take the ground game on that land, e.g. holder of shooting rights.

Scotland
The provisions of Section 6 of the 1880 Act do not apply to Scotland; but the same provisions are contained in Sections 50 and 50A of the Agriculture (Scotland) Act 1948. Briefly, this prohibits the use of spring traps except in rabbit holes and the use of poisons. Prior to 1981, it also prohibited certain night shooting of ground game, but this particular prohibition has been amended by the Wildlife and Countryside Act 1981 as follows:

Agriculture (Scotland) Act 1948 Section 50 as amended by the Wildlife and Countryside Act 1981

1 It shall not be unlawful for the owner of the shooting rights on any land or any person holding those rights from him, or the occupier of any land (subject to (2) below), to use a firearm for the purpose of killing ground game thereon at night. (Expiration of the first hour after sunset and the commencement of the last hour before sunset.)

2 The occupier of any land shall not use a firearm to kill ground game at night (except where he has exclusive right)

unless he has first obtained the written authority of the other person or one of the other persons entitled to kill ground game.

3 An occupier who is entitled to use a firearm for the purpose of killing ground game may subject to the provisions of Section 1 of the Ground Game Act 1880 authorise one other person so to use a firearm.

NIGHT SHOOTING OF HARES

England, Wales and Scotland

The amended provisions of Section 6 of the Ground Game Act 1880 and the corresponding legislation under Sections 50 and 50A of the Agriculture (Scotland) Act 1948 would appear to override the restrictions on night shooting of hares with firearms under the Hares Act and Hares (Scotland) Acts 1848 (see pages 55 and 57). However, Section 6 does not exempt in England and Wales a person who merely holds the shooting rights and who could not be deemed an 'authorised' person under the Act.

WRITTEN AUTHORITY

The form of authorisation is not laid down but should include the identity of the holder, date, land covered, signature of occupier and whether firearms may be used.

A suggested format is shown overleaf:

AUTHORITY UNDER SECTION 1 GROUND GAME
ACT 1880

NAME ....

OF ....

....

IS:

★ 1 A RESIDENT IN MY HOUSEHOLD ON THE LAND

★ 2 IN MY SERVICE ON THE LAND

★ 3 EMPLOYED TO TAKE GROUND GAME FOR REWARD

AND IS AUTHORISED TO TAKE RABBITS AND HARES
(★ WITH FIREARMS / ★ AT NIGHT)
ON THE FOLLOWING LAND:

....

. . . . SIGNATURE OF OCCUPANT

. . . . DATE

★ Delete as applicable

AUTHORITY UNDER SECTION 1 GROUND GAME
ACT 1880

NAME ....

OF ....

....

IS HEREBY AUTHORISED ON BEHALF OF ....

(* OWNER OF LAND/SHOOTING RIGHTS) TO DEMAND
THE PRODUCTION OF A WRITTEN AUTHORISATION
GRANTED TO PERSONS TAKING OR ATTEMPTING TO
TAKE GROUND GAME ON THE FOLLOWING LAND:

....

. . . . SIGNATURE OF * OWNER

OF LAND/SHOOTING

RIGHTS

. . . . DATE

* Delete where applicable

CHAPTER 4
Day and Night Poaching

TRESPASS AND POACHING

THE *TORT* OF trespass is a necessary ingredient in a number of criminal offences associated with poaching. It is essential, therefore, to understand exactly what constitutes an act of trespass under the game laws, because in many cases if the trespass on land cannot be proven the case may be lost.

In the majority of cases proving a trespass on land will present no problems since direct evidence of that fact can usually be given by the landowner, gamekeeper or whoever has seen the poacher on the land. Occasionally, this evidence is not available and an actual physical entry on the land cannot be proven.

CONSTRUCTIVE ENTRIES ONTO LAND

For daytime trespass, it is now reasonably well established that a poacher can no longer seek the protection of the public highway,[1] footpath or other right of way as a means to poach either there or on adjacent land. The principle that the highway or road should be treated as land in occupation of

[1] See Harrison v Duke of Rutland (1893) page 3.

the owner or occupier of adjacent land has been maintained over many years and has in fact been extended to include types of constructive entries onto land. In the case of R v Pratt (1855) the defendant was liable although he merely fired a gun from the highway into a field. This case was followed in Pratt v Martin (1911) in which the defendant was actually found guilty of trespass in pursuit of game on the highway.

Firing from one's own land into another's is a constructive entry.

The situation in respect of trespass changes where a constructive entry is made by anyone firing a gun into another's land whilst actually standing on land he owns or has authority to be on, other than the public highway. The act would still be a trespass although no physical entry onto the land is made; but if the act of shooting at game takes place in the daytime, he would only be liable for trespass: unless he physically enters the land to pick up the shot game, a poaching offence is not committed.[1] In the case of Horn v Raine (1898) the picking up some hours later of game shot on another's land by a man standing on his own land was held to constitute an offence of trespass in search or pursuit of game, both acts being considered close enough, in time, to constitute the offence.

ASSISTING POACHERS FROM THE HIGHWAY

Anyone assisting a poacher from the highway (e.g. a lookout) may also be guilty of poaching. For example, in R v

---

[1] If such an action is committed during the *night*, it is an offence of *unlawfully taking or destroying game or rabbits on any land* (Night Poaching Act 1828) even though the land is not entered.

Passey (1836) poachers were in a field with a look-out on the highway to give the alarm: it was held that all were guilty of poaching.

USE OF VEHICLES

The driver who sets out *deliberately* to knock down game on the road with his car commits a poaching offence because by his actions he has become a trespasser. In these circumstances, the case may be difficult to prove as the deliberate intentions of the driver to kill game by the use of his car would have to be shown.

POACHING OFFENCES

Poaching (from the French *pocher*, to encroach) has never been judicially defined, for although the word appears in the title of some Acts, it is not used to describe specific offences. However, the term *poaching* is used to mean the illegal taking or killing of game or the attempt to do so.

The most common poaching offences normally fall within the provisions of three Acts of Parliament that have changed little since their introduction in the 1880s: the Game Act 1831, the Game (Scotland) Act 1832 and the Night Poaching Act 1828.

The first two Acts deal with daytime poaching offences and each contains similar provisions. The latter, as its title suggests, deals with offences committed during the night anywhere in Great Britain. However, time of offence is by no means the sole difference between these Acts: they differ considerably in scope, with the curious result that in some circumstances the legislation in respect of daytime offences is much stronger than that concerning offences committed during the night. The definition of game also varies from Act to Act.

DAYTIME OFFENCES

ENGLAND AND WALES: GAME ACT 1831

Game Act 1831
Section 30 Under Section 30 of the Game Act 1831 an offence is committed by any person who trespasses[1] in the daytime by

entering or being upon any land in search or pursuit of game, woodcock, snipe or rabbits.

Search or pursuit does not necessarily mean that actual chasing or running after game has to be proved. The mere intention of a person looking for game while on the land would suffice. Neither is it necessary to prove that the *searching* and *pursuing* was with the intention to kill at the time or reduce the game into possession (Stiff v Billington 1901). The offence is only committed where there is pursuit of *live* game.

Provisions under the Act against trespassers found on the land do not extend to anyone hunting or coursing with hounds or greyhounds and in fresh pursuit of any hare, fox or deer already started upon any other land on which he or she was entitled to hunt or course.

Game

Game is defined in Section 2 as hares, pheasants, partridges, *Section 2* grouse, heath or moor game and black game. (Woodcock, snipe and rabbits are included in the provisions of the Act but not classed as game.)

Daytime

Daytime is defined as one hour before sunrise to one hour *Section 34* after sunset (local time).

Gang poaching

Section 30 also makes provision for a greater penalty to apply *Section 30* on conviction where five or more acting together commit the offence of gang poaching; this would include anyone assisting poachers from the highway.

A further offence is also committed when five or more *Section 32* together trespass in search or pursuit of game, woodcock, snipe or rabbits and one of them is armed with a gun and *any* of them, by violence, intimidation, or menace, prevents or endeavours to prevent any authorised persons from exercising their powers under Section 31.[2]

---

[1] Trespass is discussed in more detail on pages 2–5.
[2] See page 37.

SCOTLAND: GAME (SCOTLAND) ACT 1832

Game (Scotland) Under Section 1, an offence is committed by anyone who
Act 1832 commits any trespass by entering or being, in the daytime,
Section 1 upon any land, *without leave of the proprietor*, in search or
pursuit of game, or woodcock, snipe, *wild ducks* or conies
(rabbits). (The variations from the Game Act 1831 are
printed in italics.)

The definition of *search* and *pursuit* are the same as in
England and Wales and there are the same provisions in the
Scottish Act as in the English Act for hunting and coursing
hare or fox (but not deer) with hounds or greyhounds.

Game

Game is not defined in the Scottish Act, but in practice the
definition given under the Night Poaching Act 1828 is used.[1]
It has, however, been held to include capercaillie (Col-
quhoun's Trs. v Lee 1957) and no doubt within the spirit of
the Act ptarmigan would be included.

Section 3   Daytime is one hour before sunrise to one hour after
sunset (local time).

Gang poaching and disguise

As with the legislation covering England and Wales, provision
is made in this Act for a greater penalty to apply on
conviction where five or more persons are acting together to
commit the offence. In addition, a greater penalty also exists
should any of the poachers *have his face blackened, coloured
or otherwise disfigured for the purpose of disguise*.

Violence

Section 6 Under Section 6, an offence is committed by any trespasser
who assaults or obstructs any person acting in the execution
or by virtue of the powers and provisions of this Act.

FERRETS

Ferreting is a legitimate method of taking rabbits. Although
ferrets are often used for poaching, no additional offence is
committed through their use.

---

[1] See page 39.

RESTRICTION ON PROSECUTIONS

Under Section 11 of the Game Laws (Amendment) (Scotland) *Game Laws*
Act 1877, anyone who has been or shall be prosecuted for any *(Amendment)*
act as constituting an offence under any one or more of the *Act 1877*
Game Acts shall not be liable to be prosecuted again for the *Section 11*
same act as constituting an offence under any other Acts.

There may be many instances where multiple offences are committed under various Game Acts arising from the same set of circumstances. Section 11 effectively means that proceedings under only one Act can be taken in Scotland, with the exception of offences relating to game licences.

ENFORCEMENT OF THE 1831 AND 1832 GAME ACTS

Enforcement in England and Wales is dealt with in Section 31 of the Game Act 1831 and in Scotland in Section 2 Game (Scotland) Act 1832. Anyone found committing the offence may be asked by an authorised person to give his full name and address and to quit the land forthwith; if he gives a false name or address or refuses to give his name and address, or wilfully continues on the land, or returns to the land, he may be arrested.

The trespasser must give his real name – surname and first name. If he refuses or gives a vague description of his address or, having once quit the land, returns later, he can be arrested by an authorised person. No one can legally be arrested *unless* he has been asked to give his name and address and to quit the land.

Should a poacher, who has given his correct name and address, wilfully continue or return to the land, the power to arrest only applies if he is on the *same* land and for the purpose of pursuing game there.

Authorised persons
A person authorised to exercise the power of arrest must fall within one of the following categories:

1 Anyone having a right to kill game on the land
2 Occupiers (whether they have a right to take the game or not)
3 Anyone authorised by 1 or 2 above
4 Gamekeeper or servant

5 Wardens, rangers and others employed in a similar capacity in Royal forests and parks, etc. (England and Wales only)

Poachers arrested by anyone other than a police officer must be brought before a Justice of the Peace (Sheriff in Scotland) as soon as convenient and in any case within twelve hours. If this is not possible or reasonable in the circumstances, the person must be set free; he may nevertheless be proceeded against by summons or a warrant.

Game (Scotland) In Scotland the prosecution may be by the owner or
Act 1832 occupier or by the Procurator Fiscal for the county and a
Section 2 conviction may proceed on the evidence of a single witness.

POLICE POWERS

Game Laws In England and Wales a police officer may arrest anyone he
(Amendment) has reasonable cause to suspect of having committed an
Act 1960 offence of daytime poaching, subject to the provisions of the
Section 2 general power of arrest under the Police and Criminal Evidence Act 1984, and he may enter land to exercise this power under the Game Laws (Amendment) Act 1960.

In Scotland the Police and Criminal Evidence Act does not apply to powers of arrest and no direct power is given to the police in respect of daytime poaching. However, a Scottish constable may use his common law power of arrest if this is applicable.

POACHING AT NIGHT

The law relating to daytime poaching is much wider in scope than for offences committed during the night.

A night poacher's folding .410 shotgun. The home-made silencer gives a noise output similar to an air rifle.

Under Section 1 of the Night Poaching Act 1828, it is an offence unlawfully at night:

1   To take or destroy any game[1] or rabbits on any land, *Night Poaching* whether open or enclosed. The Night Poaching Act 1844 *Act 1828* amended Section 1 of the 1828 Act to include any public *Section 1 (a)* road, highway or path, or their verges, or at the openings, outlets or gates from any such land into a public road, highway or path.

   To constitute an offence, the game or rabbits must actually be taken or destroyed.

2   To enter or be on any land,[2] whether open or enclosed, *Section 1 (b)* with any gun, net, engine or other instrument, for the purpose of taking or destroying game.

   It must be proved that the poacher had a gun, net, engine or other instrument and that he was on land for the purpose of taking game.[3] The word *engine* has been held to include a snare (Allen v Thompson 1870).

Night time is defined in Section 12 of the 1828 Act as one *Section 12* hour after sunset to one hour before sunrise (local time).

PURSUIT OF RABBITS AND HARES AT NIGHT

The distinction between game and rabbits in the Night Poaching Act creates a legal pitfall for unwary keepers and policemen. Anyone unlawfully on land at night in search of rabbits does not commit the offence of night poaching, even if he has equipment with him for that purpose. The two offences the poacher can commit in these circumstances are the pursuit of rabbits without a game licence[4] and, if carrying a firearm, the further offence of armed trespass.[5]

However, hares *are* included in the definition of game *Section 1 (b)* under the second offence of entering for the purpose of taking or destroying game and in the vast majority of cases, particularly those involving lurcher dogs, hares are nearly always pursued as well as rabbits. Lamping equipment

---

[1] Game: hares, pheasants, partridges, grouse, heath or moor game, black game and bustards.
[2] This includes the highway.
[3] Rabbits not specified.
[4] See pages 59–61.
[5] See page 101.

The poacher in pursuit of hares or rabbits requires a game licence.

would also be deemed *instruments*. Being on land for the purpose of taking hares would, of course, have to be proved in court by verbal admission or direct evidence of a pursuit.

USE OF DOGS

The use of dogs is *not* an offence under the Night Poaching Act. Anyone searching at night for hares or rabbits with a dog and nothing else would not commit an offence of night poaching until actually taking or destroying a hare or rabbit.

USING VIOLENCE

Section 2 Under Section 2, if a poacher committing the Section 1 offences described above assaults or offers violence with gun, crossbow, firearms, bludgeon, stick, club or other offensive weapon to the owner or occupier of the land, his gamekeepers or servants or assistants, he commits a further offence.

If the assault is carried out by one poacher, a companion poacher who takes no actual part in the assault cannot be convicted of assault unless it can be proved that both were out with a common purpose – not only to poach but to resist arrest by the use of violence, if necessary (R v Pearce 1929).

GANG POACHING

Section 9 Under Section 9, where three or more together, at night, unlawfully enter any land, whether open or enclosed, for the purpose of taking or destroying game or rabbits and any of them are armed with a gun, crossbow or other offensive weapon, a further offence is committed.[1]

To commit this offence it is not necessary for all the poachers to enter the land, provided all are associated together for one common purpose and some enter while others remain near enough to assist, e.g. as lookouts (R v Whittaker and others 1848). If any of the poachers are armed, all are deemed to be armed within the meaning of the statute (R v Goodfellow 1845).

Poaching pheasants by trawling a net over a cover crop.

USE OF LAMPS AND NETS TO TAKE GAME BIRDS

Where pheasants or other game birds are taken at night by the use of lamps or artificial light (e.g. a torch strapped to the barrel of a gun), a further offence is committed under the Wildlife and Countryside Act 1981.

Wildlife and Countryside Act 1981

It is the practice in some areas to poach game birds by trawling a hand-propelled net over cover crops. This is not in itself an offence.[2]

---

[1] The inclusion or exclusion of rabbits has the effect of making it an offence for three armed men to pursue rabbits (Section 9) but not two armed men (Section 1 (b)).

[2] The use of nets to take birds is an offence in some circumstances. See page 116.

THE ENFORCEMENT OF THE NIGHT
POACHING ACTS 1828 AND 1844

The legislation recognised that poaching by night, in a gang or with offensive weapons, was a far more serious matter than daylight poaching, since a poacher caught in such circumstances was likely to fight to escape capture and recognition. Stronger powers of arrest for night poaching were therefore introduced than for day poaching.

ARREST

Night Poaching Act 1828 Section 2 Under Section 2, anyone found committing night-poaching offences may be arrested by the owner or occupier or their gamekeepers or servants or persons assisting them on the land or adjoining highway, road or path.

Anyone arrested should be delivered to a police officer as soon as possible.

The power of arrest does not specifically cover someone who holds the game rights but is neither owner nor occupier nor his assistant, and such a person arresting for night poaching may render himself liable to a claim for false imprisonment should a court decide he was not authorised by the Act.[1] However, if the holder of the game rights appoints a gamekeeper, the keeper can 'deem' or 'treat' his employer as his assistant, thus allowing him the power of arrest.

In the event of a poacher being pursued for an offence of night poaching, he may be arrested in any place to which he has escaped. This would not, of course, convey an automatic power of entry by force into private premises to effect the arrest. The poacher would also have to be arrested in hot pursuit: where the poacher had been lost for a considerable time and away from the land in question, the power to arrest would cease. In cases of this nature, it would be a question for the magistrates to decide whether the spirit of the legislation covering the power of arrest had been followed.

---

[1] See trespass pages 12–13.

POLICE POWERS – ENGLAND AND WALES

Entry on Land
Under Section 2 (1) of the Game Laws (Amendment) Act *Game Laws*
1960, where a police officer has reasonable grounds to *(Amendment)*
suspect that a person is committing an offence on any land *Act 1960*
under Section 1 or 9 of the Night Poaching Act 1828, he may *Section 2 (1)*
enter any land for the purpose of exercising his power of
arrest.

Under Section 2 (3), the power of entry conferred by *Section 2 (3)*
subsection (1) is not exercisable in relation to land occupied
by or under the management of:

1 Secretary of State for War, Secretary of State for Air or the
  Admiralty
2 Ministry of Aviation
3 United Kingdom Atomic Energy Authority

Arrest – Police and Criminal Evidence Act 1984
Under Section 25 of the Police and Criminal Evidence Act *Police and*
1984, a police officer may arrest anyone he has reasonable *Criminal Evidence*
cause to suspect of having committed an offence of night *Act 1984*
poaching, subject to the provisions of the general power of *Section 25*
arrest under this Act.

POLICE POWERS – SCOTLAND

There are no specific powers of arrest given to the police in *Game Laws*
Scotland for night-poaching offences unless called upon to *(Amendment)*
assist an owner, occupier or gamekeeper; in which case they *Act 1960*
may arrest under the power given in Section 2 as a person *Section 2*
assisting.

If necessary, they may use their common law power to
arrest night poachers, provided that certain conditions are
met, e.g. poacher gives a false name and address.

POWERS TO SEARCH AND SEIZE
FOR DAY AND NIGHT POACHING

GAME ACT 1831

Game Act 1831   The Game Act 1831 only applies to England and Wales.
Section 36   However, Section 5 of the Game (Scotland) Act 1832 contains similar provisions to the following in respect of daytime offences.

Under Section 36 where a poacher is found on any land during the day or night in search or pursuit of game and is in possession of *recently killed*[1] game, the following may demand that the game be immediately handed over and, if this demand is refused, it may be taken from the poacher by:

1 Anyone having the right to kill game on the land (the owner or holder of the game rights).
2 The occupier of the land, whether or not he has a right to kill the game.
3 Any gamekeeper or servant employed by the above.
4 Anyone assisting or acting on behalf of any of the above.

Game recently killed can be seized, but there is no legal right to search a poacher.

Only game is mentioned as being capable of being seized, although in practice all game, including rabbits, in the possession of poachers is usually seized.[2]

[1] In Scotland, there is a power to seize game whether recently killed or not.
[2] Rabbits can be seized by the police.

It would be a matter for the magistrates to decide whether or not it was *recently killed* game, if this particular point was raised.

There is no legal right to search a poacher or his belongings. Only the police are empowered to search poachers in these circumstances. There is no power to seize ferrets.

Ownership of game which is seized under this section is vested in the person(s) who are entitled to the game on that land. Obviously the game seized would be valuable evidence and normally arrangements would be made by the police for its preservation and eventual production in court, if required.

There are no powers, other than those possessed by the police, for the seizure of articles other than game (e.g. nets, snares, guns etc.) apart from certain exceptions for appointed gamekeepers in England and Wales.[1]

POLICE POWERS: GAME LAWS (AMENDMENT) ACT
1960 – ENGLAND AND WALES

Under Section 4 of the Game Laws (Amendment) Act 1960, where a poacher is arrested by a person in the presence of a police officer for day or night poaching offences or is arrested by the police officer for such offences in accordance with the Police and Criminal Evidence Act 1984, he may search him and seize and detain any game or rabbits or any gun, part of a gun or cartridges or other ammunition or nets, traps, snares or other devices used for killing or taking game or rabbits found in his possession. *Game Laws (Amendment) Act 1960 Section 4*

The searching of offenders would be subject to the search procedure under the Police and Criminal Evidence Act 1984 and relevant guidance given in the codes of practice to the Act. The Act gives a police officer the power to seize anything which is evidence of an offence, if it is necessary to prevent its loss.

POLICE POWERS: COMMON LAW – SCOTLAND

Police in Scotland have a common law power to search persons apprehended for poaching offences in order to find any game or articles which may have been used to assist them

[1] See pages 46–7.

in the course of poaching. Any game or articles found may be
seized as productions (exhibits in court).

SPECIAL POWERS OF APPOINTED
GAMEKEEPERS

GAME ACT 1831 – ENGLAND AND WALES ONLY

Game Act 1831 Under Section 13 of the Game Act 1831, gamekeepers
Section 13 appointed in writing by certain nobility may seize dogs,[1]
nets, engines (e.g. snares) or other instruments used for the
killing or taking of game on the land to which their
appointment relates, from anyone *not possessing a licence to
kill game.* The power to appoint gamekeepers in this way is
restricted to:

Lord of a Manor
Lordship
Royalty
Any steward of the Crown, of a Manor, Lordship or Royalty.

In Wales, the Act extends the power to appoint gamekeepers to owners of land to the clear annual value of £500,
provided the lands are not within any manor. By permission
of the landowner, the gamekeeper's powers can be exercised
over lands which are not the property of the person
appointing.

Such appointments will only be valid if registered with the
Clerk of the Peace for the area. The term *Clerk of the Peace* is
no longer a title of office, but by Section 56 of the Courts Act
1971 the administrative functions of this office have now
been transferred to the Clerks of the Local Authorities.

Firearms
Firearms are not specifically included amongst the property
capable of being seized. Neither are they considered to fall
within the meaning of *other instruments.* It was thought in the
case of Daddle v Hickton (1868) that the legislation had
never intended this Section to include a gun because of the
serious consequences that may arise from gamekeepers
attempting to seize such dangerous weapons. There is no
power within poaching legislation expressly authorising
gamekeepers to seize firearms.

[1] Ferrets are not included.

Dogs

Dogs or equipment seized under this power may be taken for the use of the Lord or Steward. The Act gives the power to seize all dogs without distinction provided the conditions of the power to seize are met. The implication is that anything seized becomes the property of the Lord etc. and that he would then be able to use or dispose of the property as he thinks fit.

Deputies

Persons as described may also appoint or deputise others to have the powers of an appointed gamekeeper within their manor or estates.

Registers

The provisions under the Act for enhancing gamekeepers' powers by registering appointment have largely fallen into disuse. Many local authorities no longer maintain registers of gamekeepers and for those that still do they remain no more than archive material.

The powers vested in gamekeepers appointed under this Act could be useful in combating poaching, particularly in respect of the seizure of dogs now being used extensively for taking ground game. There would appear to be no reason why, provided the conditions as to title can be met, that such appointments could not still be registered with the respective Clerks of Councils, who on application would be obliged to set up a form of register.

POACHING OFFENCES BY
OCCUPIERS OF LAND

ENGLAND AND WALES

In some instances *occupiers* of land with no rights to the game *Game Act 1831* on that land do not come within the provisions of certain *Section 12* poaching offences, simply because the act of trespass is not committed. However, where the game rights are reserved to the exclusion of the occupier, an offence is committed if the occupier pursues, kills or takes any game or gives permission for someone else to do so without authority of the person holding the game rights. The person given permission would be trespassing and committing day or night poaching offences; the occupier would be guilty of an offence under Section 12 for giving them permission. This is a specific offence within the Act solely relating to the occupier either taking game or allowing others to do so. There are no powers of apprehension in respect of such occupiers in these circumstances and the power under Section 31 of the Game Act 1831 would appear not to apply. However, this power would be applicable in respect of any person whom the occupier had given permission to take game, since under Section 30 such a person cannot use the defence that he was not a trespasser by virtue of having been given permission by the occupier.

Section 12 makes such a defence void in these circumstances by stating that the owner or other person with the game rights will himself be deemed the *legal occupier*, therefore making it impossible for the actual occupier to give such authority on the land.

Owner/occupier

An owner actually occupying the land who infringes a shooting tenant's rights by pursuing or taking game would commit the offence under Section 12, but a non-occupying owner who does so would only be liable to a civil action for breach of contract. Any person granted exclusive sporting rights has a right of action in the civil courts against anyone whose acts interfere with his enjoyment of them (Nicholls v Eley Sugarbeet Factory 1931).

CHAPTER 5

Prevention of Poaching

POACHING LEGISLATION DOES not include an effective prevent-ative law capable of dealing with the situation of a person *going equipped* to poach. The Poaching Prevention Act 1862 (see below pages 51–4) concerns only those suspected of *having been poaching* and restricts all powers to the police. If a poacher is stopped on a road or highway en route for a poaching expedition and equipped for such purposes, there is little positive action that can be taken against him.

ENGLAND AND WALES:
JUSTICE OF THE PEACE ACT 1361

Such is the inadequacy of specific preventative legislation that recently successful use of the law to prevent poaching has been made in England under the Justice of the Peace Act 1361 in conjunction with the Magistrates Courts Act 1980.

COURT ACTION BY WAY OF COMPLAINT

The Act creates grounds for complaint against a person's future conduct whereby a breach of the peace may be occasioned. It is based on an action of civil complaint in which details of a person's past conduct may be cited, including any previous convictions. The magistrates are invited to make an order on the grounds that a person's future activities need to be restrained for the public good; provided, of course, that they accept the person in question is likely to commit an offence in the future.

Magistrates have the power under Section 115 of the Magistrates' Courts Act 1980 to require the person to enter into a recognizance (a bond), with or without sureties, to keep the peace or to be of good behaviour or both. Such measures are seen as precautionary to prevent future poaching rather than a means of punishment for previous acts. The magistrates only have the power to bind over the defendant, not to fine or imprison. In the punitive sense therefore, nothing actually happens to the poacher on his first appearance before the court. Should he resume his poaching activities, he would be in breach of the binding-over order and risks being taken back to court and forfeiture of the money held as surety or even imprisonment. There are no powers of arrest or seizure under the Act.

THE DORSET CASE: R v BOND (1984)

A recent case in Dorset illustrates the measure of circumstantial evidence necessary before the Justice of the Peace Act 1361 can be used successfully.

By 1983 lamping for deer at night had become one of the commonest forms of poaching in Dorset, particularly during the winter months. It was occurring over a wide area and on a large scale, and was relatively well organised. Police and gamekeepers were powerless, unless they could actually catch the poachers in the act or in possession of deer carcases. In January 1984 some of the poachers were found in possession of a number of carcases. Further enquiries were made and, in addition to charges under the Deer Acts, proceedings by way of complaint were also preferred under the Justice of the Peace Act. On five separate occasions the defendants had been checked by the police in the early hours of the morning on what were suspected to be journeys to or from poaching expeditions. On four out of the five occasions, large lurcher-type dogs were seen in the defendants' car and on one occasion a search revealed lamping equipment. The magistrates were sufficiently convinced, having heard all the circumstances, that the defendants could well continue their poaching activities and consequently orders were made binding over the defendants in the sum of £200 to keep the peace and be of good behaviour for a period of two years. One defendant refused to consent to be bound over and subsequently appealed to the Crown Court. However, this appeal was later abandoned.

This case emphasises the need for efficient gathering of intelligence concerning the movements of poachers, their associates and activities if the Justice of the Peace Act is to be used successfully.

POACHING PREVENTION ACT 1862

The Poaching Prevention Act 1862 gives powers to the police for whom it is an important and useful means of detecting poaching offences. It was amended by the Game Laws (Amendment) Act 1960 to extend the list of articles capable of being seized in certain circumstances.

DEFINITION OF GAME

Section 1 defines game as hares, pheasants, partridges, eggs *Poaching* of pheasants and partridges, woodcock, snipe, rabbits, *Prevention Act* grouse, black or moor game and eggs of grouse, black or *1862 Section 1* moor game.

POWERS TO STOP AND SEARCH

Under Section 2, a police officer may stop and search any *Section 2* person or vehicle in any highway, street or public place, if the officer has reasonable cause to suspect him of coming from land, having been unlawfully in search of game.

Recent legislation that refers to the term *public place* generally includes anywhere to which the public have access, whether on payment or otherwise; but under the 1862 Act the term has been construed to cover only places in which police officers would be in the ordinary performance of their duties: for example, a public house to which poachers had been followed has been held not to be a public place within the meaning of the Act.

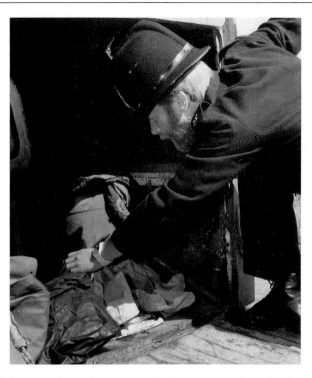

A police officer
exercising his power
to search in a public
place.

Although there is no restriction to search, whether it be
day or night time, the power does not extend to a person
suspected of *going* poaching.

In the case of Hall v Robinson (1889), the view that a
constable who actually sees a man poaching can no longer
suspect him of poaching was held to be wrong and it is now
clear that a person may still be suspected even though he has
actually been seen by the officer on the land. The poacher
who runs away does not evade any subsequent search,
provided he is followed and brought back to the highway.

POACHING OFFENCES

Section 2 Anyone found with game unlawfully obtained, or any gun,
part of a gun, cartridges or other ammunition, nets, traps,
snares or any other device of a kind used for the killing or
taking of game, commits one or more of the following
offences:

1 Obtaining game unlawfully by trespass. (If found on the
highway and subsequent search reveals possession of game
either on the poacher or in his vehicle.)

2 Using a gun, net, etc, for unlawfully killing or taking game.

3 Aiding or abetting a poacher to commit either of the above offences.

It is not necessary to prove that game has actually been taken nor is it necessary to prove, by direct evidence, either the specific land where poaching has taken place or, in the case where game is found, the unlawful means used to take it. The prosecution must satisfy the court by either direct or circumstantial evidence and not merely speculation that the defendant has been poaching.

Defence
It is a good defence for the defendant to prove that he had a bona fide belief that he had permission to go on the land together with reasonable grounds for that belief (Dickinson v Ead 1914).

ENFORCEMENT

The Act does not include a power of arrest even when game or gun is found following a search. However, in England and Wales a police officer may now exercise his general power of arrest under the Police and Criminal Evidence Act 1984, should this apply. In Scotland, the police may use their common-law power of arrest if applicable (e.g. if the poacher gives a false name).

The officer may seize any game, gun, part of a gun, any ammunition, nets, traps, snares or any other device used for killing or taking game. There is no power to seize dogs or ferrets, although a police officer may now seize *anything*, if he has reasonable grounds to believe it is evidence of an offence, providing it is necessary to prevent its loss or concealment (Section 19, Police and Criminal Evidence Act 1984).

On conviction of an offence under Section 2, the court has the discretion to direct that any game, gun or other article seized be forfeited.

PRESERVATION OF EVIDENCE

Since in 1862 the evidence could not be preserved for any *Section 2* length of time without deteriorating, provision was made in the Act for a written order to be obtained from a Justice of the Peace authorising sale of the game prior to any court proceedings. The police would not be liable for selling the game should the case not be proved, but the value of the game must be restored to the person from whom it was seized. Now game seized is usually kept in a deep freeze to be produced in court.

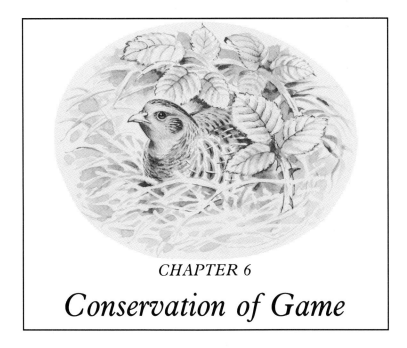

CHAPTER 6

Conservation of Game

RESTRICTIONS ON KILLING AND TAKING GAME IN ENGLAND AND WALES

UNDER THE GAME Act 1831, as amended by the Game Act 1970, game means hares, pheasants, partridges, grouse, heath or moor game and black game. As Lord Coleridge said in the case of Cooke v Trevener (1911), 'In Section 2 game must mean game of all kinds, wild or tame, dead or alive.' *Game Act 1831 (amended 1970) Section 2*

CLOSE TIMES, DAYS AND SEASONS

Night
Under the Hares Act 1848, it is an offence for anyone to use any firearm or gun of any description at night for the purpose of killing game. This is an additional offence to night poaching where game has been shot during the night, which begins one hour after sunset to one hour before sunrise. This prohibition does not apply to occupiers and persons authorised under the Ground Game Act 1880.[1] *Hares Act 1848 Section 5*

---

[1] See page 24.

Sunday and Christmas Day

Game Act 1831 It is an offence for any person to kill or take any game or use
Section 3 any dog, gun, net or other engine or instrument for the
purpose of killing or taking any game on a Sunday or
Christmas Day.

Where someone does not take or kill game, but nevertheless
uses for that purpose any of the articles described above, the
offence would be complete (e.g. an unsuccessful shot at a
bird or an attempt to take a hare by the use of a lurcher).

A snare has been held to fall within the meaning of *engine*
(Allen v Thompson 1870). In this particular case, the
defendant was convicted of the offence of taking game on a
Sunday by using snares which were found set on land on a
Sunday, two of which contained dead grouse. There was no
evidence that the defendant had been on the land on the
Sunday in question, the snares having been set the previous
day.

Where a gang are found taking game and one of them is
using a gun, all may be treated as using the gun (R v
Littlechild 1871).

Close seasons
It is an offence to kill or take any of the game listed below
between the dates shown:

GAME	CLOSE SEASONS
Partridges	1 February – 1 September
Pheasants	1 February – 1 October
Grouse	10 December – 12 August
Black game	10 December – 20 August[1]

Exceptions to close days and seasons
There are circumstances whereby the Minister of Agriculture
and Fisheries may authorise, by the issue of a Pest Control
Notice under Section 98 Agriculture Act 1947, the killing of
game which would otherwise be in contravention of the
above restrictions under Section 3 of the Game Act 1831.[2]

[1] Except in Somerset, Devon and the New Forest in Southampton when the
close season extends from 10 December to 1 September.
[2] See page 66 regarding the taking of birds for breeding, sale alive and exhibition.

Rabbits and hares
There is no close season for rabbits or prohibited times of taking under any legislation with the exception of the provisions of the Ground Game Acts 1880 and 1906 relating to the taking of rabbits and hares on moorlands and unenclosed lands.[1] Apart from this exception, there is also no close season for hares, but they are included in the definition of game and are therefore protected on Sundays and Christmas Days and by the provisions relating to the requirements for game licences.[2] There is also a restriction on the sale of hares at certain times of the year.[3]

RESTRICTIONS ON KILLING AND TAKING GAME IN SCOTLAND

CLOSE TIMES, DAYS AND SEASONS
Night shooting
The shooting of game or hares at night with any firearm is prohibited by Section 47 of the Hares (Scotland) Act 1848. This prohibition does not apply to occupiers and persons authorised under the provisions of the Ground Game Act 1880.[4]

Hares (Scotland) Act 1848

Sunday and Christmas Day
There are no statutory restrictions in Scotland, as in England and Wales, on the killing of game on Sundays during the open season and on Christmas Day. However, it is not customary to do so; when the 'Glorious Twelfth' falls on a Sunday, shooting in earnest does not begin until the following day. There is an unwritten law in Scotland that shooting on Sunday should only take place after noon in order to prevent the disturbance of church services.

Close seasons
It is an offence for any person to wilfully take, kill, destroy, carry, sell, buy or have in his or her possession any of the game listed between the dates given in the table (see overleaf):

Game (Scotland) Act 1772

[1] See page 27.
[2] See page 59.
[3] See page 58.
[4] See page 24.

GAME	CLOSE SEASONS
Partridges	1 February – 1 September
Pheasants	1 February – 1 October
Muirfowl (grouse) and Ptarmigan	10 December – 12 August
Heathfowl (black game)	10 December – 20 August

Exceptions

The provisions do not apply to pheasants or partridges caught up in the seasons allowed by the Act and then kept during the close season in any mew or breeding place. Parts of the Game Act 1831 relating to dealing in game also extend to Scotland and at certain times of the year it may be an offence to kill game but not to possess, buy or sell it.[1]

Agriculture (Scotland) Act 1948 Section 39   There are circumstances whereby the Agricultural Executive Committee can require steps to be taken to kill or destroy game during the close season under Section 39 of the Agriculture (Scotland) Act 1948. These provisions are similar to those in respect of pest control in England and Wales.

Rabbits and hares

There are no restrictions on the taking of rabbits or hares in Scotland, except on moorland and unenclosed land as restricted by the Ground Game Acts 1880 and 1906.[2]

RESTRICTIONS ON THE SALE OF HARES: HARES PRESERVATION ACT 1892

Hares Preservation Act 1892 Section 2 & 3   The Hares Preservation Act 1892 makes provision for the protection of hares during the breeding season. It applies to England, Wales and Scotland.

Under Sections 2 and 3, it is an offence to sell or expose for sale any hare or leveret between the months of March and July inclusive, but this does not apply to imported foreign hares.

[1] See pages 66–7.
[2] See page 27.

PROTECTION OF OTHER GAME

The species generally included as game in some Acts –
capercaillie, woodcock and common snipe – are protected by
the Wildlife and Countryside Act 1981 (Schedule 2 Part I).
Capercaillie were not included in the original definition of
game as they were not re-introduced until the late nineteenth
century.

GAME	CLOSE SEASONS
Capercaillie and (except in Scotland) woodcock	1 February – 30 September
Woodcock in Scotland	1 February – 31 August
Common snipe	1 February – 11 August

GAME LICENCES

The current legislation dealing with game licences dates back
to the nineteenth century. Both the Game Act 1831, which
applies in England and Wales only, and the Game Licences
Act 1860, which applies also to Scotland, deal with similar
offences concerning the taking of game without the appropriate licence. This duplication gives rise to some confusion;
although a person may be proceeded against for the same
offence under both Acts and be subject to separate penalties,
generally proceedings are only taken under one Act and the
one which best suits the circumstances of the case.

Game certificates and *licences to kill game* are synonymous in
meaning.

GAME ACT 1831: ENGLAND AND WALES

It is an offence for anyone to kill or take any game or use any *Game Act 1831*
dog, gun, net or other engine or instrument for the purpose *Section 23*
of searching for or killing or taking game without a game
certificate.

Game means hares, pheasants, partridges, grouse, heath or *Section 2*
moor game and black game. Rabbits are not included in this
definition.

GAME LICENCES ACT 1860:
ENGLAND, WALES AND SCOTLAND

Game Licences Act 1860 Section 4 It is an offence for anyone to take, kill or pursue, or assist in doing so, by any means whatsoever or use any dog, gun, net or other engine for the purpose of taking, killing or pursuing any game, woodcock, snipe, rabbit or deer, without an appropriate licence.

The Act does not define game, but would include hares which are generally treated as game, as well as capercaillie in Scotland.

The offence under the 1831 Act is wider in scope, since it includes the mere searching for game. However, the 1860 Act also includes persons assisting offenders.

A trespasser, with a gun and dog, walking over land where there is game, may be held to be in the act of *searching* for game. He does not have to reach the stage of actually pointing a gun at game although this would obviously be good evidence of the offence. The word *engine* has been held to include a snare (Allen v Thompson 1870).

Where game is found in the possession of a person who claims innocent acquisition, the onus of proof is upon him to show that this is, in fact, the case.

PERSONS EXEMPT

A game licence is not required by:

Game Licences Act 1860
1 Member of the Royal Family
2 Gamekeeper of Crown lands
3 Holder of a gamekeeper's licence on land where his employer has a right to kill game
4 Anyone assisting the holder of a game licence to take or kill game (including rabbits) provided he is in his company.

The last category exempts beaters and loaders from the necessity of holding a licence. Loaders must not carry a gun of their own or shoot their employer's gun. The certificate holder must be using his own dog, gun, or other equipment for the purpose of taking game; it is doubtful whether a beater using his own dog would be within this exemption. Anyone assisting a gamekeeper and holding his position by deputation or appointment and not possessing a licence to kill game in his own right would not be exempt under this section.

EXEMPTIONS FOR TAKING RABBITS AND HARES

A game licence is not required:

1 By occupiers of land or persons *authorised* by them under   *Ground Game Act*
the provisions of the Ground Game Act 1880[1] to take or   *1880 Section 4*
kill rabbits and hares.

2 By the proprietor of any warren or of any enclosed   *Game Licences Act*
ground or by the tenant of lands (enclosed[2] or not) either   *1860 Section 5*
by himself or by his permission to take or destroy
rabbits.

This exemption effectively means anyone not having the
appropriate authority to be on the land from either the
owner of the land or of the shooting rights or the tenant
needs a game licence to pursue or take rabbits. Poachers
committing day or night poaching offences in which
rabbits are either pursued or taken commit this offence if
they are unable to produce game licences.

3 By those pursuing and killing hares by coursing with   *Game Licences*
greyhounds or by hunting with beagles or other hounds.   *Act 1860*
(A spaniel in certain circumstances may be with the   *Section 5*
hounds.) (This exemption is also contained in Section 4 of   *Hares Act 1848*
the Hares Act (England and Wales) 1848.) The use of the   *(England &*
word *coursing* is quite wide and is not confined to organised   *Wales)*
coursing events. It has been held to include any hunting of   *Section 4*
hares with greyhounds (Dolby v Halmshaw 1848).

4 By the person in actual occupation of enclosed lands, the   *Hares Act 1848*
owner of enclosed lands having the right to kill game, any   *(England &*
person directed or authorised in writing by either of the   *Wales) and Hares*
above to take, kill or destroy hares.   *(Scotland) Act*
Section 2 of the Hares Act 1848 (England and Wales)   *1848*
limits the exemption for persons directed or authorised to   *Section 1*
only one at any one time in a particular parish. There
would appear to be no similar restrictions in Scotland. The
authority must be in writing and registered with the
Magistrates' Clerk for the area concerned. This exemption
has been largely superseded by the provisions of the
Ground Game Act 1880, but it does benefit those for
whom game rights are not derived from occupations of the
land. (Attempts to register with the Magistrates' Clerk
may be met with confusion as this procedure has fallen
into disuse.)

[1] See page 24.
[2] See page 62.

LICENCE EXEMPTIONS FOR TAKING DEER

Game Licences Act 1860 Section 5 A game licence is not required for the pursuing and killing of deer by hunting with hounds (legal in England and Wales only), or the taking and killing of deer in inclosed lands[1] by the owner or occupier of such lands or by those under his direction or with his permission.

TYPES OF GAME LICENCE

There are four types of game licence, each catering for different periods of the year taking into account the open seasons for various game birds. They are colour coded and obtainable at Crown Post Offices. The date and time of issue will be shown on the licence, which will only be valid from that particular time. The licence will, however, expire at midnight of the day on which it is stated to expire. The holder's full name and address and the amount of duty paid must also be shown on the licence.

Not all licences are readily available from stock and there may be a delay in issue, particularly in respect of the occasional licence.

DURATION	COLOUR	PURPOSE
Taken out after 31 July and expiry 31 July following year	Red	For all year sportsmen, embracing all open seasons for game birds and shooting of hares where not exempt
Taken out after 31 July and expiry 31 October same year	Green	Popular for grouse shooters
Taken out after 31 October and expiry 31 July following year	Blue	Popular for pheasant shooters
Occasional licence for any continuous period of 14 days	Black	Occasional shoot only where game is perhaps shot on one occasion only during the year

[1] *Inclosed lands* means land used for farming and enclosed by normal agricultural hedges in contrast to moorland where deer roam free. A game licence is not required where deer are shot on enclosed land with the owner's permission, but run and drop on land where the shooter does not have permission (Jemmison v Priddle 1972).

If any person, having obtained a licence to kill game, is *Game Licences Act* convicted of any offence of day poaching under Section 30 of *1860 Section 7* the Game Act 1831 or under the Game (Scotland) Act 1832, the licence immediately becomes null and void.

GAMEKEEPER'S LICENCE

A gamekeeper's employer may obtain an annual licence (at a *Game Licences Act* lower cost than the twelve-month licence above) which will *1860 Section 7* authorise the gamekeeper to take or kill game on land where his employer has the right to take game. The licence is transferable on the appointment of a new gamekeeper, should the licence still be in force, and is only valid in respect of such a person whilst he remains employed as a gamekeeper. If a gamekeeper wishes to shoot game on another's land, where his employer does not have the game rights, then the gamekeeper must take out a game licence in his own name.

POWERS TO DEMAND PRODUCTION OF A GAME LICENCE

The following may require the production of a game licence *Game Licences Act* from anyone engaged in an activity for which a game licence *1860 Section 10* is required:

1 Police officer authorised by a District Council
2 Officer of the Inland Revenue
3 Gamekeeper of land where the person is found
4 Lord of a Manor
5 Holder of a game licence
6 Owner, landlord, lessee or occupier of land where the person is found

Anyone required to produce his licence by any of the above must produce the licence and allow it to be read and copied if necessary. If he is unable to produce a licence, he is obliged to give his full name and address and state the place where the licence was taken out. If he refuses or gives false details he commits an offence, but there are no powers of arrest in these circumstances, except for the police, who may use their general power of arrest under the Police and Criminal Evidence Act 1984.

USE OF POISON AND DESTRUCTION OF EGGS

ENGLAND AND WALES

Game Act 1831 It is an offence for anyone without the appropriate authority
Section 24 to wilfully take out of the nest, or destroy in the nest, the
eggs of any game bird. There is no general power to seize
such eggs unlawfully taken, although the police may seize
them as evidence of an offence under the Police and Criminal
Evidence Act 1984.

ENGLAND, WALES AND SCOTLAND

Game Act 1831 It is an offence for anyone, with intent to destroy or injure
Section 3 game, to put or cause to be put at any time any poison or
Hares (Scotland) poisonous ingredient on any ground where game usually
Act 1848 resort or on any highway.
Section 4   Section 4 of the Hares (Scotland) Act 1848 creates an
identical offence specifically including hares as well as game.

DEALING IN GAME

One method of preserving game is to restrict free trade by
licensing people who wish to deal in it. In this way illegally
taken birds should not, in theory, enter the market, although
keepers know that there is always a ready customer for the
poacher's bag.

Game dealers need to
be licensed.

The Game Act 1831 requires dealers to be licensed in England; section 13 of the Game Licences Act 1860 extends the provisions relating to the sale of game to Wales and Scotland. The sale of venison is covered by separate legislation under the Deer Act 1980 (England and Wales) and the Deer (Scotland) Act 1959.

GAME DEALER'S LICENCE –
ENGLAND, WALES AND SCOTLAND

Two licences – a local authority licence and an excise licence – are required to trade in game (hares, pheasants, partridges, grouse, heath or moor game, black game or bustards and including imported game). A licence is not needed for conies (rabbits), woodcock, snipe, quail and landrail (corncrake). However, the sale of woodcock and snipe is restricted by the Wildlife and Countryside Act 1981 and quail and corncrake are protected species under the same Act.[1]

COUNCIL LICENCE

A local authority licence may be granted to a householder, *Game Act 1831* shop or stall-keeper, but not to an innkeeper, victualler or *Section 18 &* beer retailer. Section 18 also excludes those employed on *Game Licences* mail and stage coaches or public transport and carriers and *Act 1860* higglers. In modern terms it means that postmen, bus and *Section 13* lorry drivers cannot obtain a licence, but it is doubtful whether this would be enforced.

There may be no fee payable, as local authorities are often content to register dealers for public health purposes. Enquiries at council offices can lead to confusion at first, as applicants are often directed to the department that issues licences for gaming machines in public houses.

EXCISE LICENCE

An excise licence is obtainable from a post office; it is a *Custom & Excise* condition of issue that a council licence be produced at the *Management Act,* time of application. The council licence will specify the *1979 & Game* business premises: an excise licence is required for each one. *Licences Act 1860* Partnerships and companies require one licence per premise. *Section 15*

---

[1] See page 134–5.

Both licences expire on 31 July each year. The excise licence must be renewed; the council may not require renewal of their licence, but this should be checked on initial application.

DEALER'S SIGN

Game Act 1831 Once licensed, the holder must exhibit a sign outside his
Section 18 premises with his name and the words *Licensed to Deal in Game*.

PROHIBITED PERIODS

Game Act 1831 Game birds cannot be bought by or sold to any person ten
Section 4 days after the start of the close season for such birds. The
& Game Act prohibition includes live, dead, tame and wild birds. In spite
1970 of an appeal, a well-known department store was found guilty of offering for sale frozen pheasant during the prohibited period.

POSSESSION

Prior to the Game Act 1970, it was also an offence to *possess* game in the prohibited period; but the advent of freezers made this impractical and the restrictions on possession were removed. It would, therefore, be lawful for a dealer or other person to freeze birds obtained outside the prohibited period (or imported birds subject to import controls) which may then be sold during the following open season. Properly kept records would substantiate purchases outside the prohibited periods.

EXHIBITION AND BREEDING

Game Act 1831 It was also recognised that birds are kept for rearing, exhibition or sale alive: therefore anyone can buy live birds for these purposes at any time from a game dealer. However, anyone who keeps birds for breeding, etc., must obtain a game licence to sell them and the sale must be to a dealer.

The prohibited periods under the Game Act 1831 originally applied to England only, but in 1860 were extended to the United Kingdom. Scottish legislation created close seasons for the killing, taking and sale of game in Scotland, which differ from those in England, and these were unaffected by the Game Licences Act 1860. The extension of the Game Act 1831 to Scotland, in respect of game dealing, means that at certain times of the year in Scotland it may be an offence to kill game, but not to possess, buy or sell it. So far as the sale of game in Scotland is concerned, the close season is the same as throughout the rest of United Kingdom under the Game Act 1831.

SPENT HENS

There is a practice among some game dealers of buying up pheasants, which have been kept for egg production, at the end of the breeding season, when end-of-lay birds can be bought very cheaply; they are then killed, frozen and sold to the public after 1 October in the following open season. Sales in season are not illegal, but must be considered deceitful if the customer is expecting to buy a bird killed in that season.

Section 3 of the Game Act 1831 creates an offence of killing or taking game during the close seasons.[1] It may be supposed that in 1831 the killing of spent hens was not considered by the legislators; but if Section 3 is strictly construed, as it has been in respect of killing on Sunday and Christmas Day, the killing of spent hens outside the open season is an offence. *Game Act 1831 Section 3*

Under Section 4, the buyer and seller of birds for such a purpose would both commit offences, as transactions are only legal in respect of live birds for rearing or exhibition purposes or sale alive. This exception was introduced into the 1831 Act by the Game Act 1970, the only purpose of which was to permit *sales* for rearing and exhibition and the *possession* of live game for breeding and dead game killed in a previous season. The National Association of Game Dealers has approached Parliament to allow the sale of dead birds out of season, but even though the government has had the opportunity to insert sections in several relevant Acts, it has not done so. It may be felt that to permit such sales would open the floodgates to poachers and disreputable dealers, leading to a severe reduction in the game population. *Section 4*

---

[1] See page 56.

WHO MAY SELL AND TO WHOM

Game Act 1831 Under the Game Act 1831, a licensed game dealer may only buy game from:

Section 28 1 Another game dealer

Section 28 2 Holder of a *full* game licence

Section 17 3 Licensed gamekeeper (with the written authority of his employer, if the game is taken on his land; if taken off the land, a full game licence is required).

4 A person authorised by a magistrate to dispose of game forfeited under the Poaching Prevention Act 1862.

A licensed game dealer may also buy hares from the occupier of land, or persons authorised by him, who have taken them under the Ground Game Act 1880, as amended.[1]

Section 25 An unlicensed person may not sell any game, live, frozen or otherwise, even to a licensed dealer; a game-licence holder may only sell to a dealer, who must establish that the vendor is legally able to sell the game before purchasing. One exception to this rule is the innkeeper selling game for consumption on the premises, but it must have been

Section 26 purchased from a licensed dealer and would not include game killed or taken by himself. The term *innkeeper* would not include a store with a licence to sell alcohol.

Section 27 No one may buy or obtain game from another unless the vendor is a licensed dealer.

DEALING IN WILDFOWL

Wildfowl are not classified as game and trading is not controlled in England, Scotland or Wales by the Game Laws. However, the Wildlife and Countryside Act 1981 restricts sale by persons not registered with the Department of the Environment (D.O.E) to Schedule 3 Part II and III pest and sporting species only. Geese are not contained in Schedule 3 and consequently cannot be sold under any circumstances, even where protected geese are shot under licence.[2]

---

[1] The owner who does not occupy the land but retains the sporting rights and the shooting tenant may only sell hares to a dealer if holders of a full game licence.

[2] See page 113.

VENISON

The 1980 Deer Act restricts the sale of venison in England and Wales to licensed game dealers only. In Scotland licensed game dealers may only trade in game: trade in venison is subject to a separate licensing procedure.

SALE AND PURCHASE: ENGLAND AND WALES

It is an offence for anyone other than a licensed game dealer to sell, offer or expose for sale or possess for sale any venison during the prohibited period. The prohibited period in relation to venison from a species protected by a close season (i.e. red, fallow, roe and sika) begins ten days after the start of the close season. Therefore, a stalker may only sell or possess venison for sale during the open season and the first ten days of the relevant close season. Dealers may possess and sell during the prohibited period. *Deer Act 1980 Section 2 (1) (a)*

It is an offence for anyone other than a dealer to sell, offer or expose for sale venison at any time unless the sale is to a licensed game dealer. *Section 2 (1) (b)*

It is also an offence for anyone to sell, possess for sale, purchase or receive venison from any deer which he knows or believes has been illegally taken or killed under Section 1 Deer Act 1980 (poaching) or any provision of the 1963 Deer Act (close season or unlawful methods). *Section 2 (2) (a)*

SALE OUT OF SEASON

The Deer Act 1963 exempts the killing of deer out of season by occupiers of land to prevent crop damage.[1] But there is no provision for deer killed legally out of season to be sold by the occupier to a dealer. Section 2 (1) (a) of the 1980 Deer Act allows dealers to sell and possess venison during the close season, but makes the sale of venison during the close season by non-dealers an offence. An occupier who finds it necessary to cull deer in the close season, or a deer farmer, must either consume the venison or give it away; if he wishes to sell it, he must become a licensed game dealer, which then removes the restriction imposed by Section 2 (1) (a), but he must then comply with the conditions in respect of dealer's signs, keeping and inspection of records etc. *Deer Act 1963* *Deer Act 1980 Section 2 (1) (a)*

[1] See page 165.

Deer Act 1980   The term *deer* means any species and includes the carcase
Section 8 or part of it; *venison* means the carcase, or any edible part of
the carcase, including imported meat, but not canned or
cooked venison, allowing hotels and restaurants to include
venison on the menu. The reference to cooked meat
obviously follows the exception in the Game Act 1831 which
permits an innkeeper to sell game for consumption on his
premises, but the Deer Act 1980 is far wider in its scope in
that any person could sell cooked or canned venison which he
had obtained lawfully.

RECORDS

Deer Act 1980 A licensed dealer must keep records in a book in the format
Section 3 shown in Schedule 1 to the Act.

A council official or police officer may inspect the records,
venison in premises, vehicles, invoices and other documents
which relate to the records. The book must be retained for
three years from the last entry and other documents for three
years from the date of the entry relating to them.

It is an offence to fail to comply with Section 3, make false
entries or obstruct an official or police officer.

Transactions between English and Scottish dealers may be
made across the border, provided that they are recorded on
the prescribed forms and that both parties are licensed in
their own countries.

SCOTLAND

Anyone wishing to trade in venison is required to be licensed
by Part IIIA Deer (Scotland) Act 1959 (as amended by the
Deer (Amendment) (Scotland) Act 1982) and the Licensing
of Venison Dealers (Scotland) Orders 1984.

The main difference between England and Scotland is that
licensed game dealers in England, where the issue of a licence
is a mere formality, may deal in both game and venison;
whereas in Scotland a quite separate licence is required for
the venison dealer, who must first go through a vetting
procedure.

The licensing authority in Scotland is an Island or District
Council and may grant a licence, valid for three years, to
anyone it considers fit to deal in venison.

The application can be made by an individual or by his

agent involved in the day-to-day running of the business, perhaps the manager of one of his premises. Full names and addresses of the applicants are required. If the applicant is a company, details of the registered office, directors, partners, etc. are also needed. In both cases, the address of any premises used for handling venison within the area of the authority must be included, together with any other information which may be additionally required by the authority.

Copies of an application for grant or renewal are sent to the local Chief Constable, fire authority and the Red Deer Commission. The authority may then make enquiries as to the suitability of the applicant and may take the results into account when considering the application; but where they intend to do so, the applicant must be notified and given the opportunity to reply.

The authority may refuse an application, but must give reasons for so doing. If a licence is granted, it may be unconditional or subject to reasonable conditions which may include the inspection of venison. Where a licence is not granted or renewed, the applicant may appeal to the Sheriff; but there does not appear to be any form of appeal in respect of conditions.

RECORDS

The orders also prescribe the format of records to be kept (which are roughly similar to the English format) and they must be in a book. This prevents the use of loose sheets which may be altered and replaced.

Venison, invoices, receipts, consignment notes and other documents may be inspected by a police officer or a person authorised in writing by the Secretary of State or the Red Deer Commission in order to verify any entry made in the book.

The book shall be kept for three years from the last entry and documents for three years from the date of the entry to which they refer.

OFFENCES

Section 25D of the Deer (Scotland) Act 1959 contains a number of offences in venison dealing:

Deer (Scotland) It is an offence to sell, offer for sale, possess or transport for
Act 1959 the purpose of sale any venison unless one is (*i*) a licensed
Section 25D (1) venison dealer or (*ii*) in possession or transporting for the
purpose of selling to such a dealer (e.g. one is a stalker or
landowner) or (*iii*) one has purchased the venison from a
licensed dealer.

Section 25F Venison is defined as the carcase or any edible part of the
carcase of a deer. Unlike English legislation, canned and
cooked venison come within the Scottish definition, but (*iii*)
above permits the hotelier to serve venison to his customers if
purchased from a venison dealer.

It would appear that in (*iii*) any unlicensed person, a
butcher for example, may sell or possess any venison if
purchased from a licensed venison dealer, unlike the English
situation where only licensed game dealers may sell venison
to unlicensed persons.

In contrast with the Deer Act 1980, in Scotland the
transaction is not related to a *prohibited period*, the only
provision being that the deer was lawfully killed.

Section 25D (3) It is an offence to sell, offer for sale, possess for sale,
transport for sale, purchase or receive any carcase which one
knows or believes was unlawfully killed.

Section 25D (5) Any licensed venison dealer failing to keep records or
making false entries commits an offence.

Section 25D (6) Anyone obstructing the inspection of such records commits
an offence.

DISQUALIFIED FROM HOLDING LICENCE

Section 25D (7) Anyone convicted of an offence under Part III (illegal taking
of deer) or IIIA (licensing procedures) may be disqualified by
the court from holding a venison dealer's licence.

CHAPTER 7

Protection of Game

IN THE PAST summary justice, meted out by gamekeeper on poacher, was common. Today the average poacher is now far more aware of his civil rights and, should he receive injuries inflicted by a gamekeeper that are incompatible with the circumstances, there is every likelihood of a subsequent complaint of assault which the police would be obliged to investigate.

USE OF REASONABLE FORCE

Anyone may use such force as is reasonable in the circumstances in the prevention of crime, *or in effecting or assisting in the lawful arrest of offenders or suspected offenders*[1] or of persons unlawfully at large.

When physical restraint of poachers is necessary, only the use of reasonable force will be justified. If this is in dispute, it will be a matter for the magistrates to decide whether the force used was both reasonable and necessary in the circumstances prevailing. The use of force when dealing with trespassers can be said to relate equally to all circumstances

[1] Section 3 (1) Criminal Law Act 1967. This Act does not apply in Scotland, but the Common Law would support this principle.

where poachers are apprehended.[1] It is, of course, impossible to lay down strict guidelines regarding the amount of force which may be used; but it is the responsibility of the individual concerned to exercise his power and use of force within the law. Should his actions be subject to subsequent complaint, then he would have to show that the force used was both reasonable and no more than absolutely necessary in the circumstances. Such force may be considerable if necessary to counter severe aggression or acts likely to endanger life.

Where complaint is made by poachers against gamekeepers or others acting in a similar capacity, loyalties of the police will always be subject to scrutiny. The police must be seen to conduct a fair and unbiased investigation and accurate reporting of the facts must take place.

The risks to personal safety that gamekeepers are continually exposed to are not to be underestimated and generally the police are able to give full support and assistance in the investigation of poaching offences.

USE OF DOGS

The use of dogs by gamekeepers as an aid to enforcement of their powers or merely for self-protection has become increasingly popular. Many keepers now find kennel-room for alsatians and rottweilers – breeds noted for their courage and adaptability as guard dogs. However, unless these dogs are specifically used to protect premises, or property on premises, they do not come within the scope of the legislation controlling the use of guard dogs.[2] Such legislation does, nevertheless, underline the growing concern for public safety aroused by many incidents involving injury caused by dangerous dogs not kept under proper control.

Careful use of dogs when tackling poachers can no doubt be an asset, but the liabilities involved should be fully appreciated. A dog which attacks a person may be shot in self defence; should a poacher kill or injure a keeper's dog in these circumstances, then any claim for compensation by the

[1] See further pages 6 and 11.
[2] See page 221.

Dogs are increasingly used by gamekeepers.

keeper would be difficult to obtain, albeit the poacher may have been engaged in the unlawful pursuit of game.

Should the dog injure the poacher, it would then depend on the circumstances of the case whether any liability, civil or otherwise, would be incurred by the person in charge of the dog. In the first instance, there may be sufficient grounds for complaint that the dog is dangerous and not kept under proper control. Generally speaking, poachers trespass at their peril and should they get accidentally bitten in the process, the court may take the view that the dog was only doing its job.

It is quite another matter where there is evidence to indicate that a person in charge of the dog in some way set or urged the dog to attack, worry or put another in fear. There may be grounds for claiming assault in these circumstances and should it occur in any street, road or place of public resort under the control of the local authority in England and Wales, then a specific offence is committed under Section 28 of the Town Police Clauses Act 1847. If the facts of a particular case are in dispute and the defence put forward is one of self-defence, then the magistrates must take into account whether the use of the dog was reasonable in the circumstances.

CITIZEN'S ARREST

A citizen's arrest, quoted by many but understood by few, relates to the powers that exist for private persons to make arrests both under Common Law and Statute Law.

COMMON LAW
England and Wales
The main powers of arrest under Common Law are for
breaches of the peace. Anyone may arrest without warrant
another person who in his presence commits or is about to
commit a breach of the peace, or to prevent an immediate
renewal of a breach of the peace.

It can be unwise to
approach or tackle
suspects on one's
own, especially at
night or in an isolated
locality. A poacher on
his own may have a
look-out elsewhere.

Scotland
A private individual may arrest when he actually sees
someone commit a common-law crime. Reasonable suspicion
or acting on information received would be insufficient
grounds for such an arrest. There is no power, as in England
and Wales, to arrest for a breach of the peace, although one
may intervene in an attempt to stop the crime.

STATUTE LAW
England and Wales
Under the Police and Criminal Evidence Act 1984:

Police & Criminal
Evidence Act 1984
Section 24 (4)

1 Any person may arrest without warrant anyone who is, or
whom he has reasonable grounds for suspecting to be, in
the act of committing an *arrestable offence*.

Section 24 (5)

2 Where an arrestable offence has been committed, any
person may arrest without warrant anyone who is, or
whom he has reasonable grounds for suspecting to be,
guilty of the offence.

As can be seen this power is quite wide and covers anyone merely suspected of having committed an arrestable offence, provided the person arresting has knowledge that such an offence has been committed.

It is obviously essential to know which offences are deemed *arrestable offences*. Most serious criminal offences fall into this category, including theft and criminal damage. One of the basic criteria for deeming an offence to be arrestable is the liability to imprisonment for five years or more on first conviction of that offence.

The effects of these provisions mean that if pheasants are stolen from an enclosed breeding pen,[1] a gamekeeper may legally arrest anyone actually taking the pheasants or anyone he suspects with reasonable cause to be guilty of stealing them (e.g. a person he sees running away from the pen or a person found in possession of the pheasants at a later time).

USE OF MODERN TECHNOLOGY

The use of sophisticated equipment to warn off or detect poachers is now a necessity on many shooting estates for the preservation and protection of game. Radio alarms have become increasingly popular, with some manufacturers specifically designing systems to detect poachers by the use of trip-switch mechanisms and infra-red beams. The use of high intensity binoculars, although expensive, are of great value in locating poachers at night.

Wooden falsehood.

During the last century many gamekeepers practised traditional forms of protecting game, some involving the risk of serious injury or death to the trespasser – for example mantraps and spring-guns. These were made illegal, although the threat of their use remained, as witnessed by the erection of certain notices which became known as *wooden falsehoods*

[1] See pages 18–20.

inferring that man-traps were set and that trespassers entered
at their peril. Other falsehoods, like the one below found on a
keeper's door, are evidence of past attitudes when penalties
for poaching were extremely severe.

A keeper's warning:
'Take notice that: as
from today's date
poachers shall be shot
on first sight and if
practicable questioned
afterwards. By order:
J.R. Bramble Head
Keeper to his Grace:
The Duke of Grumby
1st November 1868'.

CHAPTER 8
Firearms

THE FIRST FIREARMS Act was introduced in 1920, prior to which there was no effective control on the possession of firearms. For, although the Gun Licences Act 1870 required all persons, subject to certain exemptions, to hold a licence to use a gun of any description including air weapons, the Act did not apply to carrying or using a gun in a house or the area around it: a licence was not considered necessary if a householder only used the gun for the protection of his own home.

However, subsequent legislation has sought to control the use of certain firearms now considered too dangerous to be possessed without strict legal control and for the purposes of legislation firearms are divided into three classes: rifles and handguns, shotguns and air weapons.

RESPONSIBLE USE OF FIREARMS

The users of firearms, whether for sport or through their occupation, have the ultimate responsibility to ensure their safe-keeping, not only to prevent crime but to prevent weapons falling into the hands of the inexperienced.

Firearms should not be left where children may be tempted to play with them.

The law in many ways reflects concern regarding the safe custody of potentially lethal weapons by placing restrictions or conditions on sale, possession or use and, in some circumstances, by ensuring proper supervision of those under the age of seventeen.

It is in everyone's interest to safeguard firearms and abide by established codes of practice. The British Association for Shooting and Conservation encourage their members to adopt high standards of safety, sportsmanship and courtesy through their codes of practice, shotgun proficiency-award scheme and sporting rifle courses. The British Shooting Sports Council also urges all firearm owners to accept the principle of personal responsibility and has its own code of practice on the safe custody of weapons.

LEGISLATION FOR THE POSSESSION, CONTROL AND USE OF FIREARMS

The Firearms Act 1968 is the main statute governing the possession, control and use of firearms. The Firearms Rules 1969 prescribe the form of firearm and shotgun certificates and detail the conditions under which firearm certificates are held. The Firearms (Dangerous Air Weapons) Rules 1969 brings certain powerful air weapons into the scope of the Firearms Act 1968. The Firearms Act 1982 (introduced on 1

November 1983) enables the provisions of the 1968 Act to be applied to imitation weapons, subject to certain conditions.

DEFINITION OF FIREARM

For the law to be applied, a weapon must fall within the basic definition of a firearm. Under Section 57 (1) of the Firearms Act 1968 a firearm is a *lethal barrelled* weapon of any description from which any shot, bullet or other missile can be *discharged*. It includes: *Firearms Act 1968 Section 57 (1)*

1 Any *prohibited weapon* (whether lethal or not).
2 Any *component part* of such a lethal or prohibited weapon.
3 Any *accessory* to any such weapon designed or adapted to diminish the noise or flash caused by firing the weapon.

Lethal
A *lethal* weapon is one capable of causing injury from which death may result. It was held in the case of Read v Donovan in 1947 that this even applied to a signal pistol despite the fact that it may never have been designed to injure or kill. An air weapon would also be considered as lethal, since even the least powerful of these weapons, if shot at close range into a vulnerable area, could cause death.

Barrelled
The weapon must be *barrelled*: that is, have some form of cylinder or tube from which the projectile can be discharged. Hence a crossbow is not a firearm because it does not have a barrel, although future legislation may impose some form of restriction on these weapons.

Discharged
A firearm can be *discharged* by any means, e.g. gas, gunpowder, spring and air pressure. It is not essential that the weapon should be capable of firing ammunition at the time, provided that it can be quickly and readily converted into firing (e.g. by the drilling out of a solid barrel). In Cafferata v Wilson (1936) a dummy revolver was held to be a firearm within the meaning of the Act. But in each case it would be for the Court to decide whether a weapon requiring substantial work on it to enable it to be fired would still be deemed a firearm. For example, the majority of starting pistols are of a design that puts them outside the definition of

The majority of starting pistols are not Section 1 firearms.

a Section 1 firearm[1] because of the considerable work and skill required for conversion: in Roche v Skerret (1964) a starting pistol was held not to be a firearm within the definition of the Act, the Court taking into account how conversion could be achieved and the amount of skill required.

Prohibited weapon
Under Section 5 (1), a *prohibited weapon* is defined as:

Section 5 (1) 1 Any firearm which is so designed or adapted that, if pressure is applied to the trigger, missiles continue to be discharged until pressure is released or the magazine is empty.[2]

2 Any weapon of whatever description designed or adapted for the discharge of any noxious liquid, gas or other thing.

Component part
Component parts are those parts of a firearm that are essential to its firing. The trigger is a component part, whereas the wooden stock may not be since it is not essential for the firing of the weapon. Sights, telescopic or otherwise, are also not essential; they merely assist the user in aiming the weapon and would therefore normally be regarded as *accessories* and not classed as firearms in their own right.

[1] See page 85 for the definition of a Section 1 firearm.
[2] For example, a machine gun.

Accessories

Accessories designed to diminish noise or flash include silencers, sound moderators and flash reducers.[1]

DEVICES NOT REGARDED AS FIREARMS

It will be seen that the definition of firearm is very wide and that in the majority of cases most weapons commonly referred to as *guns* will be covered (including all shotguns and air weapons). However, the following devices are not generally regarded as firearms within the definition of the Act:

1 Nail guns which are designed as tools
2 Alarm guns
3 Device for throwing lines to vessels in distress
4 Rocket signalling equipment
5 Devices used to propel nets to trap birds

AMMUNITION

Ammunition is the ammunition for any firearm as well as *Section 57 (2)* grenades, bombs and other like missiles, whether capable of use with a firearm or not; it also includes prohibited ammunition.

Under Section 5 (1), prohibited ammunition is defined as *Section 5 (1)* any ammunition containing or designed or adapted to contain any noxious liquid, gas or other thing.

EXEMPTIONS TO THE ACT

PROOF HOUSES

The provisions of the Firearms Act 1968 do not apply to the *Section 58 (1)* proof houses in London and Birmingham or to anyone carrying firearms to or from the proof houses for the purposes of proof or being removed after proof.

---

[1] Possession alone of component parts or accessories, such as a silencer, requires a firearms certificate, unless exempt (see page 85).

ANTIQUE FIREARMS

Section 58 (2) The provisions of the Act do not apply to *antique* firearms which are sold, transferred, purchased, acquired or possessed as a curiosity or ornament. As soon as they are used in any other way, e.g. by firing them, the exemption would cease and provisions of the Act would apply. The exemption does *not* apply to ammunition suitable for use with such a weapon.

Whilst the Act specifically exempts antique firearms, it does not define them. The common belief that a firearm would only be classed as a genuine antique if one hundred or more years old has not been upheld by the courts. In the case of Richards v Curwen (1977), firearms less than a hundred years old were held to be antiques. In the case of R v Howells (1977), a belief that a firearm was a genuine antique firearm was held to be no defence against possession without a certificate.

It must be assumed, therefore, that whether or not a weapon can be classed as an antique firearm is a question for the court to decide on the evidence given where this fact is contested. In cases of doubt over a weapon's antiquity, anyone possessing or wishing to acquire such a firearm should seek advice from the police.

IMITATION FIREARMS

Firearms Act 1982 The Firearms Act 1982 was introduced amidst growing concern over the use by criminals of firearm look-alikes. The Act extends the provisions of Section 1 of the Firearms Act 1968 to any weapon having the appearance of a Section 1 firearm, whether capable of firing any missile or not, and which is so constructed or adapted as to be readily convertible into a Section 1 firearm.

Section 1 (6) Under Section 1 (6), an imitation firearm shall be deemed as readily convertible if:

1 It can be converted without any special skill.
2 The work involved in conversion does not require equipment or tools other than those in common use by anyone carrying out works of construction and maintenance in their own homes.

FIREARM CERTIFICATES

A fundamental difference exists between the granting of a shotgun certificate and a firearm certificate: in practice, shotgun certificates are normally granted on application, unless the police have good reason to object; but applicants for firearms certificates must make out a good reason for their grant.

SECTION 1 FIREARM

Under Section 1, if you wish to acquire, possess or use a *Section 1* firearm or ammunition other than certain shotguns and air weapons, you must first obtain a firearm certificate from the Chief Officer of Police for the area in which you reside.

Possession does not necessarily imply personal possession at the time. The expression should be viewed in the widest possible sense as constructive possession: if the firearm is in a house or vehicle under the control of a person, that is sufficient to prove possession, provided he or she knew of its presence.

EXEMPTIONS FROM THE NEED FOR A FIREARM CERTIFICATE

1 *Shotguns:* a smooth bore gun having a barrel not less than *Section 1 (3)* 24in long, and not being an air gun. Component parts or accessories to a shotgun are also exempt.
It was held in the case of R v Hucklebridge (1980) that removal of the rifling from the barrel of a gun to produce a smooth bore will bring a weapon within this exemption.

2 *Airweapons:* air guns, air rifles and air pistols, unless declared specially dangerous by the Home Office.[1]

3 *Ammunition*
   (*a*) Cartridges containing five or more shot, none of which *Section 1 (4)* exceeds .36in in diameter.
   (*b*) Ammunition for an air gun, air rifle or air pistol.
   (*c*) Blank cartridges not more than 1in in diameter

[1] See page 96 for specially dangerous air weapons.

measured immediately in front of the rim or cannelure of the base of the cartridge.

4 *Silencers:* a firearm certificate is required to purchase, possess or acquire any accessory designed to diminish the noise or flash of a Section 1 firearm, but there is no restriction in respect of shotguns and airweapons exempted from the need for a firearms certificate.

5 *Occupational exemptions*

Crown servants (e.g. armed forces, police), registered firearms dealers and operators of miniature rifle ranges are allowed to possess, purchase or acquire firearms, shotguns and ammunition in connection with their business or occupation. But note that:

(a) *Crown servants* have the right to purchase and acquire weapons for carrying out official duty. Personal guns still need the relevant certificate.

(b) *Registered firearms dealer* would require a firearm or shotgun certificate to use personal guns for private purposes.

(c) *Operators of miniature rifle ranges* have exemption for rifles and ammunition not exceeding .23in for use on the range only. The exemption also covers users of the range.

It is a common misconception of keepers and stalkers that they may use their employer's rifle in the course of their employment without a firearm certificate. This is not so: a keeper, stalker or other employee who uses for the purpose of his employment any firearm belonging to his employer is required to have the details of that particular firearm registered on his own firearm certificate. His employer will also have similar details registered on his own certificate.

6 *Circumstantial exemptions*

(a) *Auctioneers:* to allow sale by auction. A permit must be obtained from the police which permits sale of firearms and ammunition.

(b) *Licensed slaughterman* may have slaughtering instrument and ammunition whilst at slaughterhouse or knacker's yard.

(c) *Proprietor of slaughterhouse* will also need a certificate to take the weapon from the premises. A free certificate is granted for purchase or acquisition.

(d) *Gun bearers* may carry a firearm and ammunition for a certificate holder's use for sporting purposes.

(e) *Officials organising races, etc.*, may possess a firearm at an athletic meeting for the purpose of starting races. Possession of ammunition not authorised except for blanks not exceeding 1in in diameter.

(f) *Rifle clubs and cadet corps* may possess firearms when engaged as members or in connection with drill or target practice. The club or corps should hold a certificate for the weapons.

(g) *Performers* and others may possess firearms for use in film, T.V. and stage productions. The exemption does not authorise purchase or acquisition by the producers without a certificate.

(h) *Ship and aircraft personnel* may possess firearms as part of ship, aircraft or aerodrome equipment. Signalling apparatus is included in this exemption.

(i) *Police permit holder* may have temporary possession where it is not necessary or desirable to issue a certificate (e.g. disposal of weapon following death of certificate holder).

APPLICATION PROCEDURE FOR FIREARM CERTIFICATE

Firearms certificates are issued by the Chief Officer of Police for the area in which the applicant lives. Once issued the certificate will last for three years when renewal will be necessary. Application forms can be obtained from any police station.

It is not necessary to state on the form of application the identification number of the firearm being acquired, since it is unlikely that this would be available at the time. Such details would subsequently be endorsed on the certificate at the time of purchase or acquisition.

Question 13 on the form relates to the disclosure of previous convictions other than minor traffic offences. This includes convictions outside Great Britain and *all* convictions irrespective of when gained.

Certificates are issued in the form of a folding booklet and specify either the number of firearms possessed or the number which may be acquired or both. Stated on the certificate will be the amount of ammunition which may be possessed at any one time and the amount which may be purchased. Subsequent purchases of firearms or ammunition over the number authorised to be acquired on the certificate must only take place following variation of the certificate.

GRANT, REFUSAL AND REVOCATION OF CERTIFICATES

Section 27 (1) & 30 (1) The Chief Officer of Police will grant a certificate if he is satisfied that the applicant has good reason for requiring the weapon and that there is no danger to public safety or the peace.

Discretion to grant or refuse an application rests with that Chief Officer in whom is vested the responsibility to ensure that a certificate is not granted to a person who is of intemperate habits or of unsound mind, or who for any reason is unfitted to be entrusted with a firearm.

In assessing whether a person is a potential danger to public safety or the peace, judgement must be largely based on the person's character. In the case of Ackers and others v Taylor (1973), a shotgun certificate was revoked on the grounds that the holder was a danger to the peace following a poaching conviction. The case gives an indication of how wide an interpretation can be given to the terms *danger to public safety or the peace*. However, more recent cases in which this terminology has been closely examined have tended to restrict the interpretation and suggest that it is wrong to refuse or revoke certificates on the basis of poaching convictions alone. Whilst there are no positive guide lines, it is clear that the police must give individual consideration to each case and that they do have a right to take into account an applicant's irresponsibility in other activities, not necessarily connected with firearms. This latter consideration was emphasised in the case of Luke v Little (1980), in which the applicant had been convicted on three occasions for drunken driving.

APPEALS

A person may appeal to the Crown Court (Sheriff in Scotland) against refusal to grant, vary or renew a certificate or against a revocation of the certificate, except in revocation following refusal to deliver a certificate to the Chief Officer of Police for variation of conditions.

An appeal must be made within twenty-one days following receipt of the Chief Officer's notice of decision.

PROHIBITION OF GRANT

Certificates cannot be granted to persons prohibited by the Act from possessing or acquiring firearms or ammunition:

1 Anyone sentenced to preventative detention or to imprisonment or corrective training for three years or more.[1] *Section 21*

2 Anyone prohibited by virtue of age (i.e. under the age of fourteen), or by being subject to a court recognizance not to possess a firearm or ammunition. *Section 22*

CONDITIONS

The Firearms Rules 1969 (Rule 11) impose the following conditions: *Firearms Rules 1969*

(*a*) The holder must, on receipt of the certificate, sign it in ink with his usual signature. This establishes an additional means of identity.

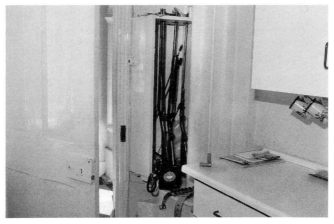

An open door for a thief: firearm owners must keep guns and ammunition securely locked up.

(*b*) The firearms and ammunition must be kept in a secure place when not in actual use.

[1] There is a five-year ban after release from borstal, prison, corrective training or detention centre, on anyone sentenced to three months or more, but less than three years.

(*c*) The holder must report at once to the Chief Officer of Police any theft or loss of any firearm to which the certificate relates.

(*d*) The holder must notify any change of permanent address to the Chief Officer of Police who granted the certificate.

Section 27 (2)   The Chief Officer of Police may impose additional conditions at his discretion to ensure effective control and minimise the risk to public safety. He may impose conditions which relate specifically to where firearms are to be kept, in what circumstances they may be used and the area of land they may be used upon, if held for sporting purposes.

Section 29   The Chief Officer of Police may at any time, by notice in writing, vary such conditions and may require the production of the certificate within twenty-one days for this purpose. A certificate may be revoked should a person fail to produce it within the prescribed period; there are no grounds for appeal against such a revocation.

CHANGE OF ADDRESS

Where a change of permanent address is within the police force area of the issuing Chief Officer, the certificate holder must comply with the condition of notification without undue delay. Certificate holders are advised to forward their certificates to the Chief Officer of Police for amendment, although this is not a condition. Police records will then be noted accordingly and the certificate amended or renewed to show the new address. In some police forces, depending on the number of weapons held, new premises may be inspected by a Crime Prevention Officer to ensure security arrangements are adequate.

When a certificate holder moves permanently into another police area, the holder must still notify the issuing Chief Officer of Police in the normal way as part of the condition of issue. In these circumstances the issuing Chief Officer of Police will, on receipt of this notification, forward all records and the existing certificate to the Chief Officer of Police for the area to which the holder has moved. The receiving force will then normally issue a new certificate free of charge and valid for the same period as the original certificate. If for any reason this is not done, a fresh certificate will be issued on renewal, the old certificate having been allowed to run its course.

Possession without certificate

It is an offence to possess, purchase or acquire a firearm to *Section 1 (1)* which this section applies without holding a valid firearm certificate, or otherwise than as authorised by such a certificate.

It is also an offence to possess, purchase or acquire any ammunition to which this section applies without holding a valid firearm certificate, or otherwise than as authorised by such a certificate, or in quantities in excess of those so authorised.

Failing to comply with conditions

It is an offence to fail to comply with the conditions subject *Section 1 (2)* to which a firearm certificate is held.

It is an offence to sell or transfer to a person other than a *Section 3 (2)* registered dealer any firearm or ammunition to which Section 1 applies, unless that other person produces a firearm certificate authorising him to purchase or acquire it or shows he is exempt from holding a certificate.

SHOTGUN CERTIFICATES

The control of shotguns is not as stringent as for Section 1 firearms.

Under Section 2, if you wish to acquire, possess or use a *Section 2* shotgun, you must first obtain a shotgun certificate from the Chief Officer of Police for the area in which you reside. This requirement applies to all shotguns declared by Section 1 not to be a firearm for which a firearm certificate would be needed, i.e. any smooth-bore gun with barrel not less than 24in long and which is not an air weapon. Component parts and accessories to diminish the noise or flash are not included in the definition, with the exception of the provisions of the Act relating to firearms dealers.[1]

---

[1] See page 95.

EXEMPTIONS

A certificate is not required for a shotgun if:

1 It has been borrowed from the occupier of private premises and used on those premises in the occupier's presence.

2 It is used at a time and place approved by the local Chief Officer of Police for shooting at artificial targets.

3 It is obtained or possessed by a person who has not been in Great Britain for more than thirty days in all in the preceding twelve months (see page 103).

4 It is used by the holder of a Northern Ireland firearm certificate.[1]

GRANT OR REFUSAL OF SHOTGUN CERTIFICATE

Unlike a firearm certificate, a shotgun certificate does not relate to a particular weapon and once granted authorises any number of weapons. A shotgun certificate is not required for the purchase or possession of shotgun ammunition.

A Chief Officer of Police should grant or renew a shotgun certificate, unless he has good reason to believe the applicant:

1 Is prohibited by the Act from possessing a gun (Section 21).
2 Would be a danger to the public safety or to the peace.

APPLICATION PROCEDURES

Application forms for shotgun certificates may be obtained from any police station and on completion should be handed to the police together with the appropriate fee. Details of specific weapons the applicant wishes to possess are not requested on the form and neither is the reason for requiring them, although the Chief Officer of Police does have to be satisfied that the applicant can possess a shotgun without danger to public safety or the peace.

The form of application is self explanatory. Previous convictions other than minor traffic offences must be

---

[1] Shotguns are covered by firearm certificates in Northern Ireland.

disclosed, irrespective of the date of any conviction. A minor traffic offence may relate to speeding but not drunken driving; if the applicant is in any doubt as to what constitutes a minor traffic offence, it is better to disclose the conviction(s) than risk prosecution for making a false declaration to obtain a certificate. If the conviction(s) do amount to minor traffic offences, they will be ignored.

The Firearms Rules 1969 require the information given on the application form to be verified by the signed statement of a British subject, who is not a member of the applicant's family and who has known the applicant personally for at least two years.

CONDITIONS FOR HOLDING A SHOTGUN CERTIFICATE

The Firearms Rules 1969 state that a shotgun certificate shall be granted or renewed subject to the following rules:

1 The holder must, on receipt of the certificate, sign it in ink with his/her usual signature.

2 The holder must immediately inform the issuing Chief Officer of Police of the theft or loss in Great Britain of any shotgun in his/her possession.

These conditions are reproduced on the certificate together with a request that the holder should notify the Chief Officer of Police of any change of address and send his certificate for amendment. Failure to do so may lead to a delay in renewal.

Chief Officers are not empowered, as with firearm certificates, to impose any additional conditions.

OFFENCES:
Possession without certificate
It is an offence to possess, purchase or acquire[1] a shotgun *Section 2 (1)* without holding a valid shotgun certificate.

Failing to comply with conditions
It is an offence to fail to comply with any of the conditions *Section 2 (2)* under which a shotgun certificate is held.

---

[1] *Acquire* is defined by the Act as meaning to hire, accept as a gift, or borrow.

Shortening barrel of shotgun

Section 4 (1) It is an offence to shorten the barrel of a shotgun to a length of less than 24in.[1]

OFFENCES: SHOTGUN AND FIREARM CERTIFICATES

False statements

Section 26 (5) It is an offence to make a false statement for the purpose of obtaining a firearm or shotgun certificate either for oneself or another.

This offence also applies to an application for the variation of a firearm certificate (Section 29 (3)).

Dealing in firearms

Section 3 (1) It is an offence, if by way of a trade or business, to manufacture, sell, transfer, repair, test or proof any Section 1 firearm, ammunition or shotgun without being registered as a firearms dealer.

Production of certificates

Section 3 (2) It is an offence to sell or transfer to anyone in the United Kingdom, other than a registered firearms dealer, any Section 1 firearm, ammunition or shotgun, unless the other person either produces the respective firearm or shotgun certificate authorising purchase or acquisition or shows he is exempt.

Section 3 (3)   It is an offence for anyone other than a registered firearms dealer to undertake repair, test or proof of any Section 1 firearm or ammunition or a shotgun for another, unless he produces a firearm or shotgun certificate authorising possession or is able to show he is exempt.

Section 3 (5)   Anyone producing false certificates in the above circumstances or personating certificate holders commit an offence.

Production to police

Section 48 (1) A police officer may demand from anyone who he believes is in possession of a Section 1 firearm or ammunition or a shotgun the respective certificate.

Section 48 (2)   A police officer may seize and detain a weapon or ammunition from anyone who fails to produce his certificate in the

[1] Registered firearms dealers are exempt if shortening a barrel to facilitate replacement of a defective part, providing on completion the barrel is not less than 24in.

above circumstances or permit the police officer to read it or otherwise show that he is exempt; the police officer may then demand the person's name and address.

It is an offence to refuse to give one's name and address or *Section 48 (3)* give a false name and address to a police officer.[1]

FIREARMS DEALERS

The 1968 Act provides that anyone who deals in firearms or ammunition by way of trade or business must be registered with the police as a firearms dealer and must keep detailed records of transactions. In general, registration can only be refused by the Chief Officer of Police if he is satisfied that the applicant cannot be permitted to carry on a business as a dealer without danger to the public safety or the peace. There is a right of appeal against such a refusal.

OFFENCES

It is an offence to carry on a business as a firearms dealer *Section 3 (1)* without being registered.

It is also an offence knowingly to make a false statement to *Section 39 (1)* obtain registration for oneself or another, or procure for oneself or another the entry of any place of business in a register of firearms dealers.

Being a registered dealer, it is an offence to have a place of *Section 39 (2)* business not entered in the police register and to carry on the business as a firearms dealer at that place.

It is an offence to fail to comply with a condition of *Section 39 (3)* registration.

AIR WEAPONS

An air weapon is any air rifle, air gun or air pistol which has not been declared specially dangerous by the Secretary of State. Most weapons are either .177 or .22 calibre, although there are a few .25 calibre barrels available to convert existing weapons.

In recent years there has been an upsurge of interest in the use of air weapons both for sporting and competition

---

[1] A police officer has the power to arrest.

The modern air rifle can be both powerful and accurate.

purposes. At the same time, manufacturers have developed very efficient, powerful and highly tuned weapons that bear little resemblance to their predecessors.

Control of air weapons is mainly directed towards their use by children and young people who represent a large percentage of users. Originally a gun licence was required for the possession of an air weapon, but today it is no longer necessary.

DANGEROUS AIR WEAPONS

Air weapons mainly operate by the compression of powerful springs. A few, however, are powered by gas (CO_2) or are of the *pump-up* type. The pump-up type can develop very high power, as can some conventional weapons if fitted with extra powerful springs or if highly tuned. Gas-operated weapons are often no more powerful than the conventional air weapon; but because they are operated by *gas* and not *air*, they do not come within the definition of an air weapon and therefore require a firearms certificate.

An air weapon may be declared specially dangerous if it exceeds a specified power output in terms of kinetic energy. Irrespective of the type of mechanism developing the power to discharge the pellet, if the kinetic energy exceeds the following limits then the weapon will automatically fall within the definition of a Section 1 firearm and a firearm certificate will be required to cover its use.

FIREARMS (DANGEROUS AIR WEAPONS) RULES 1969[1]

Under Rule 3, an air weapon will be declared specially *Rule 3* dangerous if it is capable of discharging missiles with a kinetic energy in excess of:

    6 ft/lb for an air pistol
    12 ft/lb for any other weapon

The limits do not apply to weapons designed for use only when submerged in water.

Where doubt exists as to the power of a particular weapon, it should be checked by the use of a chronograph to ensure that it is within the legal requirements (unless, of course, its possession and use is already covered by a firearm certificate).

CONSIDERATION FOR THE QUARRY

Having recognised the efficiency of the modern standard air rifle for the control of vermin, the British Association for Shooting and Conservation have made available to their members a code of practice for sporting air-rifle shooting.

To ensure clean kills, the code recommends that members voluntarily refrain from using air rifles on live quarry other than the following: crows (hooded and carrion), rook, jackdaw, magpie, jay, woodpigeon, collared dove, feral pigeon, brown rat, grey squirrel and rabbit.

FIREARMS AND YOUNG PEOPLE

Firearms are potentially dangerous and there have been many tragic accidents involving youngsters who have never been trained in the safe handling of weapons. The law recognises the dangers and imposes restrictions on the possession and use of specific types of weapon by young people under the age of seventeen.

AGE RESTRICTIONS ON BUYING OR HIRING FIREARMS

Under Section 22 (1), it is an offence for anyone under the *Firearms Act 1968* age of seventeen to buy or hire *any* firearm (including an *Section 22 (1)* air weapon) or ammunition (including blank ammunition).

---

[1] The Rules extend to Scotland under Statutory Instrument 270/1969.

Section 24 (5)   Under Section 24 (5), a statutory defence exists for the seller or hirer, if he can prove reasonable grounds for believing that the person was seventeen or over.

SECTION 1 FIREARMS AND AMMUNITION

Between the ages of fourteen and seventeen a Section 1 firearm and ammunition may be accepted as a *gift*, provided both parties possess firearm certificates authorising such a transaction.

Section 22 (2)   Below the age of fourteen, no one can *possess* a Section 1 firearm or ammunition, except in the following circumstances:

1 Carrying for the holder of a firearm certificate for sporting purposes.

2 As a member of an approved rifle club, miniature rifle club or cadet corps for drill or target practice.

3 Using at a miniature rifle range or shooting gallery, provided the calibre does not exceed .23in.

Section 24 (2)   Under Section 24 (2), it is an offence to make a gift of or lend one to a child under fourteen, or to part with possession to such a child, except in the above circumstances.

SHOTGUNS

Provided a shotgun certificate is held, there is no restriction on *possession* if aged between fifteen and under seventeen, but a shotgun may not be bought or hired.

Although there is no lower age limit for the grant of a certificate, a child under fifteen can only possess a shotgun if under the supervision of a person aged twenty-one or over and if the gun is covered with a securely fastened gun-cover to prevent firing.

Section 22 (3)   Under Section 22 (3), it is an offence for a person under fifteen to have with him an assembled shotgun other than in the above circumstances.

Section 24 (3)   Under Section 24 (3), it is an offence to make a gift of a shotgun or ammunition to a person under the age of fifteen, although it is not an offence for a youngster to possess ammunition.

AIR WEAPONS
Under seventeen
Air weapons declared specially dangerous by the Secretary of State[1] are deemed Section 1 firearms and the restrictions on young people are as for Section 1 firearms.[2] For air weapons not in this category, the following restrictions are imposed on under seventeen year olds:

1 Air weapons cannot be bought or hired.
2 Air pistols cannot be possessed in a public place.
3 Air rifles cannot be possessed in a public place unless in a cover.

It is an offence for anyone under seventeen to have with him an air weapon in a public place except: *Section 22 (5)*

1 An air gun or air rifle (but not an air pistol) which is so covered with a securely fastened gun-cover that it cannot be fired.

2 As a member of an approved rifle club or miniature rifle club engaged in target practice.

3 To use a weapon at a shooting gallery where the firearms are either air weapons or miniature rifles not exceeding .23in calibre.

Under fourteen
It is an offence for anyone under fourteen to have with him an air weapon or ammunition for an air weapon except: *Section 22 (4)*

1 Under the supervision of a person twenty-one or over. *Section 23 (1)*
   If on private premises, which includes land, the weapon may be fired within those premises. It is an offence for both the child and supervisor, if a missile is fired beyond those premises.

2 The weapon is used by a member of an approved rifle club *Section 23 (2)* or miniature rifle club engaged in target practice, or the weapon is used at a shooting gallery where rifles do not exceed .23in calibre.

[1] See page 96.
[2] See page 98.

A child may use an air rifle under supervision, but it would be an offence to fire beyond the premises.

Section 24 (4)   It is an offence to make a gift of an air weapon or ammunition to a child under fourteen or to part with the possession of an air weapon or ammunition to such a child, unless exempt under Section 23 above.

MISCELLANEOUS FIREARM OFFENCES

CARRYING FIREARMS IN PUBLIC PLACES

Section 19   Under Section 19, it is an offence for a person without lawful authority or reasonable excuse to have a loaded shotgun or loaded air weapon or any other firearm, loaded or not, together with suitable ammunition for that firearm in a public place.

The Act defines *public place* as including any highway and any other premises or place to which at the time in question the public have or are permitted to have access whether on payment or otherwise.

A shotgun or an air weapon is deemed to be *loaded* if the ammunition is in the chamber or barrel or is in a magazine or other device in a position capable of being fed into the weapon.

A valid shotgun certificate does not give a person *lawful authority* to have a loaded shotgun in a public place (Ross v Collins 1982).

Crossing of a country lane during the course of a shoot would probably be regarded as reasonable excuse for the offence of possessing a firearm in a public place.

It is not essential to establish that a person was actually carrying a firearm, provided the person has a close physical link with and immediate control of the firearm.

TRESPASSING WITH A FIREARM

Under Section 20 (1) and (2), it is an offence for a person to *Section 20 (1) (2)*
enter or be upon any land[1] or building or part of a building as
a trespasser whilst in possession of a firearm without
reasonable excuse.

SHOOTING ON OR NEAR HIGHWAYS, FOOTPATHS
AND BUILDINGS

There is no specific offence of shooting from or over a
footpath, right of way or near to buildings, etc., unless of
course it could be shown that the person was committing the
criminal offences of trespass with a firearm or possessing a
firearm or ammunition with intent to endanger life (Section
16 Firearms Act 1968). But under Section 161 of the *Highways Act*
Highways Act 1980 in England and Wales it is an offence *1980*
without lawful authority or excuse to discharge any firearm *Section 161*
within fifty feet of the centre of the highway and in
consequence of which a user of the highway is injured,
interrupted or endangered.

A person shooting from the highway may become a
trespasser under the doctrine that the highway should be
used to pass and re-pass.[2] Shooting from a footpath or other
right of way where permission on adjacent land has not been
obtained would also be trespass.

Under the Town Police Clauses Act 1847 in England and *Town Police*
Wales it is an offence to wantonly discharge any firearm in a *Clauses Act 1847*
street to the obstruction, danger or annoyance of residents or *Section 28*
passengers.

RECKLESS SHOOTING

In Scotland, it is a crime at Common Law to discharge a
firearm anywhere in a culpable and reckless manner even
though no actual injury is caused. The essence of this crime
is the wanton disregard for the safety of others.

---

[1] Land includes land covered with water.
[2] See page 3

DRUNK IN POSSESSION OF FIREARM

Licensing Act 1872 Under Section 12 of the Licensing Act 1872, it is an offence
(England & in England and Wales to be drunk in possession of a loaded
Wales) firearm of any description anywhere.
Section 12
Civic Government   Under Section 50 of the Civic Government (Scotland) Act
(Scotland) 1982, it is an offence to be drunk in possession of a firearm in
Act 1982 any public place.
Section 50

SALE OF FIREARMS NOT IN PROOF

Gun Barrel Proof Under the Gun Barrel Proof Acts 1868 to 1978, all firearms,
Acts 1868–1978 except air weapons, must bear proof marks to indicate they
have been tested as safe before being sold or exchanged. It is
an offence under the above Acts to sell, exchange, expose or
keep for sale any firearm which has not been so proofed and
marked accordingly. An attempt to part with the weapon in
any of the above circumstances would also be an offence.

IMPORT AND EXPORT OF FIREARMS

Both import and export of firearms are controlled in Great
Britain and appropriate licences may be obtained from the
Department of Trade and Industry.

In some circumstances export licences are not required:

1 When travelling abroad (for example, for a shooting
holiday), provided a valid firearm or shotgun certificate is
held. The firearm may be either with the holder or be sent
as part of personal effects. The certificate must be
presented together with the firearms and any ammunition
to a Customs and Excise officer at the place of exportation.

2 For antique firearms more than one hundred years old and
of an individual value not exceeding £8000.

3 For shotguns (barrel not less than 24in), exported as part
of personal effects by a visitor who has been in Great
Britain for not more than thirty days in any period of
twelve months.

4 For shotgun cartridges exported as personal effects (maximum of 100 allowed).

SHOOTING HOLIDAYS ABROAD

As stated above, anyone taking a shooting holiday abroad and who possesses a valid firearm or shotgun certificate can take his weapons with him. However, the country to be visited may have its own requirements for visitors.

NORTHERN IRELAND

Anyone wishing to take a firearm (including air weapons) to Northern Ireland must first obtain a certificate of approval, showing a full description of the firearm(s), from the Chief Constable of the Royal Ulster Constabulary. For Section 1 firearms and shotguns, the certificate of approval must be accompanied by the relevant firearm or shotgun certificate issued in Great Britain. Applications for a certificate of approval must be made not less than one month before the proposed date of arrival in Northern Ireland. No fee is payable and application forms for certificates may be obtained from Royal Ulster Constabulary, Firearms Licensing Department, Knocknagoney House, Knocknagoney Road, Belfast BT4 2PP.

EUROPE

Generally speaking, most European countries are more than co-operative to visiting sportsmen. Visitors should forward full particulars of the weapon to be taken when applying for a visa. A temporary import permit will then be issued with the visa and should be produced together with the firearm(s) at Customs check-points both on entering and leaving the country. The firearm(s) will then be checked against the details on the permit. The permit will normally be retained on leaving the country. Agencies specialising in shooting holidays usually make the application on behalf of their clients.

VISITORS TO GREAT BRITAIN

SECTION 1 FIREARMS

Visitors who wish to bring Section 1 firearms with them to Great Britain are advised to apply well in advance (at least 28 days) to the Chief Officer of Police for the area in which they will be residing. Either a firearm certificate or temporary permit will then be issued subject to the usual conditions being satisfied. Anyone entering the country with firearms and not having made these arrangements will find their weapons held by the Customs and Excise at the point of entry until such authority is produced.

SHOTGUNS

Visitors are not required to possess a shotgun certificate provided they do not stay for a total of more than thirty days in any twelve months. If they stay longer, visitors must obtain a Visitor's Shotgun Certificate from the Chief Officer of Police for the area in which they are to reside whilst in the country.

EXPLOSIVES

Explosive Act 1875 Under the Explosive Act 1875, anyone wishing to acquire or keep explosives, including gunpowder (black powder), must first obtain a police certificate or licence. Where the quantities required to be kept or stored are considerable, storage must be in a licensed explosive store or, for smaller quantities, in registered premises. Registration and licensing in these circumstances is by the local authority.

LOADING OF AMMUNITION

Explosives Act 1875 (Exemptions) Regulations 1979 Under the Explosives Act 1875 (Exemptions) Regulations 1979, the Health and Safety Executive grants certificates of exemption from certain requirements and provisions of the principal Act: these exemptions allow for the acquisition and storage for private use of up to 5kg of explosive (but not black powder), whether or not contained in cartridges, provided that the explosive is for sporting purposes and not for sale. Up to 4.5kg of percussion primers may also be kept in private use for reloading cartridges for sporting purposes without any form of restriction.

BLACK POWDER

Gunpowder, commonly referred to as black powder, is more *Control of*
volatile than the type of explosive powder used as a pro- *Explosives Order*
pellant for modern ammunition and can only be acquired *1953*
under the Control of Explosives Order 1953 with a licence
issued by the local Chief Officer of Police. Licences run for a
maximum of twelve months at which time they have to be
renewed. They can be refused or revoked by the Chief
Officer of Police in certain circumstances. In many areas
licences are limited to 5kg of powder, but quantities of up to
15kg can be obtained for private use, provided the Chief
Officer of Police is satisfied with the character of the
applicant and the use to which the explosive is put.

CHAPTER 9

The Protection and Conservation of Birds, Animals and Plants

THE MAJOR LEGISLATION dealing with the protection of wildlife is the Wildlife and Countryside Act 1981. Part I deals specifically with the protection of birds, animals and plants and it can be summed up by saying that it protects some birds all of the time and all birds some of the time, but only a handful of animals receive strong protection. In places the Act also overlaps with other legislation: for example, in the type and use of traps and snares.

SCHEDULES

In order to cater for varying degrees of protection for birds, animals and plants, for close seasons, the sale and ringing of birds and sale of dead birds, the species are divided into lists called Schedules, some of which are sub-divided into Parts I, II or III: for example, a Schedule 1 bird (e.g. golden eagle) is virtually untouchable, whereas the woodpigeon (Schedule 2) can be killed by certain people at any time. The Schedules are printed together at the end of this chapter (pages 132–7) for reference.

PROTECTION OF WILD BIRDS

A *wild* bird is not necessarily one that has gone feral or is living in the wild. A wild bird is a bird of any kind which in a wild state is ordinarily resident in or is a visitor to Great Britain; it does *not* include poultry[1] nor, except in Section 5, game birds.[2]

The term 'wild' therefore also includes all captive bred and tame species, live or dead, regardless of age, and only in certain circumstances can birds be killed, taken, possessed or sold. A bird is only classed as being *bred in captivity* if both parents were in lawful captivity when the egg was laid.[3]

KILLING AND TAKING OF ANY SPECIES

Section 1 creates certain offences e.g. killing a thrush in garden. It does not apply to birds bred in captivity – the keeper of legally bred birds can kill them, without causing unnecessary suffering, if he wishes – but the onus is on the defendant to show that the bird was captive bred.

Wildlife and Countryside Act 1981 Section 1 (1)

Under Section 1 (1) it is an offence to:

1 Kill, injure or take any wild bird.
2 Take, damage or destroy the nest of a wild bird whilst in use or being built.
3 Take or destroy the egg of a wild bird.

LICENCES

Section 16 permits the Department of the Environment (D.O.E.), Ministry of Agriculture, Fisheries and Food, (M.A.F.F.), Welsh Office Agricultural Department (W.O.A.D.), Department of Agriculture and Fisheries for Scotland (D.A.F.S.), Scottish Home and Health Department and the Nature Conservancy Council (N.C.C.) to issue licences to permit certain actions that would normally be illegal. Licences may apply nationally or to part of the

Section 16

---

[1] Domestic fowl, geese, ducks, guinea-fowl, pigeons, quail and turkey.
[2] Pheasant, partridge, grouse, moor game, black or heath game and ptarmigan.
[3] See registration and ringing of captive birds on page 119.

country. They may be granted to an individual for a specific purpose on one occasion (e.g. taking a bird from the wild for breeding or for a falconer to trap a falcon that has escaped from its handler) or be applicable to all persons or a class of persons (e.g. sale of feathers for fly-tying). A licence permits specified airport authorities, to take or destroy lapwings, black-headed and common gulls, their nests and eggs.

Licences are subject to variation regarding species and conditions, as circumstances change; they usually have to be renewed every three years, so before taking action it is advisable to check with the issuing authorities.

Quarry licence
Falconers can obtain a quarry licence to take wild birds with birds of prey (e.g. blackbirds with a sparrowhawk or skylarks with a merlin). A quarry licence is not required to take game birds, but a game licence must be obtained from a post office. Schedule 2 birds may also be taken without a quarry or game licence under certain circumstances (see page 111).

Aviculture

Falconry is a demanding and time-consuming pursuit. A bird cannot be laid aside like the shotgun and fishing rod.

Birds can be taken under licence for avicultural purposes, usually to enhance breeding stock. Licences have been granted to take male crossbills and a nestling peregrine falcon, for example, but licences may be granted for any species.

POSSESSION OF BIRDS AND EGGS

Under Section 1 (2), it is an offence to possess or control any *Section 1 (2)* wild bird (live or dead) or part of or something derived from a wild bird or its egg or part of an egg. This prohibition includes a bird or egg taken or killed *before* the passing of the Wildlife and Countryside Act in 1981.

Certain people, such as veterinary surgeons, taxidermists, Government officials, antique dealers, etc, may be registered to possess animals and birds in circumstances which would otherwise constitute an offence.

General licences have been issued for what would otherwise be illegal possession. For example, anyone may remove and destroy addled eggs in nesting boxes from October to January, but the eggs may not be kept or sold. Authorised persons may also take wild mallard eggs for breeding, but the young birds must be released into the wild by 31 July. Eggs and progeny of wild mallard cannot be sold. Wild eggs must not be taken later than 31 March in England and Wales or 10 April in Scotland.

It is a defence to the Section 1 (2) offence to show that the *Section 1 (3)* bird or egg had been killed or taken otherwise than in contravention of this Act or the Protection of Birds Acts 1954 to 1967 or that it had been bought otherwise than in contravention of these Acts. For example, a person who finds a dead goshawk which has been shot, and therefore illegally killed, cannot possess it without a D.O.E. licence, unlike the person who finds a bird which has died after colliding with a window.[1]

EGG COLLECTIONS

Under Section 1 (3), egg collectors may be required to show that the eggs in their possession were lawfully obtained (e.g. under licence) or form part of a collection assembled prior to 1954.

---

[1] Possession or sale of any bird which has been illegally taken or killed, or any part or derivative of such a bird, remains an offence regardless of registration or marking unless specifically licensed by the D.O.E.

DISTURBANCE OF NESTING BIRDS AND THEIR YOUNG

Section 1 (5) Under Section 1 (5), it is an offence intentionally to disturb:

1 Schedule 1 wild bird while it is building a nest, or when it is in, on, or near a nest containing young.
2 Dependent young of a Schedule 1 bird.

Nature Conservancy Council licences are needed for photography and scientific purposes. Bird watchers by *intentionally* being within one or two miles of a nest of certain species may be committing an offence.

Over-enthusiastic birdwatchers can commit the offence of disturbing a schedule 1 bird.

CLOSE SEASON

Section 1 (7) Birds in Part I of Schedule 1 are protected at all times whereas birds in Schedule 1 Part II are only protected during the close season.

CLOSE SEASON FOR PART II SCHEDULE 1 BIRDS	
Capercaillie and (except in Scotland) woodcock	1 February – 30 September
Snipe	1 February – 11 August
Wild duck and geese below high water mark of ordinary spring tides	21 February – 31 August
All other birds (including woodcock in Scotland)	1 February – 31 August

SEVERE WEATHER AND POLLUTION

Under Section 2 (6), the Department of the Environment can *Section 2 (6)* impose periods of special protection for up to fourteen days in respect of Schedule 1 Part II or Schedule 2 Part I birds. This Section of the Act is most commonly invoked for wildfowl species during severe weather or after a natural disaster, such as oil pollution, during the open season. (See Chapter 13.)

Sporting species

Under Section 2 (1), it is not an offence to take or kill a *Section 2 (1)* Schedule 2 Part I bird during the open season. Section 2 (1) (d) makes illegal such actions on a Sunday in certain areas of England and Wales (see page 217).[1]

Pest species

Under Section 2 (2), an authorised person may kill or take *Section 2 (2)* Schedule 2 Part II birds (e.g. crows, rooks, feral pigeon, etc) and take, damage or destroy their nests and eggs.[1] A licence permits such persons to sell certain gulls' eggs for human consumption.

Authorised persons
Authorised persons in this Act means:

1 Owner or occupier (or persons authorised by him) of land on which action is taken (e.g. gamekeeper, club member). Occupier of land, other than the foreshore,[2] includes a person with hunting, shooting, fishing or game rights. The authorisation need not be in writing but it is advisable.

2 Anyone authorised in writing by a local authority.

3 In relation to wild birds, anyone authorised in writing by the Nature Conservancy Council, Water Authority, District Board (Salmon Fisheries (Scotland) Act 1862), Local Fisheries Committee (Fisheries Regulation Act 1966).[3]

---

[1] Such actions are not allowed on Sunday or Christmas Day in Scotland. In parts of Scotland there is an unwritten law that shooting of any kind should only take place after noon so that Sunday worship is not disrupted.
[2] See page 211.
[3] Authorised persons do not have any power to enter land.

AREAS OF SPECIAL PROTECTION

Section 3   Under Section 3, the Secretary of State may put restrictions on a specific area. These may restrict entry to the area and make it an offence to enter the area.

An authorised person will not be guilty of an offence under such an order in respect of Schedule 2 Part II birds, nests or eggs.

The Secretary of State must notify the owner or occupier in writing, but if not practicable advertise in the local press and the order may not be made until the objections, if any, are resolved. The term *Areas of Special Protection* should not be confused with *Special Protection Areas* which is an E.E.C. designation.

PESTS AND DISEASE

Under Section 4 (1), regardless of sections 1 or 3, it is lawful to:

Section 4 (1)   1 Destroy birds, eggs or animals under section 98 Agriculture Act 1947 or Section 39 Agriculture (Scotland) Act, 1948.[1]

2 Take action under an Order made by Sections 21 or 22 Animal Health Act 1981.[2]

3 Do anything under an order or other provision of the Wildlife and Countryside Act 1981, except where such action affects Schedule 1 birds, their nests and eggs.

INJURED BIRDS

Section 4 (2)   Under Section 4 (2), a person will not be guilty of a Section 1 or 3 offence if:

1 The bird has been disabled and taken to be treated and released when fit.[3]

[1] M.A.F.F. notice to destroy pests.
[2] Prevention of animal diseases.
[3] It is advisable to take injured Schedule 4 birds to a Licensed Rehabilitation Keeper (L.R.K.), who is authorised by the D.O.E. to treat and rehabilitate such birds before releasing them back into the wild. Anyone other than a Licensed Rehabilitation Keeper must apply to register Schedule 4 birds in their possession with the D.O.E.

2 The bird was killed because it was seriously disabled with no reasonable chance of recovery.

3 The unlawful act was an incidental result of a lawful operation which could not be reasonably avoided (e.g. unknowingly destroying a nest whilst tree felling).

PROTECTION OF CROPS AND LIVESTOCK

Under Section 4 (3), it is *not* an offence for an authorised *Section 4 (3)* person to kill or injure any wild bird, *except Schedule 1 birds*, if he can show it was necessary to:

1 Preserve public health or public or air safety.
2 Prevent the spread of disease.
3 Prevent serious damage to livestock,[1] crops, vegetables, fruit, growing timber, fisheries or feed for livestock.

For crop protection in orchards owners may kill bullfinches to protect their trees; but a new licence now allows for the cage trapping and relocation of bullfinches which may then be given, but not sold, to an aviculturalist. Where a heron is taking fish, the damage must be serious: killing should be a last resort after trying all preventive methods. The D.O.E. and N.C.C. can give advice on such methods and the British Field Sports Society's booklet *Predatory Birds of Game and Fish* illustrates pond construction, fencing etc for this purpose. See also the R.S.P.B. leaflet *Protection of Fish Farms from Heron Predation*.

Licences have been issued in respect of Barnacle, Greylag, Brent and Canada geese to prevent crop damage and similar licences can be issued for other species to protect fish, especially in fish farms. Shooting of protected species under licence should not be used as a means of providing sport.

Racing pigeons
Birds of prey are seen as a potential danger by the owners of racing pigeons. But it is doubtful whether racing pigeons would come within the definition of livestock; therefore they cannot be protected from attacks by wild birds. Advice from the D.O.E. should be sought before taking action.

---

[1] Animal kept for food, wool, skin, or used for agricultural activity or improvement of shooting or fishing. Game birds come under this definition when in captivity, but not when released and probably not when in a release pen.

PROHIBITED METHODS OF KILLING AND TAKING

Section 5 prohibits a number of methods of killing and taking wild birds, including game birds.

Section 5 (1) (a)   Under Section 5 (1) (a), it is an offence to *set in position* a device of such a nature and so placed as to be calculated to cause bodily injury to any wild bird coming into contact (i.e. springe, trap, gin, snare, hook and line, electrical device for killing, stunning, frightening, or poisonous or stupefying substances).

This cage trap was set to take wild birds. The trapper was found guilty of taking a wild bullfinch, using a cage trap and confining a bird in a cage that was too small.

This would include both the illegal pole trap placed in a nest with eggs to catch jays *and* a legal trap, if used incorrectly (e.g. a fen trap set on a pole to catch birds of prey). M.A.F.F. can issue licences for the use of stupefying substances (e.g. alphachloralose for the control of pigeons).

The use of agricultural chemicals (e.g. pesticides and insecticides) in carcases and other baits as a form of predator and pest control is illegal under the Protection of Animals Act 1911 and the Food and Environment Protection Act 1985 (see page 152).

Wildlife Incident Investigation Scheme (W.I.I.S.)
Where it is suspected that a carcase or bait has been treated with agricultural chemicals or that a bird or animal has died from such poisoning, M.A.F.F. should be notified and a preliminary investigation will be carried out. Using gloves or a polythene bag to protect the skin, carcases and baits should

be placed in a polythene bag. Specimens should be forwarded to a M.A.F.F. Area Veterinary Investigation Centre for post-mortem examination.

If done in the interests of public health, agriculture, forestry, fisheries or nature conservation, it is a defence to section 5 (1) (a) to show that the device was set to kill or take any wild animal that can lawfully be killed and that reasonable precautions were taken to prevent injury to wild birds. *Section 5 (4)*

It is an offence to *use to kill or take* any wild bird any section 5 (1) (a) device whether or not of such a nature and so placed as to cause bodily injury or to use any net, baited board, birdlime or similar substance. *Section 5 (1) (b)*

It is an offence to use the following to kill or take any wild bird: *Section 5 (1) (c)*

1 Bow or crossbow.
2 Explosive (other than firearm ammunition).
3 Automatic or semi-automatic weapon.[1]
4 Shotgun with a barrel having an internal diameter of more than 1¾in at the muzzle.[2]
5 Device for illuminating the target or a sighting device for night shooting.[3]
6 Artificial light, mirror or dazzling device.[3]
7 Gas or smoke.
8 Chemical wetting agent.

Decoys

Under Section 5 (1) (d), it is an offence to use as a decoy to kill or take any wild bird, any sound recording or a live bird or animal which is tethered, secured, blind, maimed or injured. *Section 5 (1) (d)*

---

[1] A semi-automatic weapon is any weapon whose magazine is capable of holding more than two rounds of ammunition, where the depression of the trigger ejects one single shot, each subsequent shot requiring a further depression of the trigger. These weapons cannot be used for shooting any kind of wild or game bird unless licensed under the Act. A licence permits authorised persons to use semi-automatic weapons in England and Wales to kill Schedule 2 Part II species. This type of gun usually reloads itself by recoil or gas discharged from the previous cartridge and does not include hand-operated pump action weapons.
[2] For example, old punt guns.
[3] A licence permits authorised persons to use these methods in England, Scotland and Wales to kill feral pigeons, sparrows and starlings roosting on buildings or man-made structures to preserve public health and safety or prevent serious damage to crops, etc.

Use of vehicles

Section 5 (1) (e) Under Section 5 (1) (e), it is an offence to use a mechanically propelled vehicle in immediate pursuit of a wild bird to kill or take it.[1]

Trapping and netting

Section 5 (5) (a) Under Section 5 (1) (a, b, c, d, e), it is *not* unlawful for an authorised person to use a cage trap or net to take Schedule 2 Part II birds.[2]

Duck decoys

Section 5 (5) (b) It is *not* unlawful to use nets for taking wild duck in a decoy which was in use prior to the Protection of Birds Act 1954.

Cage traps

Section 5 (5) (c) It is *not* an offence to use a cage trap or net to take any game bird for breeding.

Nets

Section 5 (5) It is an offence to net birds in flight or to use a net not propelled by hand to capture birds on the ground.[3]

Unlawful shooting

Section 8 (3) Under Section 8 (3), it is an offence to promote, arrange, conduct, assist, take part in or receive money for any event where captive birds are liberated by hand or other means to be shot immediately after liberation or for the owner/occupier to permit the use of land for such events.

SALE OF LIVE BIRDS AND EGGS

Section 6 (1) Under Section 6 (1) , it is an offence to:

1 Sell, offer or expose for sale, possess or transport for the purpose of sale either live wild birds, except Schedule 3 Part I (aviary birds), or the egg or part of an egg of a wild bird.

---

[1] For example, a car or motor boat.
[2] The Game Conservancy booklet *Predator and Squirrel Control* gives practical advice on control.
[3] Certain persons, e.g. bird-ringers, may be licensed to use mist nets and cannon nets for research. Sparrows in food warehouses can also present problems and M.A.F.F. may licence the use of nets to take them.

2 Publish an advertisement indicating that the advertiser buys, sells or intends to buy or sell the above items.

This section allows the sale of ringed birds bred in captivity. The unlicensed possession for sale of any egg appears to be an absolute offence as there are no exceptions listed and no defence. Licences have been issued for:

1 Authorised persons to sell certain gulls' eggs for human *Section 2 (2)* consumption.
2 Wildfowl breeders to sell specified birds and eggs which have been bred in captivity.

SALE OF DEAD BIRDS

Under Section 6 (2), it is an offence for an unregistered *Section 6 (2)* person to:

1 Sell, offer or expose for sale, possess or transport for the purposes of sale any dead wild bird,[1] part or derivative, except Schedule 3 Part II or III birds. Part III birds may only be sold dead from 1 September to 28 February.[2]

2 Publish an advertisement indicating that the advertiser buys or sells or intends to buy or sell any of the above.

Taxidermists may mount specimens for a fee without being registered, but they may only purchase items for mounting if they are registered.

A licence permits an unregistered person in England, Scotland and Wales to sell feathers, feathered wings or skins and items made from such materials. The licence covers Schedule 2 Part II species at any time and Schedule 3 Part III species between 29 February and 31 August.

Registered persons may sell mounted birds if the specimen has a D.O.E. identifying marker fixed to it. A licence allows unregistered persons to sell such specimens if fitted with a mark by a registered person. Game birds do not come within these restrictions, but sale is subject to the game laws.

[1] A caterer who bought legally shot crows for resale as hot crow pie and an exporter who bought starlings for resale on the continent were both prosecuted, because Schedule 2 Part II species may be killed or taken but not sold.
[2] Persons registered with the D.O.E. are not restricted by these dates, but they are required to keep records to establish when the birds were killed, purchased and sold. The sale of game birds is governed by the game laws (see page 64).

SHOWS AND COMPETITIONS

Section 6 (3) Under Section 6 (3), it is an offence to show, cause or permit to be shown for purposes of competition any live wild bird (except Schedule 3 Part I species bred in captivity) or a live bird where one of its parents was such a live wild bird. The D.O.E. has issued a general licence listing birds other than those in Schedule 3 Part I which may be exhibited. The list is available on application to the D.O.E.

INSPECTION OF PREMISES

Section 6 (9) & 7 (6) Under Sections 6 (9) and 7(6), a person authorised by the Secretary of State may at any reasonable time enter premises where a registered person keeps any wild birds or where any person keeps Schedule 4 species. The D.O.E. employs inspectors to visit registered keepers and it is an offence to obstruct them.

SEIZURE

Section 19 (1) (d) Under Section 19 (1) (d), only a police officer has the power to seize and detain anything which may be evidence of an offence.

REGISTRATION OF CERTAIN CAPTIVE BIRDS

Section 7 (1) Under Section 7 (1), it is an offence to keep, possess, or control any Schedule 4 bird, if it is not registered and ringed or marked. (For registration procedure, see pages 121–3.) Licences allow vets, police, customs and excise, R.S.P.C.A. and R.S.P.B. to possess birds without registration for treatment or evidential purposes.

CAGE BIRDS

Section 8 (1) It is an offence to keep or confine any bird in a cage or receptacle which in length, breadth or height will not permit the bird to stretch its wings freely. The exceptions are:

1 Poultry.
2 When conveying birds.

3 At public show/competition for a period not exceeding 72 hours.[1]
4 When undergoing treatment by a vet.

A peregrine/saker cross on a bow perch: if kept in captivity, it must be registered and ringed. Falconers may obtain a quarry licence to take wild birds.

KEEPING, REGISTRATION AND RINGING

Regulations governing possession, ringing and registration are contained in three statutory instruments made under the Wildlife and Countryside Act 1981:

S.I. 1219 of 1982 – Selling dead wild birds
S.I. 1220 of 1982 – Ringing of certain birds
S.I. 1221 of 1982 – Registration and ringing of
                     certain birds

REGISTRATION OF BIRDS

Applications should be made to the Department of the Environment at Bristol where records are kept on computer. Changes of ownership or address must be notified and birds are required to have a numbered ring.

---

[1] A licence permits the training of birds for exhibition by confining them in a cage for one hour in 24.

POSSESSION AND SALE OF DEAD BIRDS

Certain dead birds can only be possessed or sold under licence. There is a market for any wild bird, especially mounted birds of prey, and to prevent large scale and uncontrolled trade and to restrict the taking from the wild to satisfy the demand, dealers in dead wild birds, taxidermists, museums, auctioneers, antique dealers and other sellers must be registered with the D.O.E. A successful applicant will receive a register to record details of birds received and sold, including the cause of death (e.g. natural causes, shot, poisoned, etc). Adhesive markers bearing a unique number are also supplied for fixing to each bird sold. A marker must be fixed to the outer skin, but if mounted it can be placed on the mount or base. If mounted in a sealed case, it must be fixed on the case either internally or externally; if two or more birds are mounted together, each needs an individual marker. Those who sell infrequently or deal in parts or derivatives may obtain a one-off licence instead of registration.

Every bird covered by the regulations must be marked regardless of age; an antique dealer who comes into possession of a case of antique mounted specimens must register and fix markers before he can sell them. A marker acts as a licence: if an individual acquires a marked bird, he can sell it on without the need to register. Once marked and recorded with the D.O.E. any subsequent enquiries as to origin are easily made.

A taxidermist who sets up a legally taken bird for a fee and returns it to the owner does not have to mark it; but if the owner then decides to sell it, he must apply for a licence and a marker from the D.O.E.

Under Section 1 it is an offence to possess any bird which has been unlawfully taken or killed. Someone finding and taking a short-eared owl, for example, which had been shot, would commit an offence. In these circumstances the bird should be left or destroyed, but if it is kept, the find should be registered with the curator of a local museum who may then give an authority to possess. Any subsequent sale would need a marker.

Registered persons must check whether specimens were killed or obtained lawfully and record the name and address of the supplier. Such records safeguard them from accusations of complicity if they have been led to believe that it was lawfully taken when it was not.

The taxidermist puts the finishing touches to a young goshawk.

The Act and Regulations do allow for the *keeping* of birds without restriction or ringing as long as they have been lawfully bred and not taken from the wild, but there are restrictions on *sale and exhibition.*

Only Schedule 3 birds may be sold and/or exhibited, if legally bred and fitted with the correct size close ring.

Breeders may obtain rings from the British Bird Council or International Ornithological Association for their own use only. Returns have to be made of the rings used and the data is used to decide whether to add or remove species to or from the Schedule.

POSSESSION AND REGISTRATION OF SCHEDULE 4 BIRDS

Schedule 4 birds must be registered and ringed if kept in captivity. The procedure for registration of keepers and birds is detailed below:

Registration of keepers
The applicant sends fee and registration form to the D.O.E.

Registration of birds:

1 All specimens *except* those bred in captivity in the United
   Kingdom from 1983 onwards:

Category I

Birds must be registered with D.O.E. Cable-tie rings will be
supplied and must be fitted immediately. A declaration of
ringing must be sent to the D.O.E. on completion.

Category II

Birds must be registered with D.O.E. Split-rings will be
delivered by person authorised by D.O.E. and fitted in his
presence. A declaration of ringing must be sent to the
D.O.E. on completion.

Close-ring and cable-tie issued by Department of Environment.

2 All birds bred in captivity in the United Kingdom from
   1983 onwards:

Category I and II

Keeper must apply for rings when eggs are laid, giving
D.O.E. ring numbers of parents.

D.O.E. supplies registration forms and close rings to the
breeder. For sensitive species (golden eagle, goshawk, merlin
and peregrine), the rings are sent to a D.O.E. Inspector who
will witness the ringing.

A declaration of ringing must be made no later than
sixteen days after half the cluth has hatched.

Category III

Birds must be registered, but no further action is necessary.
The birds are not required to be ringed.

CANCELLATION OF REGISTRATION

A registration is cancelled if one or more of the following apply:

1 Failure to notify change of address of the bird, date of transfer and ring number in writing.
2 Failure to notify death of bird and return ring.
3 The bird is exported without notification.[1] (The ring must be on the bird when exported.)
4 The bird is disposed of by sale or other means without notifying the D.O.E. of the date, ring number and the name and address of new keeper. All sales require a licence which is general or individual, issued by the D.O.E.
5 The bird escapes or is released into the wild without the D.O.E. being notified of date, ring number and subsequent recovery of bird. It is an offence to release certain species.
6 The ring is removed or becomes illegible. (A new ring can be supplied by the D.O.E.)

PROTECTION OF WILD ANIMALS

KILLING AND TAKING

It is an offence *intentionally* to kill, injure or take any *Section 9 (1)* Schedule 5 animal.[2]

A licence can be obtained to trap red squirrels (a Schedule 5 animal) to relocate them from areas of high population to areas of a lower density.

POSSESSION

Under Section 9 (2), it is an offence to possess or control a *Section 9 (2)* Schedule 5 animal, live or dead or part of or something derived from such an animal; *but* under section 9 (3) a person will not be guilty if he can show that the animal was not killed or taken, or was not killed or taken in contravention of 3 (a) or (b) below, or had been sold to him otherwise than in contravention of Wildlife and Countryside Act 1981 Part I or Conservation of Wild Creatures and Wild Plants Act 1975.

[1] A licence is also required to import.
[2] See page 135 for list of Schedule 5 animals.

HABITAT DESTRUCTION AND DISTURBANCE

Section 9 (4) It is an offence *intentionally* to damage, destroy or obstruct access to a structure or place which a Schedule 5 animal uses for shelter or protection or to disturb such an animal whilst occupying such a structure or place.

Stopping up an entrance or entering dogs would be such an offence. This is particularly relevant to the otter in areas where mink or coypu hunting takes place. The N.C.C. otter survey (1977) reported that such hunting, if practised on rivers which also hold otters, must cause considerable disturbance. An N.C.C. licence is required to photograph or examine protected species.

Section 10 (2) If the action is taken in a dwelling house, it is not
Section 10 (5) unlawful. In the case of bats, it is only lawful to take such action in the living area of the dwelling. If bats are in the loft it is unlawful to carry out certain operations (e.g. treatment of timber with preservative), unless the Nature Conservancy Council has been notified of the proposed action and allowed a reasonable time to advise on the necessity of the action and the method to be used. If action is permitted a licence would be issued.

Bats have been given fuller protection because of their special roosting requirements. The loss of old buildings, hollow trees and other suitable roosting sites has led to a decline in the bat population, but work by bat groups and societies in creating new roosts and the erection of bat boxes is having an effect. These groups need information about roosting sites, but sometimes cavers and potholers are reluctant to report underground roosts for fear that by entering the cave they may be accused of disturbance.

SALE

Section 9 (5)(a–b) Under Section 9 (5a–b), it is an offence to:

1 Sell or offer or expose for sale, possess or transport for sale any Schedule 5 animal, live or dead or part of or something derived from such an animal.

2 Publish an advertisement indicating that the advertiser buys, sells or intends to buy or sell such items.

PESTS AND DISEASE

Section 10 permits the following action which under section *Section 10 (1)*
9 would normally be unlawful:
1 Action required by the Minister of Agriculture, Fisheries
   and Food or Secretary of State under Section 48 Agriculture Act 1947 (Section 39 Agriculture (Scotland) Act
   1948) to kill, take or destroy specified birds, eggs or
   animals to prevent damage to crops, etc.
2 An Order made under the Animal Health Act 1981 for the
   prevention of animal disease.

INJURED ANIMALS

Under Section 10, a person will not be guilty of a Section 9 *Section 10 (3)*
offence if:
1 He took a disabled animal in order to tend and release it.

2 The animal was killed because it was seriously disabled
   and had no reasonable chance of recovery.

3 An unlawful act under Section 9 was the incidental result
   of a lawful operation which could not have been reasonably
   avoided (e.g. clearing a drainage ditch where an otter holt
   was situated).

PROTECTION OF CROPS AND LIVESTOCK

Under Section 10 (4), an authorised person, as defined,[1] will *Section 10 (4)*
not be guilty of a Section 9 offence if he kills or injures a
Schedule 5 animal and shows that the action was necessary to
prevent serious damage to:

1 Livestock[2]
2 Crops
3 Vegetables
4 Fruit
5 Growing timber
6 Other forms of property
7 Fisheries

[1] See page 111.
[2] See page 113.

Section 10 (6)   But an authorised person cannot take action under Section 10 (4) if at any time previously it had become apparent to him that such action would be necessary. He should have obtained a Section 16 licence as soon as reasonably practical after that fact had become apparent.

For example, if the owner of a trout farm becomes aware that an otter is taking his trout, he should obtain a licence before taking action. In most cases a licence will only be granted if all preventive methods have failed. It is extremely doubtful whether a licence would be granted to take an otter, but the N.C.C. or D.O.E. will give appropriate advice.

PROHIBITED METHODS OF KILLING AND TAKING
ANY WILD ANIMAL

Section 11 (1) Under Section 11 (1), it is an offence for any person to:

1 Set in position a self-locking snare of such a nature and so placed as to be calculated to cause bodily injury to any wild animal coming into contact with it.

2 Use to kill or take any wild animal any self-locking snare whether or not of such a nature or so placed as to be calculated to cause bodily injury to any wild animal.[1]

3 Use any bow or crossbow or explosive to kill or take a wild animal.

4 Use as a decoy any live mammal or bird whatever to kill or take any wild animal.

PROHIBITED METHODS OF KILLING OR TAKING
SCHEDULE 6 WILD ANIMALS

Section 11 (2) (a) In addition to the above prohibited methods for any wild animal, it is an offence under Section 11 (2) (a) to set in position a trap, snare, electrical device (for killing/stupefying), or poisonous,[1] poisoned or stupefying substance, which is of such a nature and so placed as to be calculated to cause bodily injury to a Schedule 6[2] wild animal which comes into contact.

Section 11 (6)   It is a defence to section 11 (2) (a) to show that the article was set in position to kill or take any wild animal which could

---

[1] See pages 152–4 regarding poisons and W.I.I.S.
[2] See page 136 for list of Schedule 6 animals.

be lawfully killed or taken by the above means *and* that reasonable precautions were taken to prevent injury to Schedule 6 animals *and* that the action was in the interest of nature conservation, public health, agriculture, forestry or fisheries. It is doubtful whether the term *agriculture* would include the rearing of game species, for if this had been the intention the term *livestock* would have been used.[1]

It is an offence to use such an article to kill or take a *Section 11 (2) (b)* Schedule 6 animal whether or not of such a nature and so placed or any net. Regardless of the defence to section 11 (2) (a), if a Schedule 6 animal is killed or taken an offence is committed if the article was used for that purpose.

It is an offence to *use* the following to kill or take any *Section 11 (2) (c)* Schedule 6 animal:

1 Automatic or semi-automatic weapons.[2]

2 Device for illuminating a target or a sighting device for night shooting.

3 Artificial light, mirror or dazzling device.[3]

4 Gas or smoke.

It is an offence to use as a decoy a sound recording to kill *Section 11 (2) (d)* or take a Schedule 6 wild animal.

It is an offence to use a mechanically propelled vehicle *Section 11 (2) (e)* (boat, hovercraft, car, etc.) in immediate pursuit of a Schedule 6 wild animal to kill or take that animal.

INSPECTION OF SNARES

Under Section 11 (3), it is an offence for any person to set in *Section 11 (3)* position any snare of such a nature and so placed as to be calculated to cause bodily injury to *any* wild animal coming into contact *and* while the snare is in position fail without

---

[1] See page 113.

[2] A semi-automatic weapon is any weapon whose magazine is capable of holding more than two rounds of ammunition, where the depression of the trigger ejects one single shot, each subsequent shot requiring a further depression of the trigger. Manual pump-action weapons are not included. Automatics can be used to shoot animals not included in Schedule 6 (e.g. rabbits and hares), but cannot be used to shoot *wild or game birds* unless licensed, e.g. for control of pest species.

[3] This does not affect lamping for rabbits, hares or other animals, subject to the poaching laws, which are not included in Schedule 6.

reasonable excuse to inspect it (or cause it to be inspected) at least once every day.[1]

PROTECTION OF WILD PLANTS

Section 13 (1)   Under Section 13 (1), it is an offence for:

1 Anyone *intentionally* to pick, uproot or destroy a Schedule 8 wild plant.[2] (Schedule 8 wild plants are listed on page 136.)

2 An unauthorised person *intentionally* to uproot *any* wild plant.

There are circumstances where these offences may also amount to theft or criminal damage, particularly where plants, trees or shrubs are dug up or where foliage and flowers are picked for sale or commercial purposes. The Nature Conservancy Council, however, can licence the taking of plants.

Section 13 (3)   Under Section 13 (3), it is a defence to show that the act was the incidental result of a lawful operation and could not reasonably have been avoided. This would include farming, game management, construction work, etc; but if it is known that Schedule 8 plants are on the land, advice from the N.C.C. should be sought first.

Section 13 (2)   Under Section 13 (2), it is an offence to:

1 Sell, offer or expose for sale, possess or transport for the purposes of sale any Schedule 8 plant (live or dead) or a part or derivative.

2 Publish an advertisement indicating that the advertiser buys or sells or intends to buy or sell such items.

INTRODUCTION OF NEW SPECIES

Section 14 (1)   Under Section 14 (1), it is an offence for any person to release or allow to escape into the wild any animal which is:

1 Not ordinarily resident in or a regular visitor to Great Britain.

---

[1] Similar provisions for spring traps are included in the Protection of Animals Act 1911 (see page 147).
[2] Including flower, seeds and foliage.

2 A Schedule 9 Part I species.[1] A general licence permits the release of chukar partridge and hybrids of red-legged/chukar up until October 1988.

Apart from individuals releasing animals as a means of disposal or sport, this offence would apply to such releases by animal-rights supporters. (The zander, a voracious pike-like fish, has been released illegally into various fisheries, and the damage it causes far outweighs its value as a sporting fish.)

Under Section 14 (2), it is an offence to plant or cause to grow a schedule 9 Part II plant.[2]   *Section 14 (2)*

ENFORCEMENT

If a police officer has reasonable grounds to suspect that anyone is or has been committing an offence under the Wildlife and Countryside Act 1981 he may: *Section 19 (1)*

1 Stop and search the person if he suspects he has evidence on him.

2 Search or examine anything the person is using or has in his possession.

3 Arrest, using his general power under the Police and Criminal Evidence Act 1984. In Scotland a police officer may arrest if the person fails to give his name and address to the officer's satisfaction.

4 Seize and detain anything which may be evidence or liable to be forfeited under Section 21 (6) (e.g. any vehicle, animal or weapon used to commit the offence).

In order to exercise the powers in Section 19 (1) a police officer may enter land, but not a dwelling house. D.O.E. Inspectors have the power to enter and inspect certain premises but not to arrest, search or seize; it is an offence to obstruct a D.O.E. Inspector.   *Section 19 (2)*

---

[1] Schedule 9 Part I species are listed on page 137.
[2] Schedule 9 Part II plants are listed on page 137.

WARRANTS

Section 19 (3) Search warrants can be granted by a magistrate or sheriff in respect of offences under:

1 Sections 1, 3, 5, 7 and 8 where a special penalty is involved (e.g. in respect of Schedule 1 and 4 birds, prohibited methods of killing or taking wild birds and confinement of captive birds).

2 Sections 6, 9, 11 (1) (2), 13 and 14 (e.g. the sale of wild birds, taking Schedule 5 animals, certain prohibited methods of killing or taking wild and Schedule 6 animals, taking plants and introduction of new species).

SITES OF SPECIAL SCIENTIFIC INTEREST

Sections 28–38 Under Sections 28 to 38 of the Wildlife and Countryside Act 1981 sites of Special Scientific Interest (normally referred to as triple S I's (S.S.S.I's) are areas of land or water identified as being of outstanding value for their wildlife or geology by the Nature Conservancy Council. Whilst there are other areas important for nature conservation, S.S.S.I's are exceptional and many are of international importance.

S.S.S.I's are a trust for future generations and management of such areas in the interests of wildlife can be a source of pride and pleasure to the occupier. But such management may place restrictions on certain activities and it is the N.C.C.'s view that no occupier or owner should be disadvantaged by his responsibilities for an S.S.S.I.

Selection
The N.C.C. select potential sites and carry out surveys with the occupier's or owner's permission. If the site is to be declared an S.S.S.I., the owner and/or occupier is given three months' notice, which sets out the full proposal, a list of potentially damaging operations and consultation mechanism.

Access
The existence of an S.S.S.I. is not widely publicised and there is no right of access to the site by N.C.C. staff or any other persons, other than by rights of way.

Management plan

The N.C.C. and the owner/occupier agree upon a land management plan specific to the site detailing the potentially damaging operations (e.g. modification of a watercourse, reseeding, release of feral or domestic animals, extraction of topsoil, introduction of game management, tree felling, killing or removing wild animals) which may not be carried out on the site or the extent to which they may be carried out. Actions within the agreed framework do not require day-to-day consultation and operations outside the plan can be authorised in writing without delay.

OFFENCE

It is an offence for any person who has been formally notified under Section 28 to carry out a listed operation without proper consultation or to cause or permit another (e.g. contractor) to do so.

COMPENSATION

The N.C.C. may offer an appropriate payment if loss of income is incurred through entering into a management agreement; there is also the possibility of tax benefits being available, particularly in the form of capital transfer tax and capital gains tax. Owners/occupiers may also seek grant-aid or loans from the N.C.C. to conserve and enhance the scientific interest of their land. Full details are available from any N.C.C. Regional Officer.

Schedules

The common names of birds, animals and plants are given for the species listed in the Schedules. The Wildlife and Countryside Act 1981 also identifies them by their scientific names.

SCHEDULE 1

BIRDS WHICH ARE PROTECTED BY SPECIAL PENALTIES

PART I

*PROTECTED AT
ALL TIMES*

Avocet	Grebe, Slavonian	Sandpiper, Wood
Bee-eater	Greenshank	Scaup
Bittern	Gull, Little	Scoter, Common
Bittern, Little	Gull, Mediterranean	Scoter, Velvet
Bluethroat	Harriers, all species	Serin
Brambling	Heron, Purple	Shorelark
Bunting, Cirl	Hobby	Shrike, Red-backed
Bunting, Lapland	Hoopoe	Spoonbill
Bunting, Snow	Kingfisher	Stilt, Black-winged
Buzzard, Honey	Kite, Red	Stint, Temminck's
Chough	Merlin	Swan, Bewick's
Corncrake	Oriole, Golden	Swan, Whooper
Crake, Spotted	Osprey	Tern, Black
Crossbills, all species	Owl, Barn	Tern, Little
Curlew, Stone	Owl, Snowy	Tern, Roseate
Divers, all species	Peregrine	Tit, Bearded
Dotterel	Petrel, Leach's	Tit, Crested
Duck, Long-tailed	Phalarope, Red-necked	Treecreeper, Short-toed
Eagle, Golden	Plover, Kentish	Warbler, Cetti's
Eagle, White-tailed	Plover, Little ringed	Warbler, Dartford
Falcon, Gyr	Quail, Common	Warbler, Marsh
Fieldfare	Redstart, Black	Warbler, Savi's
Firecrest	Redwing	Whimbrel
Garganey	Rosefinch, Scarlet	Woodlark
Godwit, Black-tailed	Ruff	Wryneck
Goshawk	Sandpiper, Green	
Grebe, Black-necked	Sandpiper, Purple	

PART II

*PROTECTED
DURING THE
CLOSE SEASON*

Goldeneye	Goose, Greylag (in Outer Hebrides, Caithness, Sutherland and Wester Ross only)	Pintail

SCHEDULE 2

BIRDS WHICH MAY BE KILLED OR TAKEN

PART I
OUTSIDE THE CLOSE SEASON

Capercaillie	Goose, Pink-footed	Plover, Golden
Coot	Goose, White-fronted	Pochard
Duck, Tufted	(in England and	Shoveler
Gadwell	Wales only)	Snipe, Common
Goldeneye	Mallard	Teal
Goose, Canada	Moorhen	Wigeon
Goose, Greylag	Pintail	Woodcock

PART II
BY AUTHORISED PERSONS AT ALL TIMES

Crow	Gull, Herring	Rook
Dove, Collared	Jackdaw	Sparrow, House
Gull, Great black-backed	Jay	Starling
Gull, Lesser black-backed	Magpie	Woodpigeon
	Pigeon, Feral	

SCHEDULE 3

BIRDS WHICH MAY BE SOLD

PART I
ALIVE AT ALL TIMES IF RINGED AND BRED IN CAPTIVITY

Blackbird	Greenfinch	Siskin
Brambling	Jackdaw	Starling
Bullfinch	Jay	Thrush, Song
Bunting, Reed	Linnet	Twite
Chaffinch	Magpie	Yellowhammer
Dunnock	Owl, Barn	
Goldfinch	Redpoll	

PART II
DEAD AT ALL TIMES

Pigeon, Feral	Woodpigeon

PART III

*DEAD FROM 1
SEPTEMBER TO
28 FEBRUARY*

Capercaillie	Pintail	Snipe, Common
Coot	Plover, Golden	Teal
Duck, Tufted	Pochard	Wigeon
Mallard	Shoveler	Woodcock

SCHEDULE 4

BIRDS WHICH MUST BE REGISTERED AND RINGED IF KEPT IN CAPTIVITY

Schedule 4 birds are also divided into three categories by the D.O.E. Categories I and II must be ringed and registered; Category III must be registered but do not need to be ringed.

Category I

Hawks, True (except Old World Vultures) that is to say, Buzzards, Eagles, Harriers, Hawks and Kites (all species in each case)

Osprey

Falcons (all species)

Category II

Bunting, Cirl	Shorelark
Bunting, Lapland	Shrike, Red-Backed
Bunting, Snow	Tit, Bearded
Chough	Tit, Crested
Crossbills (all species)	Warbler, Cetti's
Fieldfare	Warbler, Dartford
Firecrest	Warbler, Marsh
Oriole, Golden	Warbler, Savis
Redstart, Black	Woodlark
Redwing	Wryneck
Serin	

Category III

Avocet	Curlew, Stone
Bee-eater	Divers (all species)
Bittern	Dotterel
Bittern, Little	Duck, Long-tailed
Bluethroat	Godwit, Black-tailed
Corncrake	Grebe, Black-necked
Crake, Spotted	Grebe, Slavonian

Greenshank
Hoopoe
Kingfisher
Petrel, Leach's
Phalarope, Red-necked
Plover, Kentish
Plover, Little ringed
Quail, Common
Rosefinch, Scarlet
Ruff
Sandpiper, Green
Sandpiper, Purple

Sandpiper, Wood
Scoter, Common
Scoter, Velvet
Spoonbill
Stilt, Black-winged
Stint, Temminck's
Tern, Black
Tern, Little
Tern, Roseate
Treecreeper, Short-toed
Whimbrel

SCHEDULE 5

ANIMALS WHICH ARE PROTECTED

Adder*
Bats, Horseshoe (all
  species)
Bats, typical (all
  species)
Beetle, Rainbow leaf
Burbot
Butterfly, Chequered
  Skipper
Butterfly, Heath
  Fritillary
Butterfly, Large Blue
Butterfly, Swallowtail
Cricket, Field
Cricket, Mole
Dolphin, Bottle-nosed
Dolphin, Common
Dragonfly, Norfolk Aeshna
Frog, Common*
Grasshopper, Wart-biter
Lizard, Sand
Lizard, Viviparous*
Moth, Barberry Carpet

Moth, Black-veined
Moth, Essex Emerald
Moth, New Forest Burnet
Moth, Reddish Buff
Newt, Great Crested
or Warty Newt
Newt, Palmate*
Newt Smooth*
Otter, Common
Porpoise, Harbour or
  Common
Slow-worm*
Snail, Carthusian
Snail, Glutinous
Snail, Sandbowl
Snake, Grass*
Snake, Smooth
Spider, Fen Raft
Spider, Ladybird
Squirrel, Red
Toad, Common*
Toad, Natterjack

* Protected only in respect of Section 9 (5) in that they may
  not be sold.

SCHEDULE 6

ANIMALS WHICH MAY NOT BE KILLED OR TAKEN BY CERTAIN METHODS

Badger

Bats, Horseshoe (all species)

Bats, Typical (all species)

Cat, Wild

Dolphin, Bottle-nosed

Dolphin, Common

Dormice (all species)

Hedgehog

Marten, Pine

Otter, Common

Polecat

Porpoise, Harbour or Common

Shrews (all species)

Squirrel, Red

SCHEDULE 8

PLANTS WHICH ARE PROTECTED

Alison, Small
Broomrape, Bedstraw
Broomrape, Oxtongue
Broomrape, Thistle
Calamint, Wood
Catchfly, Alpine
Cinquefoil, Rock
Club-rush, Triangular
Cotoneaster, Wild
Cow-wheat, Field
Cudweed, Jersey
Diapensia
Eryngo, Field
Fern, Dickie's Bladder
Fern, Killarney
Galingale, Brown
Gentian, Alpine
Gentian, Spring
Germander, Water
Gladiolus, Wild
Hare's-ear, Sickle-
   leaved

Hare's-ear, Small
Heath, Blue
Helleborine, Red
Knawel, Perennial
Knotgrass, Sea
Lady's Slipper
Lavender, Sea
Leek, Round-headed
Lettuce, Least
Lily, Snowden
Marsh-mallow, Rough
Orchid, Early Spider
Orchid, Fen
Orchid, Ghost
Orchid, Late Spider
Orchid, Lizzard
Orchid, Military
Orchid, Monkey
Pear, Plymouth
Pink, Cheddar
Pink, Childling
Sandwort, Norwegian

Sandwort, Teesdale
Saxifrage, Dropping
Saxifrage, Tufted
Solomon's-seal,
   Whorled
Sow-thistle, Alpine
Spearwort,
   Adder's-tongue
Speedwell, Spiked
Spurge, Purple
Starfruit
Violet, Fen
Water-plantain,
   (Ribbon-leaved)
Wood-sedge, Starved
Woodsia, Alpine
Woodsia, Oblong
Wormwood, Field
Woundwort, Downy
Woundwort, Lime-
   stone
Yellow-rattle, Greater

SCHEDULE 9

ANIMALS AND PLANTS TO WHICH SECTION 14 APPLIES

PART I

ANIMALS WHICH ARE ESTABLISHED IN THE WILD

Bass, Large-mouthed
   Black
Bass, Rock
Bitterling
Budgerigar
Capercaillie
Coypu
Dormouse, Fat
Duck, Carolina Wood
Duck, Mandarin
Duck, Ruddy
Eagle, White-tailed
Frog, Edible
Frog, European tree or
   Common Frog
Frog, Marsh

Gerbil, Mongolian
Goose, Canada
Goose, Egyptian
Heron, Night
Lizard, common wall
Marmot (prairie dog)
Mink, American
Newt, Alpine
Parakeet, Ring-necked
Partridge, Chukar
Partridge, Rock
Pheasant, Golden
Pheasant, Lady
   Amherst's
Pheasant, Reeve's
Pheasant, Silver

Porcupine, Crested
Porcupine, Himalayan
Pumpkinseed (Sun
   Fish or Pond Perch)
Quail, Bobwhite
Rat, Black
Squirrel, Grey
Terrapin, European
   pond
Toad, African Clawed
Toad, Midwife
Toad, Yellow-bellied
Wallaby, Red-necked
Wels, European
   Catfish
Zander

PART II

PLANTS

Hogweed, Giant
Seaweed, Japanese

Kelp, Giant

Knotweed, Japanese

CHAPTER 10

Predator and Pest Control

IT WAS ONCE common practice for a gamekeeper, using any means at his disposal, to kill any bird or animal, protected or otherwise, which was thought to threaten the production or survival of game species. However, the enlightenment brought about by research into the diet and effect of predators[1] has resulted in recent years in fewer protected and unprotected species being taken, particularly birds of prey where substantial fines have also been imposed.

OCCUPIER'S RESPONSIBILITY TO CONTROL PESTS

Some species of animals and birds do need to be controlled by farmers and keepers to protect crops, livestock and game, and the occupier has a duty as well as a legal right to do so.

Although control of animal or bird pests is primarily the responsibility of the occupier, advice is available from locally based M.A.F.F. Wildlife and Storage Biologists. Failure to control pests can lead to a notice being served by Agricultural

---

[1] For example, by the Game Conservancy: *Predator and Squirrel Control*, published by the Conservancy, explains the necessity for control and the means to be used; the British Field Sports Society's *Predatory Birds of Game and Fish* has a similar purpose.

Departments on the occupier or other person having rights to deal with pests on the land requiring that specific action be taken. Failure to comply with the notice may result in the pests being destroyed by the Ministry at the occupier's expense.

PREDATORY AND PEST SPECIES

The two main groups of avian and mammalian predators and pests are:

Avian: rook, crow, magpie, jackdaw, jay, starling, moorhen, coot, certain gulls, feral pigeon, house sparrow and woodpigeon.

Mammalian: rat, mink, fox, weasel, stoat, feral cat and mice.

BIRDS

The pest species of birds, listed in Schedule 2 Part II of the Wildlife and Countryside Act 1981 (see page 133), can be killed by authorised persons at any time,[1] but some methods are prohibited, e.g. snares, spring traps, poisons, stupefying baits, bird limes, lights or dazzling devices or automatic weapons (page 114). The shotgun, air rifle or small-bore weapon and cage traps are legal methods. Where it is thought necessary to kill protected species or to use prohibited methods, a licence must be obtained from Agricultural Departments.

Under Section 74 of the Public Health Act 1961, local authorities in England and Wales may take steps to deal with nuisance or damage caused in built-up areas by pigeons, house doves, starlings or sparrows. Precautions must be taken to prevent unnecessary suffering and nothing may be done contrary to the Wildlife and Countryside Act 1981, although licences are being issued to allow the conditional use of doped grain and artificial lights. *Public Health Act 1961 Section 74*

RACING PIGEONS

The feral pigeon, collared dove and woodpigeon are classed as a pest species in the Wildlife and Countryside Act; but

---

[1] Except moorhen and coot which have a close season: see page 110.

care must be taken in identifying the species so that racing pigeons are not killed or injured. The racing pigeon is not a wild bird: it has an owner; it is often of considerable value; and it is classed as property under the Theft and Criminal Damage Acts. Intentional or reckless killing or injuring of a racing pigeon may lead to prosecution in the Magistrates Court or a claim for civil damages.

When racing pigeons are shot out in the open when mixed with feral pigeons and woodpigeons, it can be difficult to prove that the action was intentional or reckless. But a farmer does not have an absolute right to shoot racing pigeons when they are fielding. The courts would have to decide whether he had acted reasonably to protect his crops and whether the racing variety were causing a significant amount of damage. The onus is on the shooter to be able to identify the quarry species from the racing pigeon.

A lost racing pigeon remains the property of its owner until he abandons all rights to it, but no time limit can be put on such circumstances. It is doubtful whether any owner would totally abandon his rights as his bird carries an identifying ring and if found they can be reunited.

A racing pigeon may be valued at several thousands of pounds; if found, it should be treated with care. The bird is best kept in a box or cage and should be fed on corn or rice but not bread. The Royal Pigeon Racing Association (telephone 0452 713529) should be informed of the bird's ring number. A reward is given to the finder.

MAMMALS

Mammals are protected by the Wildlife and Countryside Act 1981 and the Deer Acts, but these Acts also provide for the control of both protected and pest species.

The badger is protected by the Badgers Act 1973, as amended,[1] and any necessary trapping, killing or relocation for the purpose of preventing damage may only be done under licence.

[1] See Chapter 1.

BADGER CONTROL AREA

The Badger (Control Areas) Order 1977 designated areas in Wiltshire, Devon, Cornwall, Avon and Gloucester where M.A.F.F. may take steps to secure the destruction of badgers, if it is deemed necessary in order to eliminate or reduce the incidence of tuberculosis in cattle.

Initially, M.A.F.F. used hydrocyanic acid gas (e.g. Cymag) for badger control; as a result of research undertaken following the Zucherman Report, this method was superseded by cage trapping. Following the Dunnett Report on badgers and bovine T.B., M.A.F.F. has altered its badger control strategy and control operations are now limited to infected farms.

Carcases of badgers destroyed in the control areas are the property of the Minister of Agriculture and may not be removed from the premises on which they have been destroyed without his authority.

It is an offence to harbour, conceal or take into captivity any badger in the areas to prevent its destruction or to obstruct or interfere with anything which has been, is being, or is to be done or used in connection with the destruction.

Outside the statutory control areas badger-removal operations by M.A.F.F. may be undertaken by voluntary agreement with the occupier of the land. The Crown is exempt from the Badgers Act and Wildlife and Countryside Act, in that M.A.F.F. employees do not require licences to kill or take badgers to prevent the spread of disease, if there is a voluntary agreement with the occupier. Failure to obtain the occupier's full and voluntary consent means that action can only be taken under licence.

Where an individual feels that it is necessary for badgers to be relocated or killed in order to prevent damage, a licence must be obtained from Agricultural Departments. In many cases local badger groups are able to advise and assist in preventive action rendering the need to take more drastic measures unnecessary. For example, following damage to a green on a golf course caused by badgers grubbing for worms, an application of worm-killer rectified the situation.

SNARES

The setting or use of a self-locking snare to take any wild animal is illegal under the Wildlife and Countryside Act

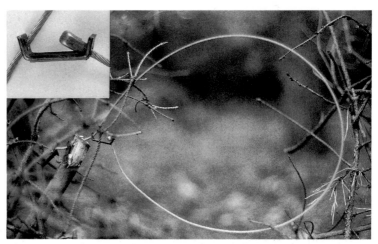

A self-locking snare.

1981. The self-locking snare is a wire-loop device which
continues to tighten as the animal struggles to escape and
unlike the common bootlace or free-running snare the self-
lock will not slacken off. Some dual-purpose snares can be
rigged to be either free running or self-locking and are not
specified in the Act; but they were considered in a debate on
the Wildlife and Countryside Bill when it was stated that as
the dual-purpose snare was a potential self-locking snare, it,
too, could be illegal. Although no longer on sale, self-lock
snares are still used, often made up from the standard free-
running fox snare by re-routing the noose wire through the
catch.

Basically, free running snares can be used to take any wild
animal not included in Schedule 6 of the Wildlife and
Countryside Act 1981, nor protected by other legislation
(e.g. Deer Acts). There is an argument that snares can be
indiscriminate and it is essential that they are set in such a
way as to prevent injury to domestic and non-target animals.
In addition, extreme care must be taken to ensure that
Schedule 6 animals cannot come into contact with snares: an
offence would be committed if all reasonable precautions
were not taken to prevent injury to them. In a prosecution it
is a defence to show that the snares were set in the interests of
public health, agriculture, forestry, fisheries or nature
conservation.[1] It is unlikely that the rearing of game birds

[1] See Section 11 (2) (a) (b) and (6) of the Wildlife and Countryside Act 1981, page
126.

will come under the term *agriculture* as in other parts of the
Act the term *livestock,* which incorporates captive game, is
specifically included but is omitted from this section.

Snares should never be set in or attached to fences, set
along public footpaths, in the vicinity of houses or other
places where offence may be caused or where there is a
danger to pets and domestic animals. Fox snares should also *Wildlife and*
be lifted when a meet of hounds is in the area. Section 11 (3) *Countryside Act*
of the Wildlife and Countryside Act 1981 also requires that *1981*
snares be inspected daily. Snares should be inspected just *Section 11 (3)*
after dawn to limit suffering.

Two simple modifications to snares to prevent unnecessary
suffering can be made:

1 Put a kink in the beginning of the noose to prevent it from
  becoming too big and thereby capturing the animal round
  the chest or middle.
2 Coil a strand of wire round the noose wire to form a stop,
  thereby creating a minimum diameter and preventing
  closure on the foot of a deer or other large mammal.

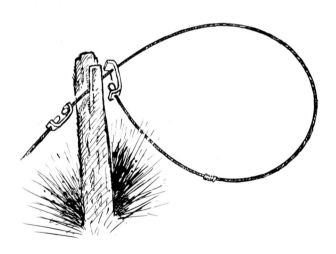

A free-running fox
snare.

Deer
Deer can be protected from snares with a deer leap or jump
by placing a horizontal stout branch, about 14in (350mm)
from ground level, in front of the snare which will cause deer
to jump over the danger. Particular care is needed where the
diminutive Muntjac or Chinese water deer are present.

Domestic cat and dog

Domestic cats and dogs are classed as property under the
Theft and Criminal Damage Acts or equivalent legislation in
Scotland and consequently it could be an offence under
either or both of these Acts to set snares intentionally or
recklessly to kill or injure these or other domestic animals. In
some circumstances, however, dog owners may be liable for
damage caused by their animals.[1] If cats and dogs are caught
in snares set to take wild animals which may be lawfully
snared, then it is possible that Schedule 6 wild animals could
also be caught in these same snares and an offence under
Section 11 (2) (a) (b) could be committed. For the
destruction of dogs and cats to protect game see pages 226–8.

Feral cats

Feral cats are prolific killers of nesting game and young
chicks and are not, as wild animals, protected by the criminal

Baited with a dead
pigeon, this type of
trap is often used for
taking feral cats.

or civil law. The best method of control, however, is by cage
trapping. The wild cat listed in Schedule 6 (*Felis sylvestris*),
found in the Scottish Highlands, is not the domestic variety
(*Felis catus*) which has gone feral.

[1] See pages 8–10.

TRAPS

The setting or use of cage or spring traps for wild birds and *Wildlife and*
Schedule 6 wild animals is prohibited by Sections 5 and 11 of *Countryside Act*
the Wildlife and Countryside Act 1981. The comments above *1981*
on the use of snares also apply to traps. *Section 5 & 11*

SPRING TRAPS

Under Section 8 Pests Act 1954 it is an offence, in respect of *Pests Act 1954*
any animal, to use or permit the use of: *Section 8*

1 Unapproved spring trap (e.g. a gin trap which is a form of
  spring trap with toothed jaws banned in 1958).
2 Approved trap in unapproved circumstances (e.g. a Fenn
  trap placed on a pole to catch birds of prey).

It is also an offence to sell, offer for sale or possess any
spring trap for such an unlawful purpose.

The prohibition in Section 8 does not apply to break-back *Small Ground*
traps designed and used to catch small ground vermin (e.g. *Vermin Trap*
rats and mice) or the type commonly used for taking moles in *Order 1958*
their runs as these are made an exception under the Small
Ground Vermin Trap Order 1958.

APPROVED SPRING TRAPS

Approved spring traps and their conditions of use are laid *Spring Trap*
down in the Spring Trap Approval Orders 1975 and 1982. *Approval Orders*
1975 & 1982

The Fenn trap being
used illegally to catch
birds of prey landing
on the post.

TRAPS	CONDITIONS OF USE
Imbra Mark I and II	To take rabbits in their holes or grey squirrels, stoats, weasels, rats, mice or other small ground vermin in artificial tunnels.
Fenn Vermin Trap Mark I, II, III and IV	To take grey squirrels, stoats, weasels, rats, mice or other small ground vermin. They must be set in artificial tunnels; the Mark IV may also be set in natural tunnels. All versions may be set in the open on rat and mice runs.
Fenn Vermin Trap Mark VI Dual-Purpose	To take rabbits in rabbit holes or grey squirrels, mink, stoats, weasels, rats, mice or other small vermin in natural or artificial tunnels.
Fenn Rabbit Trap Mark I	To take rabbits in rabbit holes.
Juby Trap	As for Imbra Traps.
Fuller Trap	To take grey squirrels only.
Sawyer Trap Lloyd Trap	To take grey squirrels, stoats, weasels, rats, mice or other small ground vermin in natural or artificial tunnels; to take rats or mice in the open on their runs.

Where there is a requirement to set traps in tunnels, twigs should be placed across the entrances to prevent birds being caught; the trap should be set well into the tunnel to avoid danger to domestic animals and game.

Pest Act 1954
Section 9   Section 9 specifies that traps set for rabbits and hares must be in rabbit holes. The courts have held that a rabbit hole is that part of a burrow which is inside the ground and covered by the roof, not the ground which is scraped away outside; the trap must be wholly within the overhang of the burrow.

The use of spring traps in the open is not permitted for rabbits and hares, but may be permitted under regulations or licence; no such regulations have yet been made and a licence will not be issued until such time as a trap suitable for open trapping has been approved. There are no traps approved at the present time to take hares.

Section 10 of the Protection of Animals Act 1911 and Section 9 of the Protection of Animals (Scotland) Act 1912 require that where spring traps are used, they should be inspected at reasonable intervals and at least once every day between sunrise and sunset. Failure to do so is an offence.

Protection of Animals Act 1911 Section 10

BAITING

Non-poisonous bait can be used in traps, but if through being placed too near an adjoining field, it attracts animals which would not otherwise have been likely to have entered the land, and those animals are injured or destroyed, the person setting the trap could be liable to pay compensation and possibly be prosecuted under the Criminal Damage Act 1971 or Criminal Justice (Scotland) Act 1980. The use of live animals and birds as bait or decoys is totally prohibited.

CATCH-ALIVE TRAPS

Catch-alive or cage traps can be used to take:

1 Any animal which is not protected (e.g. feral cat).
2 Schedule 2 Part II birds.
3 Wild duck in a duck decoy which was in use prior to 1954.
4 Game birds for breeding.

PEST CONTROL

RATS AND MICE

Under Section 2 of the Prevention of Damage by Pests Act 1949, a local authority is responsible for securing, as far as is practicable, that its district is kept free from rats and mice. It is expected to:

Prevention of Damage by Pests Act 1949 Section 2

1 Carry out periodic inspections.
2 Destroy rats and mice on land occupied by the authority.
3 Enforce the duties under the Act of owners and occupiers of land.

Under Section 3, the occupier of non-agricultural land must notify the local council of the presence, *in substantial*

Section 3

numbers, of rats and mice. Failure to notify may render him liable to a fine.

Section 4 & 5   Under Sections 4 and 5, the owner and/or occupier may be required by the local authority to take specified action. Failure to comply with the notice may result in the authority carrying out the destruction and recovering the expense from the owner and/or occupier.

NOTIFICATION OF IMPORTED PESTS

Destructive The Destructive Imported Animals Act 1932 requires the
Imported Animals occupier of any land to notify Agricultural Departments of
Act 1932 the presence of musk rats, grey squirrels, rabbits other than the European rabbit, mink or coypus, regardless of the numbers involved. Failure to notify their presence, keeping without authority or turning loose such species are offences.

Importation of mammals, including mink and coypu, is controlled by the Rabies (Importation of Dogs, Cats and Other Mammals) Order 1974 as amended. Specified animals may only be imported under a licence issued in advance.

RABBIT CLEARANCE ORDERS

Pests Act 1954 Under Section 1 of the Pests Act 1954, the whole of Britain
Section 1 (except for the City of London, the Scilly Isles and Skokholm Island, the Outer Isles and Jura) has been declared a rabbit clearance area: the occupier of any land has a continuing obligation to kill or take rabbits on his land and if this is not reasonably practicable, then to prevent damage being caused by them (e.g. by fencing). Failure to fulfill his obligations may lead to the occupier being prosecuted or the work carried out at his expense.

The occupier's right to kill rabbits is only restricted by the Ground Game Act 1880 in respect of the use of firearms and night shooting[1]. He is not given further powers by the Order, but can apply to Agricultural Departments to authorise more than one other person to use firearms, if the landowner is unwilling to permit such authorisations. The occupier would have to show that: it is necessary to employ more than the one gun he has power to authorise; he has attempted to obtain the sanction of the owner of the shooting

[1] See pages 23–31.

rights; the owner is not proposing to do the shooting himself
and his sanction has been unreasonably withheld.

Myxomatosis

Under Section 12 of the Pests Act 1954, it is an offence to use *Pests Act 1954*
an infected rabbit to spread the disease. *Section 12*

FORESTRY COMMISSION LAND

The Forestry Act 1967 gives the Forestry Commission *Forestry Act 1967*
powers to prevent damage to trees by any animal, but
in particular rabbits, hares and squirrels. They include
authorising a competent person to enter the land and destroy
them.

STATUTORY NOTICES

Under Sections 98 and 99 of the Agriculture Act 1947 and
Agriculture (Scotland) Act 1948, Agricultural Departments
can serve a notice requiring any person having the responsibility to do so to take, destroy or prevent the escape of certain
pest species on his land (i.e. rabbits, hares, rats, mice and
other rodents, deer, foxes, moles and birds which are not
listed in Schedule 1 of the Wildlife and Countryside Act
1981). Other species may be included. The notice may also
include the destruction or reduction of breeding places for
rabbits. The notice does not apply to marauding deer in
Scotland as measures are available through the Red Deer
Commission and the Deer (Scotland) Act 1959, as amended.[1]

The purpose of the notice is to prevent damage to crops,
pasture, foodstuffs, livestock, trees, banks, hedges or works
on any land. A provisional notice is served on the person
having the right to kill the kind of animal detailed in the
notice and could include the occupier, shooting tenant or
owner with reserved sporting rights. In respect of rabbits,
the notice can be served on the occupier as he still has rights
to ground game under the Ground Game Act 1880.

The notice comes into effect when confirmed by a further
notice which is issued when all objections have been
considered. If the occupier is a tenant, copies of the notices
are also sent to the landlord.

[1] See page 175.

The execution of the notice must be by lawful means with the following exceptions:

1 Game may be killed out of season.
2 Game licence is not required to take or sell game, but the Game Act 1831 requires that game be sold to a licensed game dealer.[1]
3 Poisonous gas or substances which generate such a gas can be used in the burrows, holes or earths of animals specified in the notice.

POISON AND POISON GAS

Protection of Animals Act 1911 Section 8 of the Protection of Animals Act 1911 and Protection of Animals (Scotland) Act 1912 make it unlawful, knowingly, to put or place in a building or upon land any poison or poisonous fluid or edible matter, except in the circumstances given below. Where a gamekeeper commits this offence by laying poison illegally and it is done with the landowner's knowledge, consent or on his instructions, then the landowner is also guilty.

Exceptions
The exceptions are: to destroy insects, invertebrates and rats, mice or other small ground vermin[2] where this is necessary in the interests of public health, agriculture, the preservation of domestic or wild animals, or for the purpose of manuring the land, and provided that all reasonable precautions are taken to prevent injury[3] to dogs, cats, fowls, domestic animals or wild birds.

Two further exceptions are the sowing of treated seed or grain and the use of pesticide approved under the Food and Environment Protection Act 1985.

PROHIBITED POISONS

Animal (Cruel Poisons) Act 1962 Even in the above exceptions, it is still an offence to use certain types of poison under the Animal (Cruel Poisons) Act 1962. Regulations made in 1963 banned the use of elementary yellow phosphorus and red squill in all cases and restricted the use of strychnine to killing moles.

[1] See page 64.
[2] Small ground vermin are not included in the Scottish Act.
[3] The term *access* is used instead of *injury* in the Scottish Act.

The Poisons Act of 1972 and the Poison Rules of 1982 *Poisons Act 1972*
regulate the sale and supply of poisons. Permits may be
issued, for example, for the express purpose of purchasing
strychnine for killing moles, fluoroacetic acid as a roden-
ticide for killing rats, mice or moles. Although the sale of
zinc phosphide is regulated, no permit is required for its
purchase.

Squirrels
The Grey Squirrels (Warfarin) Order 1973 allows the use of
warfarin outdoors (in special hoppers), but is restricted to
certain counties in England and Wales; it cannot be used in
Scotland and so prevents the poisoning of red squirrels.
Where warfarin is used near nature reserves, Naturalists
Trusts, Wardens, etc. should be notified.

Poisoning game
Under the Game Act 1831 and the Hares (Scotland) Act
1848, it is an offence to put poison on a highway or ground
with intent to destroy or injure game.
    The illegal use of poison is also included in the Deer Act
1963, Deer (Scotland) Act 1959 as amended, Badgers Act
1973 as amended and the Wildlife and Countryside Act 1981.

POISON APPLICATION

The Game Conservancy booklet, *Predator and Squirrel
Control*, gives advice on the strategy to be adopted, bait
mixing and application, handling of poison and carcases,
uneaten bait etc. Additional assistance is also available from
M.A.F.F. officers.

POISON GAS

Initially, poison gas could only be employed in rabbit holes
for the extermination of rabbits under Section 4 of the
Prevention of Damage by Rabbits Act 1939, but its use has
been extended to animals listed in Section 98 of the
Agriculture Act 1947.[1]
    Hydrocyanic gas sold in the form of Cymag is commonly
used on subterranean predators and pests – especially foxes –

[1] See Statutory Notices page 149.

although the use of gas is not a practice recommended by
M.A.F.F. It is also possible to obtain licences for the use of
poison and poison gas under Section 9 (1) (d) (e) of the
Badgers Act 1973 as amended and Section 16 (3) Wildlife and
Countryside Act, but it is unlikely that such licences would
ever be granted.

Care should be taken when using gas as there is a
possibility of seepage into drains and buildings and therefore
its use should be restricted to open land. It is also advisable
not to work alone.

CONTROL OF AGRICULTURAL CHEMICALS

The Food and Environment Protection Act 1985 came into
force in September 1985 and the aims of Part III are to:

Food and 1 Ensure the continuous development of means to protect
Environment   the health of human beings, creatures and plants, to safe-
Protection Act   guard the environment, and to secure safe, efficient and
1985   humane methods of controlling pests.

2 Make information about pesticides available to the public.

REGULATIONS

The Food and Environment Protection Act forms the basis
of regulations and codes of practice which will control the
sale, supply, storage, use and advertisement of pesticides; set
maximum levels of pesticide residues in food, crops and
feeding stuffs; make information on pesticides available to
the public and establish an advisory committee. These
provisions will be enforced through powers of seizure,
disposal or remedial action. The regulations will be introduced
in stages, becoming fully operative towards the end of 1987
and be enforced by various agencies (e.g. Health and Safety
Executive, Factory Inspectorate, Trading Standards,
Environmental Health and Agricultural Departments)
authorised to enter land, buildings and vehicles. They will be
able to require information about the use of substances, serve
prohibition notices and cause remedial or preventive measures
to be taken.

Prior to the Act, the safety screening of pesticides was
achieved under the Pesticide Safety Precautions Scheme
where any potential risk to users, bystanders, consumers,

livestock, wildlife, domestic animals and the environment was evaluated before a safety clearance was granted. The scheme required co-operation between manufacturers and Government Departments and progressed on a non-statutory basis. However, a safety clearance is of no value if the user does not follow the recommended precautions and uses for that product. The new Act and Regulations will make it an offence not to follow the precautions specified as part of the approval of the particular pesticide.

It is a common practice to lay on the land animal and bird carcases, eggs or other baits laced with poisonous substances in order to kill scavenging predators. This highly dangerous practice is illegal under the Protection of Animals Acts 1911 and 1912 (Scotland), Sections 5 and 11 of the Wildlife and Countryside Act 1981, Section 3 Deer Act 1963 and Section 23 Deer (Scotland) Act 1959 and will become so under the Food and Environment Protection Act and associated regulations.

Accidental injection and ingestion have led to a number of human deaths and many domestic, farm and wild animals and birds are poisoned each year. Children are particularly vulnerable when picking up carcases and eggs left lying in a wood or field. In one case, a boy took an egg home and cooked it, but on seeing it turn green, gave it to his dog which later died. In addition, the amount of poison used is usually excessive with instances of a single egg containing

Once injected with poison, the egg is placed as bait for the unwary bird or animal – a dangerous, in-discriminate and illegal practice.

sufficient poison to kill forty human beings. It should also be remembered that poisoned animals, especially game species, may enter the human food chain.

When fully in operation, the Food and Environment Protection Act 1985 will require that all pesticides be submitted by manufacturers for approval which will only be granted to specified formulations of products with specified uses and conditions of use (e.g. product X may only be sprayed on lettuces which cannot be harvested for a period of ten days after application). To spray the same product on carrots or to inject it into carcases would be an unapproved and hence, illegal, use.

WILDLIFE INCIDENT INVESTIGATION SCHEME

Where it is suspected that a carcase or bait has been treated with agricultural chemicals or that a bird or animal has died from such poison, the M.A.F.F., W.O.A.D. or D.A.F.S. should be notified of all the circumstances and a preliminary investigation will be carried out. Carcases and baits should be placed in a polythene bag, using gloves or a polythene bag to protect the skin. In England and Wales specimens should be forwarded to an area Veterinary Investigation Centre for examination and analysis and in Scotland to the Agricultural Scientific Services, East Craigs, Edinburgh.

SQUIRREL-DREY POKING

Drey poking is an effective means of squirrel control, but care should be taken to deal only with grey squirrel dreys which are roughly made of twigs-in-leaf as opposed to those of the red squirrel made of leafless twigs, disturbance of which is an offence under Section 9 (4) of the Wildlife and Countryside Act 1981.[1]

BIRD SCARERS

A variety of scarers are available and there is a M.A.F.F. advisory leaflet on their use and a N.F.U. code of practice. Part III of the Control of Pollution Act 1974 gives local authorities and magistrates courts powers to control noise

---

[1] See page 124.

nuisance. Regular complaints from local residents may result in a local authority notice being served requiring abatement of the noise and specifying steps to be taken to that end.

Failure to comply with the notice may lead to enforcement by the courts. In addition a court, on receipt of a complaint, may issue and enforce a similar notice, but in both cases it is a defence to show the noise is being made in the course of a trade or business and that the best practicable means have been adopted to prevent or counteract the effects of noise.

COMPENSATION FOR CROP DAMAGE

Animals are capable of trespass[1] and it is possible to make a claim against the owner for the damage they cause. The position with wild animals is different, since they have no owner to make claims against.

If the tenant of an agricultural holding suffers crop damage from wild animals and birds and his tenancy agreement restricts his rights to shoot or take certain species, in particular game, and for this reason he is unable to carry out control measures, he may claim compensation from the landlord for the damage under the Agricultural Holdings Act 1986.[2] *Agricultural Holdings Act 1986*

To claim compensation, a tenant must give his landlord written notice within one month of the damage becoming evident and give him the opportunity of making an inspection of a growing crop before it is harvested or, if damaged after harvest, before it is removed from the land. A written notice of the claim is then sent to the landlord within one month after the expiry of the year in respect of which the claim is made. A year normally ends on 29 September or other date agreed with the landlord. Where the shooting rights are held by a third person (e.g. shooting tenant or syndicate), the landlord is entitled to be indemnified by the third party against such claims. Claims may be settled by arbitration under this Act.

PEST CONTROL ORGANISATIONS

There are now a number of pest control societies, organisations and companies, as well as private individuals, who will

[1] See pages 8–10.
[2] There are also provisions under the Deer Acts: see page 167.

undertake control measures for payment. Where the control measures are inadequate or not successful, there is no automatic right to compensation. The situation is similar to employing a plumber or joiner whose workmanship is not up to the required standard and much will depend on the initial agreement or contract. Following legal advice, claims for compensation or damages may be made through the civil courts. It is essential that, where relevant, operatives are properly authorised to carry out the action required (for example, through written authority under the Ground Game Act).

The British Association for Shooting and Conservation provide a free wood pigeon control service, supported by the N.F.U.

The long lines of decomposing vermin on the keeper's gibbet used to be regarded as evidence of his ability. The Game Conservancy now recommend that pests be burned or buried.

CHAPTER 11

Deer

For hundreds of years deer roamed the royal forests and were hunted solely by the king or his court. Deer were a valuable asset providing food for the royal pantry, and the right to hunt or take deer was often granted as a privilege or favour for services rendered. The forest laws were draconian, but even then did not deter poachers or the farmer taking action to stop marauding deer damaging his crops.

Today, venison is a popular and profitable meat; deer farms and parks are on the increase; the poacher is ever present and legislation provides for the protection of both deer and crops. Deer remain a quarry species, but whilst stalking is a growing sport, hunting with hounds is limited now to southern England.

HUNTING

There are four packs of hounds that hunt deer in England today: the Tiverton, Quantock, Devon and Somerset Staghounds and the New Forest Buckhounds. Modern hounds are built for stamina rather than speed and consequently the chase may take several hours; when at bay, the deer is shot.

GREYHOUNDS AND LURCHERS

Taking deer with dogs, other than by hunting, is not a sport recognised by the field sport organisations, although dogs are invaluable for finding injured animals or flushing deer, particularly in woodland. Only in Scotland does legislation prohibit the use of dogs to take or kill deer under any circumstances. In England and Wales it is only an offence to do so at night; although in practice, since permission from the landowner is needed and would be unlikely to be granted, poaching offences may also be committed.

Deer poachers commonly use dogs. Although the greyhound has been used since the fourteenth century, the lurcher – a cross-breed of greyhound, saluki or whippet with a deerhound, collie or doberman – is said to be the ideal dog. Lurcher breeding has become a trade as lucrative as poaching itself; 'big, fast and a good worker in all conditions' is the advertiser's coded message extolling a dog's deer-killing abilities.

STALKING

There are now no large animal predators other than man to control deer in the British Isles. Hunting accounts for only a small percentage of the deer cull; to keep damage from deer to an acceptable level and to ensure healthy populations, the most humane, efficient and safe method is by an experienced stalker armed with an adequate high velocity rifle.

Stalking of deer is closely regulated through restrictions on firearms and close seasons. Organisations such as the Forestry Commission, B.A.S.C., British Deer Society, St Hubert Club and Game Conservancy foster high standards in the sport and in practice there is a code of conduct (a joint B.A.S.C./B.D.S. publication) which advises how deer should be shot.

In the past, it was common practice on many recognised shoots to have a go at the deer when flushed with other game. Consequently, it was not unusual for deer to be shot and wounded using the standard 12-bore game gun and cartridge with the deer making good its escape and then being subject to a painfully slow death in the undergrowth. Prior to the 1963 Deer Act, it was not uncommon for over seventy per cent of culled deer to be carrying shot of some kind. Today that number is in the region of four per cent.

Shooting from a high seat in the forest.

The species of wild deer that live in Britain range in size from Muntjac and Chinese Water Deer through to Roe, Fallow, Sika and the largest of them all, Red Deer. The legislation controlling the shooting of deer takes into account breeding seasons and size of the species and specifies the calibre of rifle and size of ammunition most suitable for their effective despatch. Even the small Roe and Muntjac deer require a projectile with substantial energy to kill cleanly.

An excellent identification chart is available from the British Deer Society. It gives six species of deer, with illustrations of front, rear and side views, including seasonal variations, sexes and young.

CHOICE OF WEAPON

The choice of weapon to shoot deer is governed by Schedule 2 Deer Act 1963 in England and Wales, and the Deer (Firearms) (Scotland) Order 1985. The firearms permitted for killing deer in England, Wales and Scotland are laid out below and include the specifications for stalking rifles and ammunition and the use of shotguns in specified circumstances. Exceptions are fully covered later under the relevant Act.

FIREARMS PERMITTED FOR KILLING DEER
IN ENGLAND, WALES AND SCOTLAND

	ENGLAND AND WALES	SCOTLAND
RIFLES	Calibre of not less than .240ins or Muzzle energy of not less than 1,700ft/lb	
RIFLE AMMU-NITION	Bullet must be soft-nosed or hollow-nosed	*Roe deer:* Bullet of not less than 50 grains AND Muzzle velocity of not less than 2,450ft per sec AND Muzzle energy of not less than 1,000ft/lb *All deer:* Bullet of not less than 100 grains AND Muzzle velocity of not less than 2,450ft per sec AND Muzzle energy of not less than 1,750ft/lb All bullets must be designed to expand on impact
SHOT-GUNS	Not less than 12 bore	Not less than 12 bore
SHOTGUN AMMU-NITION	Rifled slug of not less than 350 grains or AAA shot	*All deer:* Rifled slug of not less than 380 grains or Shot not smaller than SSG *Roe deer*: Shot not smaller than AAA
PROHIB-ITIONS	Any air gun, air rifle or air pistol	Any sight specially designed for night shooting (The above ballistic requirements eliminate all handguns and all air and gas weapons)
	A shotgun may be used only by the occupier and certain others, who must be able to prove serious damage (see Deer Act 1963, as amended, Section 10A)	A shotgun may be used only on arable or enclosed land and only by the occupier and certain others, who must be able to prove serious damage (see Deer (Firearms) (Scotland) Order 1985, No 1168).

A fundamental difference exists between the English and Scottish legislation on the method of specifying rifles and ammunition for use in deer stalking and control. In England and Wales, it is the *calibre* of the rifle itself that is the main criterion for lawful use; in Scotland, the criteria relate to the ammunition only, it being lawful to use any rifle capable of firing such ammunition. In Scotland, therefore, the regulations mean that the use of the .22 centrefire rifle against roe deer is legal (effectively starting with the .222 Remington). However, it does not include the .22 centrefire Hornet which falls short of the requirements in respect of muzzle velocity, energy and bullet weight. All .22 rimfire rifles fail to reach the required performance.

A range of ammunition, some of which falls short of the legal requirements: *from left to right*: .22 long rifle, .22 magnum, .22 centrefire, .222, .223, .243, .270, .308 super, .308, 7 × 57.

If a bullet/cartridge combination does not comfortably meet the required standard, it should not be used. Where the muzzle velocity of a particular combination of rifle and cartridge is in doubt, it should be checked with a chronograph to ensure the performance is within the legal requirements.

In England and Wales the minimum calibre for rifles is laid down as .240; consequently, it is illegal to use any .22 centrefire rifle against any species of deer, including roe and muntjac. Not all experienced, and in some cases very professional, stalkers would agree that the banning of such rifles (which were used against roe in England and Wales prior to the Deer Act 1963) contributes to the humane treatment of deer. But it is generally accepted that the use of such rifles in the hands of the inexperienced shot can be a problem and lead to considerable suffering if the bullet is not placed sufficiently accurately to strike a vital organ.

Muntjac and Chinese Water Deer

The muntjac, found only in England and Wales at the present time, is a very small deer which colonises dense cover. Their timidity, size and very rapid alarm flight make them a difficult target for the rifle, unless through regular disturbance they can be encouraged to cross well-mown forest rides. Although fox-sized, the muntjac cannot be shot with the same size of guns and calibre as are used for fox control. Similarly, the Chinese Water Deer, which is gradually becoming established as a quarry species, must be shot with the correct weapon and calibre of ammunition.

NIGHT SHOOTING

Night shooting of deer is not permitted in England and Wales. It is permitted in specified circumstances in Scotland and, in most cases, must be carried out under the Red Deer Commission's Code of Practice.[1]

SIGHTS

The only restriction on sights is in Scotland where Article 5 of the Deer (Firearms) (Scotland) Order 1985 makes it lawful to use a sight so long as it is not a light-intensifying, heat-sensitive or other special device for night shooting.

Although telescopic sights are a vital part of a stalker's equipment and once fitted tend to become a permanent fixture on the rifle, they are not classed as a component part of the rifle in terms of the legal requirement of a firearm certificate and therefore their purchase and possession are unrestricted.

RESPONSIBLE SHOOTING

Current legislation goes some way towards ensuring that both weapons and ammunition used against deer are capable of effective despatch in order to minimise unnecessary harm or suffering. However, deer can suffer irrespective of the calibre of the weapon or the suitability of ammunition, if the shot is not accurate. It should be the aim of all sportsmen to kill efficiently and humanely and when deer are wounded inexperience is not a justifiable excuse.

[1] See page 177.

To improve standards of stalking, the British Deer Society has for some time been promoting Stalker's Competence Tests. The British Deer Society also organises deer stalking courses, as do B.A.S.C. and the Game Conservancy.

FIREARM CERTIFICATES

A stalker does not have to own land or have written proof of access to land in order to obtain a firearm certificate, but he must be able to satisfy the police that he has some opportunity of using the rifle for stalking purposes. The British Deer Society does not advocate that membership of the Society should be used as a means to obtain a firearm certificate; however, attendance at a British Deer Society, Forestry Commission or B.A.S.C. stalking course should be beneficial to an application, particularly in establishing the proficiency and safety of the applicant.

There are obvious practical difficulties for the stalker in specifying where stalking is to take place, but it is the responsibility of individual Chief Constables to ensure that stalking rifles do not present a risk to public safety and the applicant may be required to be specific about the area to be stalked to establish that the land is suitable for the safe use of rifles. It is argued that land cannot be safe – only people. It is obviously difficult to establish every applicant's ability and experience, particularly as stalking courses provide the only formal qualifications. Whilst the argument has a lot to

Zeroing is an essential task prior to a stalking expedition.

commend it, certain areas of land can be used with less potential risk than others, based on the topography, population etc. The police deal with each case on its merits.

The firearm certificate would also normally cover the use of the rifle on approved ranges or land for zeroing purposes (sight adjustment) and target practice.

GAME LICENCES

As a general rule, a stalker is required to obtain a game licence,[1] the only exception being the taking of deer on enclosed lands.[2] An annual licence[3] can be bought from any main Crown Post Office.

Should the stalker intend to sell any deer shot, he must ensure that sale is restricted to a licensed game dealer, if in England, or a licensed venison dealer, if sold in Scotland.[4]

DEALING WITH INJURED DEER

Deer legislation makes provision for the despatch of an injured or diseased deer: for example, road casualties or the result of a badly taken shot, snaring and the cruel methods of the poacher. It is recognised that awaiting the arrival of a humane killer or other suitable firearm would only prolong pain and suffering, and consequently any shotgun or rifle with any ammunition can be used.

A rope, to prevent the animal from running away, and a powerful torch can be invaluable. Ensure that people are moved to a safe distance and place the animal where there is no risk of ricochet from the road surface, etc.

PROTECTION AND CONSERVATION: ENGLAND AND WALES

In England and Wales deer are protected by the Deer Act 1963 as amended by the Deer Act 1980 and the Wildlife and Countryside Act 1981.

---

[1] See page 62.
[2] See page 62.
[3] Or for a shorter period if required.
[4] See page 69.

CLOSE SEASONS

It is an offence to take or wilfully kill any red, fallow, roe or sika deer in the close season.[1] *Deer Act 1963 Section 1*

SPECIES	1 MAY – 31 JULY	1 MARCH – 31 OCTOBER	1 NOVEMBER 31 MARCH
Red	male	female	
Fallow	male	female	
Roe		female	male
Sika	male	female	

The close seasons are applicable to both wild and farm deer.

Red/sika hybrids are not included in the Schedule detailing the close seasons and consequently it can be argued that there is no close season. However, it can also be argued that a hybrid is a form of red or sika deer and is covered by a close season. There is no answer to this point until a case is decided in the courts.

There is no legal close season for Muntjac and Chinese water deer but an advisory close season from 1 March to 31 October is recommended.

KILLING DEER AT NIGHT

Under Section 2 it is an offence to take or wilfully kill deer, or take a carcase, of *any species* between one hour after sunset and one hour before sunrise. *Section 2*

EXCEPTIONS TO CLOSE SEASONS AND NIGHT CLOSE TIMES

Under Section 10 it is *not* an offence under the close seasons and night close times legislation to kill or take a deer to prevent suffering of an injured or diseased animal.[2] In these circumstances a trap or net, normally prohibited by section 3 (1) (a) (b), may also be used, but not poison. *Section 10*

Deer may also be killed during the close season and at night under Section 98 of the Agriculture Act 1947 (the

[1] See pages 168–9 for exemptions.
[2] See pages 166–7 regarding use of shotguns.

prevention of damage under an Order issued by a Government Minister).

UNLAWFUL WEAPONS

The poacher's arsenal is a mixture of modern and medieval technology, ranging from infra-red sights, light-intensifying devices and sophisticated firearms (including gas-operated guns) to the crossbow, snare and hunting dog.

Frozen in the lamper's beam, deer are easy prey for a firearm or crossbow bolt shot indiscriminately into the herd. Silent and powerful, the crossbow can be bought cheaply and requires no certificate. Another favoured method is to use piano wire strung across forest paths, thus acting as a knife or garrotte to catch stampeding deer, the unfortunate animals being cut to the bone. The noose of a snare set at the right height can sometimes be lethal but is invariably cruel, as is apparent by the signs of the strangled animal thrashing about.

Traps, snares, poison and nets

Section 3 (1) (a) Under Section 3 (1) (a), it is an offence to set in position any trap, snare, poisoned or stupefying bait so placed as to be calculated to injure any deer coming into contact.[1]

Section 3 (1) (b) Under Section 3 (1) (b), it is an offence to use any trap, snare, poisoned or stupefying bait or a net to kill or take any deer.[2]

It is also an offence under Section 4 to *attempt* to commit these offences.

Firearms and drugs

Section 3 (1) (c) Under Section 3 (1) (c), it is an offence to use any of the following to injure or kill any deer:

1 Rifle less than .240 or with a muzzle energy less than 1700 ft/lb.

2 Rifle bullet other than soft or hollow-nosed.

3 Air weapon.

4 Shotgun or shotgun ammunition.

[1] See page 143.
[2] Under Section 4 possession of these items to commit an offence is an offence in itself.

A shotgun may be used as a slaughtering instrument if it is not less than 12-bore, has a barrel less than 24in and is loaded with AAA shot or larger. This kind of weapon is carried by deer hunts and, because of the short barrel, requires a firearm certificate.

A deer may also be killed with any shotgun if it is seriously injured or in such a condition that to kill it would be an act of mercy; but the person would have to show that the injury was not caused by his own unlawful act. An unlawful act is any offence under any Act and could include the use of a rifle without a certificate or whilst poaching (Section 10 (3) (4)).

5 Arrow, spear or similar missile.

6 Missile containing poison, stupefying drug or muscle relaxant.

It is also an offence under Section 4 to *attempt* to commit any of these offences.

MOTOR VEHICLES

Under Section 3 (2) (a) and (b), it is an offence to discharge a firearm or project any missile at any deer from a powered vehicle (e.g. car, boat, helicopter or hovercraft) or to use such a vehicle to drive deer. *Section 3 (2) (a) & (b)*

It is also an offence under Section 4 to *attempt* to carry out any of these offences.

Under Section 3 (3) such actions are not illegal, however, if carried out by, or with the written authority of, the occupier of any enclosed land where deer are usually kept. *Section 3 (3)*

EXCEPTIONS FOR AUTHORISED PERSONS

Under the Deer Act 1963, there are exceptions for *authorised persons*. In this Act an authorised person is:

1 Occupier of land.
2 Resident member of his household.[1]
3 Person in his service (e.g. an employee).[1]
4 Person having the right to take or kill deer or a person authorised in writing by the occupier (includes the shooting tenant, his gamekeeper and invited guns).

---

[1] Must be authorised in writing by the occupier.

Damage

Section 10A If deer are causing damage, under Section 10A an authorised person may:

1 Take or kill deer by shooting during the close season on cultivated land, pasture or enclosed woodland.[1]

2 Use a shotgun to kill deer on any land, at any time,[1] if it is not less than a 12-bore and is loaded with either AAA shot or a single non-spherical bullet, not less than 350 grains, (i.e. a rifled slug).

However, the authorised person must be able to show that:

1 He had reason to believe that deer of the same species were causing or had caused damage to crops, vegetables, fruit, growing timber or other form of property on the land.

2 It was likely that further serious damage would be caused.

3 His action was necessary to prevent it.

This exception provides a loophole for *legalised poaching* in that some farmers plant crops close to woods or land containing deer with the intention of attracting deer through an open gate or broken down fence on to their land.

TRAILL V BUCKINGHAM (1972)

Where an authorised person takes action against marauding deer to protect his crops etc., the killing must take place on the land where the damage is occurring, not the land where the deer come from.

In the case of Traill v Buckingham, damage was being caused to crops on Buckingham's land. It was believed that the deer responsible were to be found in a wood adjoining his land, but occupied by Traill. The wood had previously belonged to Buckingham's father who sold it, but in the contract retained the right to shoot deer and other animals in the wood. During the close season Buckingham entered the wood and shot a red hind. Although found not guilty of killing out of season at the magistrates court, the Queen's Bench Division decided otherwise, on the basis that although he had the shooting rights in the wood, under the Deer Act

[1] See also the case of Traill v Buckingham (page 168).

1963 he was only entitled to deal with marauding deer on land where the damage was caused and not on adjoining land. In addition the retention of shooting rights in the contract by Buckingham did not make him an occupier of the wood or a person with the written authority of the occupier, who would be entitled to kill deer in the wood causing damage to the trees.

DEER ACT 1980

The 1963 Act did not contain any substantive anti-poaching measures: these were introduced in the Deer Act 1980 which made deer poaching a criminal offence, put controls on the sale of venison, gave the police powers to enforce the 1963 and 1980 Acts and the courts power to confiscate deer, animals (e.g. lurchers), weapons, equipment and vehicles.

POACHING

Under Section 1, it is an offence, without the consent of the occupier, owner or other lawful authority, to:

1 Enter any land in search or pursuit of any deer with the intention of taking, killing or injuring it. *Deer Act 1980 Section 1 (1)*
2 While on the land, take, kill or injure any deer or attempt to do so, search for or pursue any deer with such intent or remove the carcase of any deer: *Section 1 (2)*

Poachers' dogs about to bring down a deer.

Section 1 (3) But under Section 1 (3), a person will not be guilty if:

1 He believed he would have had the owner's or occupier's consent, if the owner or occupier had known of the circumstances (e.g. a farmer removes from a neighbour's land the carcase of a deer shot on his own land).

2 He believed he had a lawful authority (e.g. an authorised stalker enters by mistake land where he is not authorised to shoot).

TRESPASS BY A HUNT

Game Act 1831 Section 35 Section 35 of the Game Act 1831 provides that the offences of daytime poaching will not apply to a person hunting or coursing on any land with hounds or greyhounds, if in fresh pursuit of deer, hare or fox already started on other land.[1]

However, although no criminal offence is committed, there is still civil trespass,[2] for Section 35 does not give a hunt or anyone else the right to follow quarry on to another's land. The Game (Scotland) Act 1832 contains similar provisions, but only in respect of fox and hare; the 1959 Deer (Scotland) Act (which amended the 1832 Act) prohibits the hunting of deer with dogs.

Several deer sanctuaries are strategically situated in hunting country, and a number of private and council landowners have refused hunts permission to go on their land. Signs placed on the boundaries and written correspondence inform hunts of the landowner's wishes, and it is possible that where a hunt knowingly enters land without the consent of the owner or occupier in search or pursuit of deer, an offence under Section 1 (1) or (2) of the Deer Act 1980 would be committed, with no protection from Section 35 of the Game Act 1831.

Following several invasions of one such sanctuary, the League Against Cruel Sports took a civil action for trespass against the Devon and Somerset Staghounds at Bristol High Court in 1985. An injunction was granted, damages awarded and trespass by hunts defined. The Judge stated: 'The Master will be liable for trespass if he intended to cause

[1] See page 35.
[2] See page 2.

hounds to enter such land, or if by his failure to exercise proper control over them he caused them to enter such land.'

Whilst this case has obvious implications for hunting generally, it may also be applied to any individual who allows dogs to enter another's land and may result in criminal or civil proceedings; although it is doubtful whether civil action would be taken against a man exercising his dog or similar minor trespasses.

ENFORCEMENT OF DEER ACTS 1963 AND 1980

There are no provisions in the 1963 Act for the land owner or occupier to deal with anyone committing offences under the 1963 Act, but there are limited powers for him to deal with offences under the 1980 Act. Only a police officer can enforce the 1963 Act: his powers are identical with those under the 1980 Act.[1]

ENFORCEMENT BY AUTHORISED PERSON

For the purposes of the Deer Act 1980, an authorised person is the owner or occupier of land or someone authorised by him or having the right to take or kill deer on that land. If such an authorised person reasonably suspects that someone is or has been committing offences under the Deer Act 1980, he may require the person to give his name and address and quit the land forthwith. Failure to comply with such a request is an offence, but only a police officer has a power of arrest or the means of obtaining the name or address if refused. The owner or occupier or his employee may treat the suspected person as a trespasser and eject him from the land using reasonable force.[2]

Where deer are considered to be captive, tamed or domestic (e.g. deer enclosed in a deer park), they may be classed as property; in which case the offence of theft under the Theft Act 1968 may be committed and a citizen's arrest made.[3]

[1] See page 172.
[2] See page 6.
[3] See page 75.

ENFORCEMENT BY POLICE

Under Section 5 of the Deer Act 1963 and Section 4 of the
Deer Act 1980, the police are given additional powers of
enforcement which apply to both Deer Acts. If a police
officer reasonably suspects that someone is or has been
committing an offence, he may enter any land (but not a
dwelling house), and, if he suspects that evidence may be
found, he may:

1 Stop and search the suspect.
2 Search or examine any vehicle, animal, weapon or other
  equipment.
3 Arrest under the Police and Criminal Evidence Act 1984.
4 Seize and detain anything that is evidence or liable to be
  confiscated by the court.
5 Sell deer or venison and retain the proceeds until the case
  is decided at court.

FORFEITURES AND DISQUALIFICATION

Deer Act 1963 On conviction for an offence under either Act, the court may
Section 6 (4) order the confiscation of deer or venison, and vehicles,
Deer Act 1980 animals (e.g. lurcher), weapons or other things used to
Section 5 commit the offence. The Canine Defence League is prepared
to take into its care, re-train and re-home dogs forfeited by a
court.

For offences under the 1980 Act, the court may also
disqualify a person from holding a game dealer's licence and
cancel his firearm or shotgun certificate.

DEER IN SCOTLAND

The legislation covering deer in Scotland is the Deer
(Scotland) Act 1959 (amended by the Deer (Amendment)
(Scotland) Act 1982) and a number of Orders made under
the Act. For the two Orders relating to venison dealing, see
pages 70–72.

The Act, as amended, is divided into five parts:

I   Conservation and control
II   Close seasons
III Unlawful taking and killing
IIIA Dealing in venison
IV   Enforcement

Stalking in the High-lands.

The basis of the legislation is that deer may only be taken or killed by shooting in the daytime during the open season. Obviously, such strict criteria would cause many problems for farmers and occupiers of land and so the law also allows for culling in specified circumstances. Each Part of the Act is virtually self-contained, but exceptions are covered together in Section 33.

CONSERVATION

RED DEER COMMISSION

The Deer (Scotland) Act 1959 created the Red Deer Commission to conserve and control red and sika deer, their hybrids, and to a lesser extent roe and fallow.

The Commission advises the Secretary of State for Scotland on any deer-related matter, has the power to advise landowners regarding open hill management, stocking and culling levels and is able to support and assist in research.

On a more general basis, the Commission co-ordinates the different interests of land managers for the benefit and more effective management of an important wildlife resource. It considers the broad problems of land use, the effects of forestry planting programmes, deer farming, legislation and scientific research on deer in Scotland and is regularly consulted by the Forestry Commission, private individuals and companies regarding Forestry Grant Schemes and forestry protection.

Land below the 450-metre contour is in great demand for a number of uses, especially forestry; in order that all interests are protected, deer control carries a high priority. In this respect it is vitally important to balance numbers with available winter range. Deer managers have a responsibility to minimise the risk of deer damage and cannot expect farmers and crofters to over-winter their deer; consequently the law makes provision for agricultural occupiers to protect their crops.

Deer (Scotland) Act 1959 Section 5   To carry out its functions the Commission requires information. Under Section 5 occupiers are obliged to provide returns of the numbers of deer killed on their ground. Failure to supply the information is an offence.

CLOSE SEASONS

Deer (Scotland) Act 1959 Section 21 & Deer (Close Seasons) (Scotland) Order 1984   Under Section 21, no person shall take or wilfully kill or injure specified deer in the following close seasons:

SPECIES	MALE	FEMALE
Red Deer Sika Deer and Red/Sika hybrids	21 October – 30 June	16 February – 20 October
Fallow Deer	1 May – 31 July	16 February – 20 October
Roe Deer	21 October – 31 March	1 April – 20 October

Deer (Scotland) Act 1959 Section 21 (5A)   Under Section 21 (5A), close seasons do not apply to farmers who keep deer on land for the production of meat, skins or other by-products, or breeding stock. The land must be enclosed by a deer-proof barrier and the deer conspicuously marked.

CONTROL

The Act recognises that occupiers should be able to protect their livelihood from the ravages of wandering deer.

MARAUDING DEER (RED AND SIKA)

Under Section 6, the Commission has the power to authorise *Section 6* a competent person to follow and kill on any land specified in the authorisation red or sika deer and their hybrids which are causing:

1 Serious damage to forestry or to agricultural production, including crops or foodstuffs.

2 Injury to farm animals (including serious overgrazing of pasture and competing for supplementary feeding).

The damage or injury must be on agricultural land, woodland or garden ground and the killing can only be authorised to prevent further serious damage or injury.

Under Section 6 (2), if the deer which appear to be causing *Section 6 (2)* the damage originate from elsewhere, the Commission may request the person with the shooting rights to undertake the killing of deer on that land.

Under Section 6 (3), the person with the right to take deer *Section 6 (3)* on the land will be approached to undertake the cull, but where he is unable or unwilling to do so the Commission may employ some other competent person or its own stalkers. Landowners are notified of the authorisation and warned of any possible danger.

MARAUDING DEER (OTHER THAN RED OR SIKA)

Under Section 6A, where species of deer other than red or *Section 6A* sika and their hybrids are causing serious damage to agricultural land or woodland, the Commission, with the consent of the occupier, may kill such deer to prevent further damage. In these circumstances, the provisions relating to *Section 6A (3)* close seasons and night shooting do not apply, but night shooting may only be undertaken with written permission from the Commission (Section 6A (3)).

CONTROL IN THE CLOSE SEASON

To prevent serious damage at any time of the year, an *Section 33 (3)* occupier of agricultural land or enclosed woodlands is entitled under Section 33 (3) to take or kill and sell or dispose of the carcases of any species of deer found on any arable land, garden ground, permanent grass (other than moorland

and unenclosed land) which forms part of his agricultural land or on enclosed woodlands. He may also authorise in writing his own full-time employees or anyone normally resident on the land; if the occupier is a tenant, he may authorise the owner of the ground and his full-time employees. Any other person must be authorised by the Red Deer Commission.

Section 33 (3) (b)　　Under Section 33 (3) (b), anyone authorised in writing by the Secretary of State for Scotland may take or kill any deer during the close season for a scientific purpose.

Section 33 (4) (c)　　Under Section 33 (4) (c), the owner of land may request the occupier to supply the numbers of red or sika deer killed in the previous twelve months.

USE OF SHOTGUNS

Article 4 of the Firearms Order 1985 and Section 33 (3) of the Deer (Scotland) Act 1959 provide for the restricted use of shotguns where the occupier of agricultural land or enclosed woodlands believes serious damage will be caused to crops, pasture, trees or human or animal feedstuffs on that land, if the deer are not killed.

Section 33 (3) (c) (d) & (e)　　In this case the occupier, his servants or persons normally resident on the land (both must be authorised in writing by him) or a person authorised in writing by the Red Deer Commission may use a shotgun with a gauge not less than 12-bore loaded with:

1 *For shooting any deer*: a single rifled non-spherical slug not less than 380 grains or a cartridge loaded with S.S.G. or larger.

2 *For shooting roe deer:* a cartridge loaded with AAA or larger.

The killing or taking of deer may be carried out on arable land, garden grounds or land under permanent grass (other than moorland or unenclosed land) which forms part of the occupier's agricultural land or on enclosed woodlands.

NIGHT SHOOTING

Section 23　　Under Section 23, the shooting of deer at night, between one hour after sunset to one hour before sunrise, is an offence except in the following circumstances:

A range of ammunition: *from left to right*: AAA, SSG and the rifled slug.

Red Deer Commission staff may shoot at night when *Section 33 (2)* acting under Section 6 (but not in a control scheme[1]). No one else is allowed to shoot at night unless specifically authorised by the Commission or under Section 33 (4).

Section 33 (4) permits the occupier of agricultural land or *Section 33 (4)* of enclosed woodlands, in person, to shoot on his land red *(4A) (4C)* and sika deer at night to prevent serious damage to crops, trees etc. on that land. The occupier is not required to comply with the Red Deer Commission's Code of practice or obtain their permission, but he is required to pull the trigger. The Commission may also authorise in writing a competent person nominated by the occupier to shoot any species of deer at night, in accordance with the Commission's Code of Practice on Night Shooting, if the shooting is necessary and there is no other adequate method of control available. The landowner may request the occupier to supply numbers of red or sika deer killed in the previous twelve months.

Red Deer Commission's Code of Practice

Persons authorised to shoot deer at night must comply with the Commission's Code of Practice. The code gives advice on general principles, method and equipment and also specifies a number of obligatory conditions regarding:

1 Safety precautions (e.g. field of view; landowner and police to be informed).

---

[1] See page 178.

2 Target area (i.e. forward shoulder shot).
3 Vehicle operating teams (e.g. driver, spotlight operator and marksman).
4 Recommended bullet weight (e.g. 130–150 grain soft-nosed bullet with a muzzle velocity of not less than 2450ft per second and a muzzle energy of not less than 2250ft/lb for red, sika and fallow; the combination for roe deer is similar to or greater than a .243 and is the same as laid down in the Firearms Order for shooting red, sika and fallow in the daytime).

CONTROL SCHEMES

Section 7 Under Section 7, if the Commission is satisfied that red or sika deer or their hybrids have caused damage to agriculture or forestry in any locality, it may institute certain measures, having regard to the nature and character of the land, to reduce, or indeed exterminate, numbers of deer to prevent further damage.

Owners and occupiers will be consulted to secure a voluntary agreement to the measures to be implemented, but where consultations fail a control scheme may be introduced with the permission of the Secretary of State.

Section 8 Under Section 8, the scheme will specify a control area and the number of deer to be culled. The sex or class of animals may also be stipulated. Owners or occupiers may be required to undertake action within a prescribed time limit, but they cannot be required to erect a deer fence or other artificial obstruction.

Sections 9, Under Sections 9, 10 and 11, failure to comply with the *10 & 11* requirements of a control scheme may result in a prosecution. The Commission would undertake the necessary work and any expense incurred in excess of the proceeds from the sale of carcases may be recovered from the occupier or owner.

INJURED AND DISEASED DEER

Section 33 (1) Under Section 33 (1), no one shall be guilty of an offence under the Act in respect of any action taken to prevent suffering by an injured or diseased deer or by any calf, fawn or kid deprived of its mother.[1]

---

[1] See further on page 164.

UNLAWFUL TAKING OR KILLING

POACHING

Under Section 22, it is an offence: *Section 22*

1 Without legal right or permission to take, wilfully kill or injure deer on any land.
2 To remove the carcase of any deer from any land without permission from someone having such legal right.

A person will not commit an offence under Section 22 if the statutory exceptions under Section 33 apply;[1] or the deer is taken or killed on his neighbour's land, provided he first shot and wounded the animal on his own land or over land on which he has permission to shoot.

GANG POACHING

If two or more persons act together to commit any offence *Section 24* under Section 22, 23 or 23A,[2] the offences become aggravated and the penalties are increased.

UNLAWFUL METHODS

Section 23 creates the following offences of taking or wilfully *Section 23* killing or injuring deer:

1 During the night (end of first hour after sunset to the start *Section 23 (1)* of the first hour before sunrise).[3]

2 By any means other than shooting – e.g. traps, snares, *Section 23 (2)* crossbows, dogs, etc. Firearms and ammunition must comply with the requirements of the Deer (Firearms) (Scotland) Order 1985.[4]

AIRCRAFT AND VEHICLES

Under Section 23, it is an offence to:

1 Discharge a firearm or project a missile at any deer from an *Section 23 (2A) (a)* aircraft.

---

[1] See pages 175–7 for exceptions.
[2] See pages 179–80 (poaching and prohibited times and methods).
[3] See pages 176–7 for exceptions.
[4] See page 159.

Section 23 (2A) (b) 2 Use an aircraft to transport live deer except in the interior of the aircraft or under veterinary supervision.

Section 23 (3A) 3 Use a vehicle to drive deer on unenclosed land with the intention of taking, killing or injuring the deer.

Shooting from a vehicle or using it to drive deer can be illegal.

Section 23 (5)   Section 23 does not prevent persons having the legal right to take deer alive in a manner which does not cause unnecessary suffering. Section 25 (5) therefore allows deer farmers, estate managers, etc to round up live deer.

FIREARMS AND AMMUNITION

Section 23A of the amended Deer (Scotland) Act 1959 and the Deer (Firearms etc) (Scotland) Order 1985 prescribe bullet/cartridge combinations for particular deer and can therefore greatly influence the choice of weapon and firearm certificate applications. Rifle and ammunition specifications can be found on pages 159–161.

Section 23A Section 23A (3) makes it an offence to fail to comply with
(3) & (5) the Order containing the specifications; Section 23A (5) creates an offence of wilfully injuring any deer with a firearm.

UNLAWFUL POSSESSION OF DEER AND FIREARMS

Section 25 (1) Under Section 25 (1), a person may be charged with the unlawful possession of a deer, if it is suspected that it was obtained as a result of an offence under Section 21 (close seasons) or an order made thereunder or Sections 22 to 24.[1]

Under Section 25 (2), where it is suspected that a firearm *Section 25 (2)* or ammunition has been used to commit offences under sections 22 to 24,[1] the person may also be charged with unlawful possession of such firearms or ammunition.

ENFORCEMENT

EVIDENCE OF ONE WITNESS

Under Section 25 (4), contrary to the normal procedure in *Section 25 (4)* Scotland of requiring corroborative evidence by two witnesses, convictions under Section 25 may be made on the evidence of one person.

POLICE POWERS

Search and seizure   *Section 27*

1 A police officer may seize any deer, firearm, ammunition, vehicle or boat liable to be confiscated on conviction for an offence under the Act.

2 A Sheriff or Justice of the Peace may grant a search warrant to the police, if satisfied there is reasonable suspicion that a certain offence[2] has been committed and evidence of it is to be found on any premises, vehicle or boat.

3 The police authorised by such a warrant, in addition to searching the premises etc., may also search every person found therein or whom they reasonably suspect of having recently left or to be about to enter, and seize any article they have reasonable grounds to believe is evidence relating to the offence.

4 In cases of urgency the police, having reasonable suspicion that an offence has been committed, may stop and search without warrant any vehicle or boat where they believe evidence may be found. The power does not extend to premises.

[1] Section 22 (Poaching), Section 23 (Prohibited times and methods), Section 24 (Gang Poaching).
[2] Under Sections 22, 23, 23A, 24, 25, 25D (1) and (3).

Arrest

Section 28 A police officer may arrest any person found committing an offence under section 22, 23, 23A, 24, 25 or 26.

CANCELLATION OF FIREARM CERTIFICATE

Section 28A On conviction for offences under sections 22 to 25, the court may cancel a firearm or shotgun certificate.

DISPOSAL OF DEER

Section 30 Where a deer is seized under the Act and is liable to forfeiture, it may be sold and the net profits will then be liable to forfeiture.

CHAPTER 12

Fish

FISHING RIGHTS

Fishing rights are a complex subject embracing many aspects of the civil and criminal law and the responsible angler should ensure through local enquiries that he is in the right place at the right time with the right equipment.

Originally there were three forms of fishing rights:

1 Free fisheries – where anyone could fish on tidal reaches of rivers.
2 Several or private fisheries – where the rights belonged to the owner of the land under the water.
3 Commons of fishing – where the lord had the right to fish water belonging to his tenants.

These basic principles remain today and in fact are similar to sporting rights where the rights to game derive from the ownership of land. Fishing rights derive from the ownership of land forming the banks of rivers or other water, tidal and non-tidal; such land is known as riparian land and its owner, in addition to fishing rights, has the right of access to and use of the water and to receive unpolluted water.

The riparian owner, angler and navigator may all have rights to the same water.

In the same way that a landowner can sell his sporting rights, the riparian owner can sell his fishing rights. On certain rivers the public have a right of navigation and there may be situations where the riparian owner, the owner of the fishing rights and the navigator all have different rights connected with the same water; each should exercise his rights with due consideration for the rights of the others. In addition, the riparian owner should exercise his rights in a way which does not interfere with the rights of other riparian owners (e.g. by not polluting or restricting the water or preventing the passage of fish).

POLLUTION

A water authority can give consent to an individual or organisation (e.g. factory, mine etc.) to discharge material into a watercourse within specified levels. The Control of Pollution Act 1974 puts a responsibility on water authorities[1] to maintain a register of these consents, details of samples taken under the Water Resources Act 1963, the results of sample analysis and the action taken in consequence of consent violation. Since August 1985 the public has had the right to inspect these registers free of charge at all reasonable hours, which is a useful facility for anyone with an interest in the purity of water for consumption, fishing or conservation.

LEAD WEIGHTS

In January 1987 the Control of Pollution (Anglers' Lead Weights) Regulations 1986 came into force in England, Wales and Scotland.

[1] In Scotland River Purification Boards are the relevant authorities. Rivers (Prevention of Pollution) (Scotland) Act 1951.

Regulation 3 prohibits the importation of lead fishing weights and Regulation 4 bans the supply of lead weights for the purpose of weighting fishing lines. Anyone supplying split shot is presumed to be supplying it for fishing unless he can show to the contrary. Anyone who contravenes Regulation 4 commits an offence punishable by a fine of up to £2000. However, the Regulations do not apply to the importation or supply of a leadweight of 0.06 grams or less, or of more than 28.35 grams, or to the export of weights.

Lead weight means split-shot or any other thing suitable for weighting fishing lines, which is neither fully enclosed in the core of a fishing line nor incorporated in the construction of a swim-feeder, self-cocking float or fishing fly. Lead includes any alloy or compound of lead.

The Regulations do not ban the use of lead weights, but a number of water authorities have already made byelaws prohibiting their use.

DEALING IN SALMON

The Salmon Act 1986 contains provisions for the licensing of salmon dealers, in England and Wales and/or Scotland, which may be implemented through regulations which have yet to be made.

STEALING FISH

Fish, like other wild creatures, do not belong to any person but can be treated in the same way as game, in that an individual may have certain rights to take the fish, but he does not exercise rights of ownership over them until they are killed, captured or tamed, when they may then be defined as property and capable of being stolen. Taking wild fish from a river is poaching, but removing a dead fish from a fisherman's car boot is theft.[1]

Earthworms are also wild creatures; consequently, digging them up in a field is not theft, but it is theft to take captive worms from another angler's bait box.

Where there is some measure of control over fish, in that their freedom is restricted to an area of water, they can be defined as property and capable of being stolen (e.g. in a

---

[1] See page 19.

garden pond, breeding and rearing tanks). The taking of fish from a lake stocked for an angling society could be theft, but would depend on whether the fish had a sufficient element of freedom in a large lake to be considered wild. On the other hand, fish confined by fences to a small section of running water might be subject to theft.

Removal of fish from keepnets, fishing nets and traps is also theft, as is the taking of lobsters caught in a pot.

In England and Wales stealing fish is contrary to Section 1 of the Theft Act 1968. The Act also creates poaching offences to cover situations where wild fish are taken. In Scotland stealing fish is contrary to the common law offence of theft (similar to the Theft Act 1968). There is also a statutory offence under the Theft Act 1607 of taking a fish from a stank, an enclosed water.

HANDLING SALMON

Salmon Act 1986
Section 32　A person commits an offence if, at a time when he believes or reasonably suspects that a relevant offence has at any time been committed in relation to any salmon, he receives the salmon, or undertakes or assists in its retention, removal or disposal. A relevant offence is one committed by killing, taking or landing salmon in England, Wales or Scotland, contrary to the law applicable to the place where the salmon was killed, taken or landed.

LEGISLATION IN ENGLAND AND WALES

THEFT ACT 1968
Taking or destroying fish
Section 1 of the Theft Act 1968 creates the ordinary offence of theft as discussed above but Section 32 and Schedule 1 of the Theft Act 1968 create poaching offences in which there is no necessity to show that the fish were capable of being stolen or whether any fish were actually taken.

Theft Act
Schedule 1　It is an offence to take[1] or destroy, or attempt to do so, any fish[2] in water which is private property or in which there is any private right of fishery.

---

[1] Catch fish by any method regardless of whether the fish are carried away, put in a keep net or returned immediately to the water.
[2] All species of fish including crayfish and winkles.

Enforcement is governed by the time of day and means adopted to take the fish:

1 If the offence is committed at night[1] by using *any method*, any person may arrest anyone he finds committing the offence or whom he suspects with reasonable cause to be committing the offence.

2 In the daytime,[2] the same power of arrest exists if the offence is committed by a method *other than* angling, e.g. set line.

If the offence is committed by angling in the daytime, there is no power of arrest under Schedule 1.

Since there is no power of arrest for angling in the daytime, occupiers and bailiffs can only try to obtain the offender's name and address in order to obtain a summons. If, however, the circumstances of the offence also amount to an offence of theft, e.g. by angling in the daytime in a stocked or rearing pond,[3] a citizen's arrest could be made.[4]

Anything which at the time of committing offences the offender had with him for taking or destroying fish may be seized. The items may be forfeited by the court on conviction.

Police officers have additional powers of arrest and seizure under the Police and Criminal Evidence Act 1984.

CONFISCATION OF TACKLE

Prior to the Theft Act 1968, fishing tackle could be confiscated and kept by the landowner or his bailiff instead of prosecuting the person found fishing illegally. This often suited both parties and was a good deterrent, but the power is no longer available.

SALMON AND FRESHWATER FISHERIES ACT 1975

The Salmon and Freshwater Fisheries Act 1975 consolidated previous legislation dating from 1923; it covers prohibited

[1] One hour after sunset to one hour before sunrise (local time).
[2] One hour before sunrise to one hour after sunset (local time).
[3] See pages 185–6.
[4] A water authority bailiff has new powers to deal with this situation and these are discussed in the section on enforcement of the Salmon and Freshwater Fisheries Act.

methods of taking fish, obstructions to passage of fish, times of fishing, sale and export, licensing and enforcement.

REGULATION OF FISHERIES

Salmon and Freshwater Fisheries Act 1975 Section 28 Section 28 imposes a duty on every water authority to maintain, improve and develop salmon, trout, freshwater and eel fisheries in their area and to establish advisory committees of those interested in the fisheries.

'Fishery' is not defined: it could extend from a garden pond to the sea, depending on how the water is used.

For the purposes of the Act, fish are defined as follows:

Section 41 *Salmon:* all fish of the salmon species.

Trout: any fish of the salmon family commonly known as trout, including migratory trout and char.

Freshwater fish: any fish living in freshwater exclusive of salmon and trout and of any kinds of fish which migrate to and from tidal waters and of eels. Eels: includes elvers and fry of eels.

CLOSE SEASONS

Section 19 & Schedule 1 Water authorities are obliged to make byelaws fixing annual close seasons and weekly close times of salmon and trout other than rainbow trout. The following table is a basic requirement which can be altered, by byelaws, to suit local needs. Byelaws can also be made which dispense with close seasons for freshwater fish or rainbow trout.

FISH		CLOSE SEASON/TIME
Salmon	Annual	31 August – 1 February
	For rods	31 October – 1 February
	For putts & putchers	31 August – 1 May
	Weekly	6am Saturday – 6am Monday
Trout	Annual	31 August – 1 March
	For rods	30 September – 1 March
	Weekly	6am Saturday – 6am Monday
Freshwater fish	Annual	14 March – 16 June

Under Section 19 it is an offence to fish for, take or kill fish during the close season. The seasons for each species vary according to the method used, as can be seen from the table. In addition the seasons may differ, by several weeks, from the basic requirement above and from one water authority to another.

SALE AND POSSESSION

It is an offence to buy, sell or possess for sale salmon between *Section 22 (1)* 31 August and 1 February or trout (other than rainbow) between 31 August and 1 March.

Under Section 22 (2), Section 22 (1) does not apply to the *Section 22 (2)* sale of salmon preserved by various means outside the United Kingdom at any time or within the United Kingdom between 1 February and 31 August. Trout may be bought and sold if preserved within the United Kingdom between 1 March and 31 August. The exception also extends to salmon or trout caught outside the United Kingdom and likewise to salmon and trout legally caught at a time and place within the United Kingdom by any net, instrument or device.

Trout may be bought and sold at any time for the purposes *Section 22 (3)* of stocking, restocking, artificial propagation and science.

EXPORT

It is an offence to export salmon or trout which are unclean *Section 23 (1)* or caught at a time when their sale is prohibited where they were caught.

All salmon and trout for export between 31 August and 1 *Section 23 (2) – (5)* May must be entered with the Customs and Excise and the exporter must be able to furnish proof that they were not entered in contravention of this section. Customs may examine, forfeit, detain and, if necessary, destroy consignments if the requirements are not met.

PACKAGES

It is an offence to send consignments of salmon or trout at *Section 24 (1) – (6)* any time unless the package is conspicuously marked *salmon* or *trout* on the outside. Packets suspected of containing salmon or trout may be inspected by a police officer, water authority official, ministry official, officer of a market authority or the Fishmongers Company and they may detain the contents until it is shown that all is in order. The power to detain is also extended to salmon and trout not contained in a package, and if a person obstructs officers exercising their powers under this Section an offence is committed.

FISHING LICENCES

Sections 25 & 26 A water authority is obliged to regulate fishing for salmon and trout in their area through the issue of fishing licences. Sections 25 and 26 stipulate what a licence may allow, put limits on the number of licences and selection of holders.

Section 27 A person commits an offence if, in any place in which fishing of any description is regulated by a system of licensing, he:

1 Fishes for or takes fish without a licence, or uses a means prohibited by licence, or contrary to the licence conditions.

2 Has in his possession, for the purpose of taking or killing fish, an instrument other than one which he is authorised to use by licence.

Section 29 Licences may be obtained from the Minister of Agriculture, Fisheries and Food to artificially propagate or rear salmon or trout.

INTRODUCTION OF FISH AND SPAWN

Section 30 It is an offence to introduce fish or fish spawn into an inland water, or possess them for that purpose, unless the water authority has given written permission. It is also an offence under the Wildlife and Countryside Act 1981 to release or allow to escape into the wild certain species of fish.[1]

OBSTRUCTIONS TO PASSAGE OF FISH

Since the twelfth century there has been legislation preventing the total obstruction of rivers for the purpose of taking fish. There has to be a minimum gap to allow fish to pass and initially the standard was set at the length of a well-fed, three-year-old pig standing sideways in the mid-stream channel. Modern provisions are far more complicated as custom and practice over hundreds of years have created numerous ingenious devices for taking fish.

---

[1] See page 128.

It is an offence to:

1 Take or obstruct migratory fish by fixed engines or weirs. *Section 6–7*

2 Use an unauthorised fishing mill dam to take salmon or migratory trout. *Section 8*

3 Fail to make and maintain a fish pass. *Section 9*

4 Alter or injure a fish pass and take or hinder the passage of migratory fish through a fish pass or free gap. The minimum requirement for a free gap is not less than three feet – about the length of a pig. *Section 12*

5 Fail to use gratings at inlets to protect fish. *Section 14*

6 Fish within certain limits close to dams or obstructions. *Section 17*

PROHIBITED METHODS

It is an offence to use, or possess with intent to use, the following prohibited implements to take or kill salmon, trout or freshwater fish: *Section 1 (1) (a) & (b)*

1 A firearm as defined by the Firearms Act 1968.[1]

2 An otter-lath or jack, wire or snare: an otter-lath or jack is a floating device for running out lures, and is often a board to which baited lines are attached, usually moored to or trailed by a boat. There is no connection with a live otter, although in one case it was contested unsuccessfully that the prohibition was on the use of the animal. One enterprising poacher spent many a happy hour sailing his model boat under the bailiff's nose with baited lines fixed to the keel. In the days when pike were more valuable than salmon, they were snared with a noose at the end of a long pole. Another method of taking pike was to use roach on a line wound round a spindle or trimmer and attached to an inflated bladder. The hooked pike would pull out the line and then fight against the bladder until exhausted. It has been known for lines to be tied to the legs of a number of geese to take pike and perch, the geese usually staggering ashore weary but victorious.

---

[1] See page 81.

3 A crossline or set-line: these are commonly used by poachers and consist of a simple, weighted, line tied to a stick with baited hooks attached. An unattended rod and line could also be classed as a set-line. A crossline goes from bank to bank and a setline is cast into the water and secured at one end. If a court considered that a hand-held

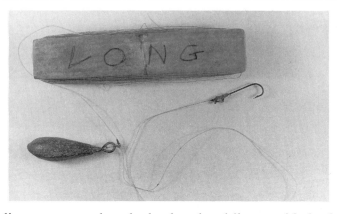

A simple but very effective set line.

line was secured to the bank, a hand-line would also be a set-line. A tree-lined bank is often favoured as it gives cover to the poacher who will secure the end of the line under a stone or branch at the water's edge; in order to find the line on his return he may mark its position with some object. Crosslines may also be set between two stones in a stream with several droppers attached and are almost impossible to detect. A fly-spoon may also be attached to a whippy branch at the edge of a fast-flowing stream allowing the fish to play itself until exhausted.

4 A spear, gaff, stroke-haul, snatch or other like instrument. A stroke-haul and snatch are implements used for foul-hooking by dropping weighted lines into the water and jerking the hooks into a body of the fish. A weighted treble hook cast by a rod is sometimes used in this way. Byelaws may require the return to water of foul-hooked fish. Sub-section 4 allows the use or possession of a gaff with a plain metal hook without a barb, or a tailer as an auxiliary to angling.

5 A light.

Section 1 (2)   To escape conviction, anyone contravening Section 1 would have to show that his actions were in connection with the preservation or development of a private fishery and he had previously obtained written permission from the water authority.

STONES AND MISSILES

It is an offence to throw or discharge any stone or other *Section 1 (1) (c)* missile to take, kill, or facilitate the taking or killing of salmon, trout and freshwater fish.

ROE

A person commits an offence if, for the purpose of fishing for *Section 2 (1)* salmon, trout or freshwater fish, he:

1 Uses any fish roe.
2 Buys, sells, or exposes for sale, or has in his possession any salmon or trout roe.

UNCLEAN AND IMMATURE FISH

A person commits an offence if he knowingly takes, kills, or *Section 2* injures any salmon, trout or freshwater fish which is unclean *(2) & (3)* or immature, or attempts to do so; this section does not apply to taking fish accidentally and then returning them to the water with the least possible injury.

An immature salmon is one of a length less than twelve inches from the tip of the snout to the fork or cleft of the tail. The length of other fish is determined by byelaws.

An unclean fish is any fish about to spawn, or has recently spawned and has not recovered from spawning. Unclean fish are not saleable or eatable, but their roe is a devastating bait for salmon and trout.

SPAWN

It is an offence to wilfully disturb fish spawn or spawning *Section 2* fish or any bed, bank or shallow on which any spawn or *(4) & (5)* spawning fish may be. This offence has been successfully used to prosecute poaching on spawning beds. There are exceptions for those with a legal right to take materials from waters for scientific purposes, artificial propagation, or the preservation or development of a private fishery.

NETS

Section 3 (1) It is an offence to shoot or work a seine or draft net for salmon or migratory trout across more than three-quarters the width of any waters.

Section 3 (2) & (3) It is illegal, unless authorised by a byelaw, to take salmon or migratory trout with any net which has a mesh measuring less than two inches from knot to knot (along each side of a square) or eight inches round each mesh when wet, but does not include a landing net used as auxiliary to rod and line.

Section 3 (4) The placing of two or more nets close together, effectively reducing the mesh size, or the covering of nets with canvas or other device in order to evade Section 3 (1) and (2) above is also a contravention.

POLLUTION

Section 4 (1) It is an offence to cause or knowingly permit to flow, or put or knowingly permit to be put, any liquid or solid matter into any waters containing fish of any kind, to such an extent as to cause the waters to be poisonous or injurious to fish, spawning grounds, spawn or food of fish.[1] No offence is committed if the person is authorised in accordance with section 5 (2) below.

EXPLOSIVES, POISON AND ELECTRIC FISHING

Section 5 (1) & (4) It is an offence for any person in or near any waters (including those adjoining the coast of England and Wales to a distance of six nautical miles) to use any explosive, poison or other noxious substance, or electrical device with intent to take or destroy fish. It is also an offence to possess the above items for the purpose of contravening Section 5 (1).

Section 5 (2) Section 5 (1) does not apply where a person is authorised in writing by the water authority (or the Minister in respect of noxious substances) for scientific purposes, protection, improvement or replacing of fishing stocks.

---

[1] See page 184 regarding the examination of water-sample analysis records. Other pollution offences may be committed under the Control of Pollution Act 1974.

DESTRUCTION OF DAMS

It is an offence for anyone without lawful excuse to destroy or *Section 5* damage any dam, flood-gate, or sluice with intent to take or *(3) & (4)* destroy fish. This would also be an offence under the Criminal Damage Act 1971.

ENFORCEMENT OF FISHING LAWS

Offences under the Salmon and Freshwater Fisheries Act 1975 and the byelaws are normally enforced by official water bailiffs appointed by a water authority (or M.A.F.F.) under the Water Resources Act 1963. These official bailiffs carry a Warrant of Appointment which shows that they have certain powers of inspection, arrest, search, seizure and entry on to land, derived from Sections 31 to 36 of the Salmon and Freshwater Fisheries Act 1975. For the purpose of enforcing these provisions they are deemed to be constables who now have additional powers under the Police and Criminal Evidence Act 1984 and are required to comply with certain procedures in the exercise of those powers.

BAILIFFS AS CONSTABLES

Section 36 of the Salmon and Freshwater Fisheries Act states that a water-authority bailiff *shall be deemed a constable* for the purpose of the enforcement of the Act and byelaws made under it, and he shall have all the same powers and privileges, and be subject to the same liabilities as a police constable. The production of the bailiff's Warrant of Appointment is a pre-requisite to the exercise of his powers. The Warrant of Appointment is similar to a police constable's warrant card.

Anyone who assaults or obstructs a bailiff in the execution of his duty commits an offence equivalent to assaulting or obstructing a police officer.

PRIVATE WATER BAILIFFS

A bailiff employed by the owner of a fishery or angling club does not have the powers granted to a bailiff appointed by a water authority. The private bailiff may only act upon the land or waters owned by his employer or club. He may turn trespassers off the land using reasonable force and exercise the power of arrest and seizure of tackle under the Theft Act 1968.

A private bailiff may apply to a water authority to be officially appointed as a bailiff and receive a Warrant of Appointment to exercise a bailiff's powers on his club waters only.

INSPECTION OF LICENCES

Section 35 (1) & (2) A bailiff or constable may require the following to produce their licence for inspection and state their name and address:

1 Anyone fishing.
2 Anyone he reasonably suspects of being about to fish or of having fished in the preceding half hour.

The holder of a fishing licence (e.g. club member or private bailiff) may also require *anyone fishing* to produce his licence and give his name and address.

It is an offence to fail to produce one's licence or to give one's name and address; but if the licence is produced within the following seven days to the water authority, no action can be taken in respect of the failure to produce the licence.

POWERS OF SEARCH AND SEIZURE

A water bailiff may:

Section 31 (1) (a) 1 Examine any dam, fishing weir, fishing mill dam, fixed engine or obstruction, or any artificial watercourse, and for that purpose enter on any land.

Section 31 (1) (b) 2 Examine any instrument or bait which he has reasonable cause to suspect of having been or being used or likely to be used in taking fish unlawfully. He may also examine any container he reasonably suspects of having been or being used or likely to be used for holding any such instrument, bait or fish.

Section 31 (1) (c) 3 Stop and search any boat or other vessel used in fishing in a water authority area or any vessel or vehicle which he has reasonable cause to suspect of containing:
(*a*) fish caught unlawfully,
(*b*) any such instrument, bait or container under Section 31 (1) (b).

4 Seize any fish, instrument, vessel, vehicle or other thing *Section 31 (1 (d)*
   liable to be forfeited by a court.

Under paragraph 5, Schedule 4 Part II, a court, on
conviction for any offence under the Act, may order the
forfeiture of:

1 Illegally taken fish, or fish in the offender's possession at
   the time of committing the offence.

2 Any instrument, bait or other thing used in commission of
   the offence.

3 Any substance or device unlawfully possessed in contravention of Section 5.

4 On conviction on indictment,[1] any vessel or vehicle used
   in connection with the commission of the offence, or in
   which any substance or device unlawfully in the person's
   possession was contained at the time of the offence.

SEARCH PROCEDURE

The Police and Criminal Evidence Act 1984 requires that
where a *constable* searches a person who has not been arrested
a certain procedure must be followed. This now also applies
to official water bailiffs carrying out searches under the
Salmon and Freshwater Fisheries Act and guidance should
be sought from the relevant water authority as policies
relating to implementation vary.

ENTRY TO LAND AND DWELLINGS

If a bailiff or water authority official possess a special written *Section 32*
order from the authority they may enter, remain upon and
traverse any lands adjoining or near to waters within a water
authority area for the purpose of preventing any offence
under the Salmon and Freshwater Fisheries Act. They may
not, however, enter a dwelling or its immediate surroundings,
or decoys or land used exclusively for the preservation of
wildfowl. Additional entry powers are provided by the Water
Resources Act 1963.

    A magistrate can grant a bailiff or official authority to enter *Section 33*
and remain on any land to detect persons committing

[1] Part I of Schedule 4 details the offences which may lead to a conviction on
indictment.

offences under the Act and can grant a warrant to a bailiff, official or police officer to enter and search premises (e.g. the freezers of a hotel suspected of buying illegally taken fish). The Police and Criminal Evidence Act 1984 lays down certain procedural requirements relating to the application for and execution of search warrants.

Under the Police and Criminal Evidence Act a bailiff *who is deemed to be a constable* may enter premises, including a dwelling, to recapture a person unlawfully at large, if he has reasonable grounds to suspect that the person is on the premises. This would cover situations where an arrest has been made, but the offender escapes from the bailiff's custody and is chased into a building or land where the bailiff would not normally have access.

ARREST

Section 34 A bailiff with assistants may arrest and deliver to a police officer anyone who at night:

1 Illegally takes or kills salmon, trout, freshwater fish or eels.
2 Is found on or near any waters with intent to illegally take or kill such fish.
3 Has in his possession a prohibited instrument for the capture of such fish.

FISHING IN SCOTLAND

DISTRICT FISHERY BOARDS

Statutory provisions have been made for the formation of District Fishery Boards to represent the proprietors of the salmon fishing of a certain area. The duties of the boards are multifarious and include administration and fish conservation and they are empowered to appoint water bailiffs.

DEFINITIONS OF FISH

In most Scottish fisheries legislation sea trout fall within the meaning of the term salmon and in this chapter references to salmon include sea trout. Trout means brown trout and does not include rainbow or brook trout. Freshwater fish means any fish living in freshwater, including trout and eels, but excluding salmon and fish such as flounders which migrate between the open sea and tidal freshwater. The word fish, if unqualified, means all kinds of fish.

LEGISLATION

Scottish fishing law has not been streamlined into one Act but is a complex maze of interrelated statutes dating from 1607 to the present day. Additionally, certain rivers have their own individual Acts. For this reason, presentation of the main offences and provisions is in the form of an annotated list. In case of doubt reference should be made to the relevant Act quoted. For brevity, Acts are cited by the year only, e.g. 1951 Act. The main statutes are:

Theft Act 1607
Solway Act 1804
Tweed Fisheries Acts 1857 to 1969
Salmon Fisheries (Scotland) Act 1868
Fresh Water Fish (Scotland) Act 1902
Trout (Scotland) Act 1933
Diseases of Fish Act 1937
Salmon and Fresh Water Fisheries (Protection) (Scotland) Act 1951
Sea Fish (Conservation) Act 1967
Freshwater and Salmon Fisheries (Scotland) Act 1976
Inshore Fishing (Scotland) Act 1984
Salmon Act 1986

Most of the Salmon Act 1986 came into force in January 1987, and broadly does three things: it creates a new constitution for District Fishery Boards; it provides new powers for improving the management of fisheries; and it attacks poaching by providing for dealer-licensing and tightening up the law on possession of salmon. The Act makes some changes to the above statutes and these have been included in the text.

The English Salmon and Freshwater Fisheries Act 1975 does not extend to Scotland except in respect of the banks and tributary streams of the Border Esk.[1] The English side of the Solway Firth, as defined, is also covered by this Act.

[1] The Border Esk also comes within the Salmon and Freshwater Fisheries (Protection) (Scotland) Act 1951.

FISH FARMS

Fish farming operations on fish farms, as defined by the Diseases of Fish Act 1937, are subject to many exceptions in respect of fishing offences under Scottish law.

GENERAL EXEMPTION

1986 Act Anyone who contravenes any enactment relating to the
Section 27 taking of or fishing for salmon will not be guilty of an offence if his act or omission has been exempted by the Secretary of State. An exemption can only be granted if the proprietors of the affected salmon fisheries, including the Tweed, and the district salmon fishery board have previously consented to the action or omission.

EXEMPTION FOR SCIENTIFIC AND CONSERVATION PURPOSES

1986 Act Anyone who contravenes an enactment relating to salmon,
Section 28 salmon roe or eggs will not be guilty of an offence if his act or omission is for: a scientific purpose or for protecting, improving or developing fish stocks or conserving any creature or living thing, and he had previous permission in writing from the District Fishery Board or Secretary of State. Only the Secretary of State can give permission for certain actions.

FISHING WITHOUT PERMISSION

1951 Act It is an offence to fish for salmon without legal right or
Section 1 written permission in inland waters and the sea up to one statute mile from the low water mark.
1976 Act   It is an offence to fish for freshwater fish in an area
Section 1 (2) (b) proscribed in a Protection Order.

PROHIBITED METHODS

It is an offence for anyone to:

1868 Act 1 Fish for salmon with a net of less than 3½in stretched
Section 15 (4)   mesh. See also Tweed offences (page 206).

1868 Act 2 Use a net to catch salmon at falls.
Section 15 (5)

Poachers netting a
salmon pool.

3 Catch any salmon at a fish pass. See also Tweed offences   *1868 Act*
   (page 206).   *Section 15 (6)*

4 Fish for salmon with nets at mill dams.   *1696 Act*

5 Fish for salmon in the sea by drift net or other gill net, *1967 Act*
   trawl net, seine net, (other than beach seining or fishing *Section 5*
   from shore by net and coble), troll or long-line. This
   offence applies only to fishing from a boat. However,
   it is also an offence to fish for salmon with a gill net within
   half a mile of the Scottish shore, whether or not a boat is
   used, under the Inshore Fishing (Salmon and Migratory
   Trout) (Prohibition of Gill Nets) (Scotland) Order 1986.

6 Fish for salmon in inland waters other than by rod and   *1951 Act*
   line[1] or net and coble.[2] But even fishing by net and coble *Section 2 (1)*
   may be illegal if, for example, the net remains stationary
   across the river for longer than is necessary for the coble to
   tow it round. Prior to this Act there were certain rights in
   existence which were included as exceptions (e.g. certi-
   ficated fixed nets in the Solway and cruive rights). The
   Salmon Act 1986 will allow the use of a bag net, fly net or
   other stake net (and may define their method of use) or net
   and coble, but this provision is not yet in force.

---

[1] Rod and line means a single rod and line with such bait or lure as is lawful.
Prohibited lures and methods include: fish roe, double-rod fishing, cross-lines and
set-lines, use of an otter, striking the fish with a hook (foul-hooking, sniggering or
dragging). See page 191 for the use of these methods and explanation of terms.
[2] Does not apply in Tweed District: see page 206.

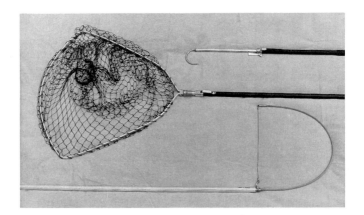

A gaff, landing net or tailer are normally permitted when fishing with rod and line.

1951 Act 7 Fish for or take trout in inland waters other than by rod
Section 2 (2)   rod and line.[1] By mutual agreement the proprietors of a loch may use a net.

1951 Act 8 Fish for or take freshwater fish in inland waters other
Section 2 (2)   than by rod and line, net or trap.

1951 Act 9 Use explosives with intent to take or destroy fish.
Section 4

     10 Use poison or other noxious substance with intent to take or destroy fish.[2]

     11 Use an electric device to stun or destroy salmon or freshwater fish.

CLOSE TIMES FOR SALMON

Annual

The annual close season for every district continues for 168 days, but the actual period varies from district to district and is set by byelaw. The Salmon Act 1986 permits the Secretary of State, on application from a district salmon fishery board, to set the annual close season in any district and the periods within it when rod and line fishing is permitted. Byelaws and lists of dates are available from the Department of Agriculture and Fisheries for Scotland.

1868 Act   It is an offence to fish for salmon during the annual close
Section 15 (1) time other than by rod and line.[3]

---

[1] The use of a gaff, tailer or landing net in conjunction with a rod and line is permitted.
[2] Section 4 also applies in the sea up to twelve nautical miles from the baselines.
[3] Does not apply in Tweed District: see page 206.

It is an offence to fish for salmon during the annual close time by rod and line, except as allowed for by byelaw.[1] *1868 Act Section 15 (3)*

It is an offence to fail to remove boats, nets and other tackle from a salmon fishery within 36 hours of the start of the annual close time.[1] *1868 Act Section 23*

It is an offence to buy, sell or possess any salmon taken during the close time.[1] It has been decided that the close time for this purpose is the period between the beginning of the latest and the end of the earliest close time in Scotland (currently 15 September – 10 February). *1868 Act Section 21*

Weekly close season

It is an offence to fish for or take salmon on a Sunday or during the weekly close time other than by rod and line. *1951 Act Section 13*

It is also an offence to fail to comply with weekly close time byelaws relating to putting fixed salmon nets out of fishing order.[1] *1868 Act Section 24*

CLOSE TIME FOR TAKING AND POSSESSION OF TROUT

It is an offence to fish for, take or have possession of trout in the close season. *1902 Act Section 1*

PURCHASE AND SALE OF TROUT

It is an offence to purchase or sell any trout between 1 September and 31 March. This does not apply to stocking or prohibit the taking of fish. *1933 Act Section 2*

OBSTRUCTION AND DISTURBANCE

It is an offence to:

1 Prevent the passage of salmon through a fish pass. The Tweed District has its own legislation. *1868 Act Section 15 (5)*

2 Fail to comply with byelaws relating to fish passes, screens, sluices, etc at mill dams and lades. *1868 Act Section 15 (8)*

3 Fail to comply with byelaws relating to cruives. Does not apply in the Tweed District. *1868 Act Section 15 (8)*

---

[1] Does not apply in Tweed District: see page 206.

1868 Act 4 Use any device for the purpose of obstructing the passage
Section 19   of juvenile salmon.

1868 Act 5 Disturb any salmon spawn or spawning bed.
Section 19

1868 Act 6 Obstruct the passage of salmon to the spawning grounds
Section 19   during the annual close season.

UNCLEAN AND UNSEASONABLE SALMON

1868 Act It is an offence to buy, sell, take, or possess any unclean or
Section 20 unseasonable salmon. Close-times offences are independent
of this section. Unclean salmon are commonly known as kelt,
a fish which has recently spawned, and an unseasonable
salmon is a gravid fish on the point of spawning.

IMMATURE FISH

It is an offence to:

1868 Act 1 Buy, sell, or possess salmon roe. A person will not be
Section 18   guilty of the offence if he can show a court that he had a
satisfactory reason for possession.

1868 Act 2 Knowingly take, destroy, buy, sell, possess or injure
Section 19   juvenile salmon. There are exceptions for the cleaning or
repairing of a dam or mill lade or work done in the exercise
of rights of property in the bed of a river.

1933 Act 3 Purchase or sell trout of less than eight inches. This does
Section 2   not apply to stocking or prohibit the taking of fish.

PACKAGES AND EXPORT

1951 Act   Packages containing salmon, sea trout, or trout must be
Section 16 marked conspicuously on the outside with the word
SALMON, SEATROUT or *TROUT* as the case may be and
the name and address of the sender.

1951 Act   If a District Bailiff (Secretary-of-State bailiff if authorised)
Section 16 (2) suspects that a package consigned to a carrier has been dealt
with contrary to law, or is not properly marked, he may open
and detain the package and contents pending proceedings
and destroy the fish if they become unfit for human
consumption.

It is an offence to:

1 Export salmon during the annual close time without proof of legal capture.[1]

1868 Act Section 22

2 Export salmon caught by rod and line during the close time for net fishing.[1]

1868 Act Section 22

3 Export unclean or unseasonable salmon. This offence is independent of the close times.

1863 Act Section 3

UNLAWFUL POSSESSION OF FISH AND IMPLEMENTS

If anyone is found in possession of any salmon or trout or any instrument, explosive, poison or noxious substance, which could be used for the taking of salmon or trout, in circumstances which afford reasonable grounds for suspecting that he has obtained possession of such salmon or trout or such instruments as the result of or for the purposes of committing an offence under Sections 1–4 of the Act (i.e. poaching, using illegal methods, two or more acting together, use of explosives etc.) that person may be charged with illegal possession. An offender may be convicted on the evidence of one witness.

1951 Act Section 7

It is an offence to be in possession of salmon in circumstances in which the possessor believes, or reasonably suspects, that the salmon had been taken or killed in Scotland, England or Wales contrary to the law applicable to the place where it was killed or taken.

1951 Act Section 7A

INTRODUCTION OF SALMON OR SALMON EGGS

It is an offence to introduce salmon or salmon eggs into inland waters without written permission of a district salmon fishery board.

1986 Act Section 24

MISCELLANEOUS OFFENCES

It is an offence for any person other than a water bailiff or constable in the exercise of his duty, or a person having the right to fish therein, to take or remove dead salmon or trout from any water.

1951 Act Section 6

It is an offence to land salmon caught in contravention of an Order made under the 1967 Act.

1967 Act Section 6

[1] Does not apply in the Tweed District.

TWEED AND SOLWAY

The River Tweed and the Scottish Solway are now subject to most of the general Scottish salmon fishery legislation, but some special local provisions still apply (e.g. fishing without permission in the Solway for fish other than salmon or sea trout). Provision for enforcement of the Tweed Acts is basically similar to that for the general Scottish Acts, but enforcement of the Solway Act can be effected by 'any person' (which includes bailiffs) (1804 Act, Section 18). Although the Solway Act has not been explicitly repealed (except insofar as it applied to England and the Annan District), most of its provisions have been superseded by general Scottish Acts and are implicitly repealed. 'Any person' should therefore be especially careful when seeking to enforce the Solway Act.

OFFENCES RELATING SPECIFICALLY TO THE TWEED

Tweed Fishery Act 1857 It is an offence under the Tweed Fishery Act 1857 to:

Section 45 1 Use nets during the annual close time.
Section 52 2 Use a ferry boat for fishing.
Section 52 3 Possess or use ferry boats unless marked.
Section 52 4 Neglect to lock up a ferry boat when not in use.
Section 53 5 Use a boat without the name or number painted on it.
Section 53 6 Use a net-fishing boat for angling.
Section 54 7 Use a net-fishing boat without such marks as the Commissioners direct.
Section 60 8 Beat the water or obstruct the movement of salmon up or down the river.
Section 62 9 Use a wear-shot net within thirty yards of another until the latter is fully landed.
Section 70 10 Take foul or unseasonable salmon.
Section 72 11 Neglect to return foul or unseasonable salmon to the river.
Section 73 12 Neglect to deliver to the owner of the fishery any salmon caught while trout fishing.
Section 74 13 Wilfully take or possess salmon smolts, fry etc.

It is an offence under the Tweed Fishery Act 1859 to: *Tweed Fishery Act 1859*

1 Fish for salmon during the annual close time. There is an *Section 6* exception for fly fishing from 15 September to 30 November and 1–14 February and a provision for taking salmon with permission, for artificial propagation.

2 Possess salmon caught during the annual close time. *Section 10*

3 Sell salmon caught by rod and line during the extension of time allowed for rod and line fishing.

4 Fail to remove boats or nets, etc. from the fishery by 17 *Section 11* September.

5 Breach the provisions with regard to construction of stake *Section 12* nets and bag nets and the way in which they are to be put out of fishing order during the weekly close time.

6 Use or possess nets less than 3½in stretched mesh. There *Section 13* is an exception for nets used solely for taking herring or shrimps and landing nets used with rod and line. The possession offence extends to any place within five miles of the river.

7 Use cleeks between 15 September and 1 May. *Section 16*

OFFENCES RELATING SPECIFICALLY TO THE SOLWAY

Under the Solway Act 1804 it is an offence to: *Solway Act 1804*
1 Neglect to place hecks at cuts used to irrigate lands. *Section 7*
2 Fish for salmon or other fish without permission. *Section 9*
3 Enter a fishery with face blackened or disguised with *Section 16* intent to take salmon or other fish.

Under section 7B of the 1951 Act it is an offence to *Salmon & Fresh-* obstruct the passage of salmon in the Solway Firth by placing *Water Fisheries* or using an uncertificated fixed engine. *(Protection) (Scotland) Act 1951*

ENFORCEMENT

Apart from the police and British Sea Fishery officers there are three other categories of persons with powers to enforce fishing legislation: water bailiffs appointed by the District Boards, and bailiffs and wardens authorised by the Secretary of State under the 1951 and 1976 Acts respectively. Wardens are nominated by the occupier or owner of freshwater fishing rights within an area covered by a Protection Order made under the 1976 Act.

The production of the bailiff's or warden's letter of appointment or badge is sufficient authority to exercise his powers.

The District Bailiff's powers extend to the whole of the district of the board appointing him and to any adjoining salmon fishery district. The coastal limits of such districts extend for three miles seawards from the low water mark. The primary concern of District Boards is the protection of salmon, but bailiffs also have some powers in respect of trout. The powers of a Secretary-of-State bailiff extend only to the waters for which he is authorised and could extend to areas of sea. Wardens may exercise their powers only within an area covered by a Protection Order.

Power of entry

1868 Act Section 27 — A District Bailiff, at any hour, may enter and remain on any land in the vicinity of a river or the sea coast to prevent breaches or detect persons guilty of a breach of the 1862–68 or 1951 Acts. If asked to leave the land by the owner or occupier, a District bailiff; must do so: he may be liable to trespass, if he refuses, unless he can show that he had reason to believe that an offence had been or was about to be committed.

1951 Act Section 10 (1) — District, Secretary-of-State bailiffs and police officers may enter land to examine a dam, fixed engine, obstruction or lade. Land includes land covered by water, but not a dwelling or any associated yard, garden or outhouse. A lade is an artificial channel diverting water from inland water containing salmon or trout.

1976 Act Section 2 & 3 — Wardens may enter land, but not buildings in the vicinity of water, for the purpose of establishing if persons have a legal right or written permission to fish and may cause them to produce written evidence within fourteen days.

Power of search

1951 Act Section 11 — A Sheriff or Justice of the Peace, if satisfied that there are reasonable grounds for suspecting that someone has committed an offence under Sections 1–4, 7 and 7A of the 1951 Act (i.e. fishing without permission, fishing other than by rod and line or net and coble, gang poaching, use of explosives, electrical devices and poisons and unlawful possession) and that evidence of the offence is to be found in any premises or in any vehicle, may grant a warrant to a District or Secretary-of-State bailiff or constable to enter, at any time within one week, by force if necessary, the vehicle or premises. The warrant also authorises the holder to search those persons who are on the premises, about to enter or who have recently left the premises.

In cases of urgency, a police officer may stop and search a vehicle, anyone in the vehicle, or who has recently left it or is about to enter it. The power only extends to premises for the offence under section 7A (unlawful possession), but does not include dwellings or adjoining yard, garden, outhouses, etc.

A warrant may also empower a District Bailiff to enter *1868 Act* premises where it is suspected that a breach of the 1868 or *Section 26* 1951 Acts has been committed, or that illegally caught salmon, illegal nets or instruments are concealed.

Search and seizure
Any District or Secretary-of-State bailiff or police officer may:
1 Stop and search any boat used in fishing or any boat which *1951 Act* there is reasonable cause to suspect of containing salmon *Section 10* or trout.
2 Search and examine nets or other instruments used in fishing or any basket, pocket or other receptacle capable of carrying fish, which there is reasonable cause to suspect of containing salmon or trout illegally taken.
3 Seize any fish, instrument, article, boat or vehicle which is liable to be fortfeited under the 1951 Act. This power has been extended to cover fish, instruments and articles liable to forfeiture in connection with salmon offences under Section 18 of the 1967 and Section 7 of the 1984 Acts.

In addition, where a bailiff has reasonable grounds for *1951 Act* suspecting that evidence of an offence against Section 1–4, 7 *Section 11 (4)* or 7A is to be found in a vehicle on private land adjoining water or in a stationary vehicle on a road adjoining such water or land, he may search that vehicle.

Bailiffs may sell fish they seize as being liable to forfeiture. *1951 Act Section 20*

District bailiffs may also seize illegally taken salmon, *1868 Act* illegal nets, engines or other instruments found in the course *Section 26* of a search made under a search warrant. In addition, if any bailiff has reasonable grounds to suspect that evidence of an offence under Section 3 or 4 of the 1951 Act (gang poaching or use of explosives, poisons or electrical devices) is to be found in a vehicle on private land adjoining the water he may search the vehicle.

1976 Act   A Warden may seize equipment being used or about to be
Section 2 (2) used by persons without a legal right or permission to fish.

Arrest
Any bailiff may arrest anyone found committing offences under the following sections:
    1868 Act: Sections 15 (1)–(6), 18–22
    1951 Act: Sections 1–8
    1967 and 1984 Acts: salmon related offences
    Tweed bailiffs have similar powers in respect of offences contrary to the Tweed Acts (Section 38, 1857 Act).

Obstruction
It is an offence to obstruct a:
1 District Bailiff in the exercise of his powers under the 1857, 1859, 1862–68 or 1951 Acts, and by extension under the 1967 or 1984 Acts.

1951 Act   2 Secretary-of-State bailiff in the exercise of his powers.
Section 10 (6)

1976 Act   3 Warden in the exercise of his powers or rights.
Section 3 (3)

CHAPTER 13

Wildfowl

Wildfowl legislation covers both traditional wildfowling – the shooting of ducks, geese and waders on coastal foreshore and river estuaries – and the shooting of wildfowl on inland marshes, lakes and flight-ponds throughout the country.

RIGHTS OF ACCESS AND SHOOTING ON FORESHORE

Historically, restrictions governing access and shooting on the foreshore were few, but more recently such areas have increasingly fallen under the control of bodies such as local authorities, conservation organisations and wildfowling clubs.

Foreshore is defined differently in England and Wales than in Scotland; restrictions on wildfowling also vary.

ENGLAND AND WALES

In England and Wales, the foreshore is defined as *that part of the sea shore covered by the ebb and flow of the four ordinary tides midway between the springs and the neaps.* In some areas the definition excludes a good deal of marsh or saltings on the seaward side of the sea wall.

The sea wall should not be regarded as the foreshore boundary.

Much of the foreshore in England and Wales belongs to the Crown (as part of the Crown Estate) or the Duchy of Lancaster and consequently some of these areas are subject to control by the holders of regulating leases. The remaining areas are in private ownership. Irrespective of ownership and certain public rights of fishing and navigation, there is no general public right to use the foreshore, or gain access to or egress from it, for the purpose of wildfowling, despite custom or past usage, and therefore authority must always be obtained. This view was underlined in the case of Beckett v Lyons in 1967 in which it was held that the defendants had no right to go onto the foreshore for the purpose of collecting coal and taking it away.

Certain areas of Crown foreshore are under the control of wildfowling clubs affiliated to the British Association for Shooting and Conservation. On behalf of its members, the Association has negotiated a form of authority entitling members to be on foreshore in the ownership of the Crown for the purpose of wildfowling. This privilege could be withdrawn at any time by the Crown Estate Commissioners. It should also be noted that a considerable amount of foreshore for which the authority applies is controlled by clubs affiliated to the B.A.S.C. and an appropriate pass or club membership must first be gained before visiting the foreshore.

Members of wildfowling clubs affiliated to B.A.S.C. and covered by the authority agreed with the Crown Estate Commissioners and Duchy of Lancaster are not entitled to shoot species other than legitimate wildfowl quarry. Should they do so, they would be deemed to be trespassers and the authority would have no effect. Consequently, offences of civil trespass, trespass with a firearm and perhaps poaching offences may be committed if other quarry is pursued.

SCOTLAND

In Scotland the foreshore is defined as *that area lying between the high and low-water marks of ordinary spring tides*. This definition is, by comparison to that which applies to England and Wales, more favourable to the wildfowler in Scotland in that it embraces a greater area of the foreshore.

In Scotland, except in Orkney and Shetland, the public have the right to recreation (which includes wildfowling) on the foreshore unless that right to recreation has been taken away by Statute; for example, where a declaration has been made for an area considered worthy of special protection under the Wildlife and Countryside Act 1981 or the establishment of a national or local nature reserve or countryside park. As in England and Wales, there is no access or egress other than by public right of way. Permission must always be obtained to cross private land.

LIABILITIES OF WILDFOWLING

The responsibility lies with the individual wildfowler to ensure that he has lawful authority to be on a particular area of land or foreshore and that what he shoots is legitimate quarry and in season. Quarry identification is an important aspect of wildfowling, for legitimate quarry and protected species can often be found together (e.g. greylag and white-fronted geese in Scotland).

ACCESS

Wherever inland wildfowling is sought, permission must first be obtained, whether it be to shoot wildfowl on private land or merely to cross it as a means of access to or egress from other land where shooting can legally take place. In the case of the latter, it is advisable that when crossing private land guns should be placed in slips and dogs kept at heel or on a lead.

Where access and egress to and from the foreshore is gained via a public right of way, if shooting takes place while on that right of way the wildfowler may well be treated as a trespasser.[1] Failure to obtain lawful authority to be on land may render the wildfowler liable to civil action for trespass or the more serious offence of trespassing with a firearm.[2]

POACHING

Wildfowlers shooting wild duck on land where they do not have authority may commit a poaching offence in Scotland since wild duck are included in the Game Laws.[3] In England, however, wild duck are not included in the Game Laws: apart from taking birds during the close season, or

Wildfowlers should ensure that they have lawful access to the foreshore.

protected species, or trespass with a firearm, no offence is committed. If wildfowl are shot by owners, occupiers of land or other persons with legitimate access but where the shooting rights are vested in others, grounds for civil action may apply.

POWERED BOATS

It is illegal to shoot from a mechanically propelled boat in pursuit of wildfowl and this is of particular importance to those fowlers still practising puntgunning. Traditionally, there has never been a place for an engine in the sport and even today the use of powered craft is viewed as being unsporting. The use of an engine, apart from bringing the sport into disrepute, may well lead to a prosecution under the Wildlife and Countryside Act 1981.[4]

[1] See page 3
[2] See page 101.
[3] See page 36.
[4] See page 116.

B.A.S.C. maintains a register of practising punt gunners.

There is no specific licence required for puntgunning, provided that the appropriate shotgun certificate is held. However, B.A.S.C. do keep a voluntary register of practising puntgunners.

SHOTGUNS

There are restrictions placed on the use of automatic shotguns and on the size of punt-guns.[1]

WILDFOWLER'S CODE

More than ever before wildfowlers are placed in a position of trust by those in society who wish the sport to continue. They must always observe the law and shoot responsibly in order to maintain the standards of the sport and a good reputation.

The B.A.S.C. has available to their members a Wild-fowler's Code which sets the standard expected of all wildfowlers. It is in the individual's interest to learn and practice the code.

[1] See page 115.

CONSERVATION AND PROTECTION
OF WILDFOWL

Open seasons and quarry species are defined by the Wildlife and Countryside Act 1981.

OPEN SEASONS

Wild geese and duck

Below the mean high water of ordinary spring tides	1 September – 20 February (inclusive)
Inland	1 September – 31 January (inclusive)

Waders[1]

Above or below mean high-water mark	1 September – 31 January (inclusive)

The wildfowl that may be taken during the open seasons are given below:

WILDFOWL THAT MAY BE TAKEN DURING OPEN SEASON

Geese :	Canada, Greylag, Pink-footed and White-fronted[2]
Duck:	Mallard, Teal, Wigeon, Pintail, Shoveler, Tufted Duck, Gadwall, Common Pochard and Goldeneye
Waders:	Golden Plover

---

[1] Golden Plover only: Snipe and Woodcock are subject to the Game Laws: see page 59.
[2] In England and Wales only: the Whitefronted is a protected species in Scotland.

RESTRICTIONS ON SUNDAY AND CHRISTMAS DAY

Before the passing of the Wildlife and Countryside Act 1981, Orders prohibiting the shooting of wildfowl on Sundays could be made under the provisions of Sections 2 and 13 of the Protection of Birds Act 1954. Although Sunday Orders can still be made under Section 2 (3), none have been made. However, some Sunday Orders made prior to the Wildlife and Countryside Act 1981 have not been repealed and are still in existence. They have the effect of making it illegal to shoot wildfowl on a Sunday in the following counties (or parts of counties in existence before the 1974 re-organisation):

Anglesey, Brecknock, Caernarvon, Carmarthen, Cardigan, Cornwall, Denbigh, Devon, Doncaster, Glamorgan, Great Yarmouth County Borough, Isle of Ely, Leeds County Borough, Merioneth, Norfolk, Pembroke, Somerset, North and West Ridings of Yorkshire.

In Scotland, the shooting of wildfowl anywhere on Sundays or Christmas Day is illegal.

SALE OF WILDFOWL

The sale of wildfowl is restricted by the Wildlife and Countryside Act 1981.[1] However, some wildfowling clubs prohibit the selling of any wildfowl taken on land they control.

SHOOTING OF WILDFOWL UNDER SPECIAL LICENCE

In certain circumstances (e.g. serious crop damage), the shooting of wildfowl, whether of a protected or quarry species, can be done at any time under the provisions of a special licence.[2] It is under such licences that Barnacle, Brent and Canada geese are shot in some areas. Those invited to shoot under the licence must be fully aware of the licence conditions and it should not be used as a means of providing sport.

[1] See page 117.
[2] See page 113.

SUSPENSIONS OF WILDFOWLING DURING SEVERE WEATHER

Severe weather over a prolonged period can have a harmful effect on wildfowl. Feeding becomes difficult and birds quickly lose body weight. They tend to congregate in tidal areas free from ice; as they become desperate for food they are less wary of man and are easy quarry for a minority of unscrupulous wildfowlers.

Whilst responsible wildfowlers exercise voluntary restraint in these conditions, there remains provision under Section 2 (6) of the Wildlife and Countryside Act 1981 for the Secretary of State to impose, if certain criteria are met, a Statutory Order suspending the shooting of all wildfowl.[1] The Order may cover the whole or a specified area of Great Britain for a period not exceeding fourteen days.

The state-of-ground data collected daily by coastal meteorological stations around the country provide the criteria for the Nature Conservancy Council, in consultation with other organisations, including the B.A.S.C., to advise the Secretaries of State whether a statutory suspension of shooting of wildfowl should be signed. For the purposes of Suspension Orders the term *severe weather* is taken as meaning that the ground is frozen or covered with snow to varying degrees over a substantial area of the country. Statutory Orders are normally signed on the 13th day of severe weather, with a two-day publicity period before the Order comes into force at 0900 hours of the 15th day. Where severe weather continues throughout the fourteen-day suspension and looks likely to continue, the Secretaries of State may be advised to renew their Orders for a further maximum period of fourteen days.

[1] And any wild bird included in Part II of Schedule 1 or Part I of Schedule 2 outside the close season.

CHAPTER 14

Dogs

Dogs have featured in the laws of the land for centuries. Legislation has caused dogs to be banned from the Royal forests, mutilated to prevent them from chasing deer and their owners taxed to raise funds for the Napoleonic wars. Current legislation mainly covers their licensing, control and the protection of livestock.

DOG LICENCES

Since 1796 there has been an excise duty on the keeping of a dog. It is the *keeper's* responsibility to take out a licence, which lasts for twelve months, in respect of each dog. The term *keeper* is wider than *owner* and includes anyone in whose custody, possession or charge a dog is seen or found, even if he is only looking after it temporarily. A new licence must be bought when the dog changes hands.

It is an offence under the Dog Licences Act 1959 to keep a dog without a licence, but there are some exceptions: *Dog Licences Act 1959*

1 Dogs kept and used solely for tending sheep or cattle. The onus is on the keeper to show that this is the case; personal pets, gun dogs, etc, must be licensed.

2 Dogs kept by a shepherd in the exercise of his calling. An unemployed shepherd may need to keep dogs in order to obtain work.

3 Dogs under six months old. The onus of proving the dog's age rests with the owner.

4 Hound dogs under twelve months not having run with a pack. (This permits puppy walkers and others to look after hounds in their first year.) The master of the hounds is deemed the keeper.

5 Guide dogs for the blind. (A pet that is not a guide dog must be licensed.)

A police officer may demand production of a licence.

COLLARS

Control of Dogs Order 1930 The Control of Dogs Order 1930 (as amended) requires that every dog in a public place must wear a collar with the owner's name and address on it. The owner and the person in charge of the dog commit offences if the dog is not wearing a collar, but there are exceptions where a dog is being used for sporting purposes, driving or tending cattle or sheep, destruction of vermin or is one of a pack of hounds.

DOGS ON ROADS

Road Traffic Act 1972 Section 31 (1) Section 31 (1) of the Road Traffic Act 1972 gives local authorities in England and Wales the power to designate roads and make it an offence to permit a dog to be on such a road without being on a lead. Designation is often applied to main and busy roads and there should be some form of notice on lamp-posts indicating that the road is so designated. There are exceptions for dogs used for a sporting purpose under control and driving cattle or sheep.

DANGEROUS DOGS

Dogs Act 1871 & 1906 It is not a criminal offence to keep a dangerous dog, but under the Dogs Act 1871 and 1906 a court can order the owner to keep the dog under proper control or to have it destroyed. A dangerous dog is one that attacks people or animals. Proceedings are taken by way of a complaint at a Magistrates' Court where the case is heard in the same way as a criminal offence with evidence being given by both sides; accurate identification of the dog is obviously essential. If the dog is destroyed prior to the hearing, the proceedings cease.

GUARD DOGS

Under the Guard Dogs Act 1975, the use of a guard dog at any premises (which does not include agricultural land or dwelling houses) is not permitted unless a handler is present on the premises and controls the dog at all times and a warning notice is exhibited at each entrance to the premises. If the handler is not present, the dog must be secured so that it is not at liberty to go freely about the premises.

Guard Dogs Act 1975

STRAY DOGS

The Dogs Act 1906 requires the finder of a stray dog to return it to its owner or take it to the nearest police station.

Dogs Act 1906

DOGS IN THE COUNTRYSIDE

Those who walk or work their dogs in the country must take great care to ensure they are always under close control and are not given the opportunity to worry livestock or game. Before going on any land, particularly if controlled by a public body, enquiries should be made as to the existence of byelaws which may prohibit certain activities. For example, under the Forestry Commission Byelaws 1982 (which are typical of byelaws applied to country parks and council property throughout the country) it is an offence to:

Forestry Commission Byelaws 1982 (vii), (xiv), (xviii), (xx)

1 Dig up or remove any soil.
2 Permit a dog to disturb, worry or chase any bird or animal.
3 Wilfully disturb, injure, catch, net, destroy or take any bird, fish or animal.
4 Wilfully disturb, damage or destroy the burrow, den, set or lair of any wild animal.

DOGS WORRYING LIVESTOCK

Dogs (Protection of Livestock) Act 1953 Section 1 Under Section 1 of the Dogs (Protection of Livestock) Act 1953, the owner of a dog and, if it is in the charge of a person other than its owner, that person also, commit an offence if the dog worries[1] livestock[2] on agricultural land.[3]

A farmer may be justified in shooting a dog to protect his livestock.

Control of Dogs Order 1930 In addition, the Control of Dogs Order 1930 gives local authorities the power to make regulations for the control of all dogs, or classes of dogs, between sunset and sunrise to prevent worrying of cattle, horses, mules, asses, sheep, goats and swine.

Wildlife and Countryside Act 1981 The Wildlife and Countryside Act 1981 extended the definition of worrying to include the situation where a dog is at large (i.e. not on a lead or under close control) in an enclosure in which there are sheep. The dog merely has to be free to roam about in the field and need not be chasing or attacking the sheep for the offence to be committed. Close control is not defined, but the majority of sheep farmers would expect the dog to be within a yard or two of its owner and this may well be the interpretation applied by a court.

This extended definition of worrying to include dogs at large in an enclosure of sheep does not apply to a:

1 Dog owned by, or in the charge of, the occupier of the field or enclosure or the owner of the sheep or anyone authorised by either of those persons.

[1] Attacking or chasing livestock in a way likely to cause injury, suffering, abortion, loss or diminution of their produce.
[2] Cattle, sheep, goats, swine, horses, asses, mules, domestic fowls, turkeys, geese and ducks. Game is not included.
3 *Agricultural land* includes land used as arable, meadow or grazing land or for the purpose of pig or poultry farming, market gardens, allotments, nursery grounds and orchards.

2 Police dog, guide dog, trained sheep dog, working gun dog or a pack of hounds.

LIABILITY

The owner and person in charge of the dog are both liable to prosecution, but if the owner can satisfy the court that at the time of the incident the dog was in the charge of a fit and proper person, then the owner will not be held liable. *Dogs (Protection of Livestock) Act 1953*

Where livestock trespass on to land and are worried by a dog belonging to or in the charge of the occupier of the land, an offence is only committed if he causes the dog to attack the livestock (see liability under Animals Act 1971 on page 224).

ENFORCEMENT

Proceedings can be instigated by the police, occupier of the land or the livestock owner.

If a police officer finds a dog on agricultural land and has cause to believe the dog has been worrying livestock, he may seize it to establish its ownership. If the dog is not claimed within seven days, it may be disposed of as a stray.

IDENTIFICATION

A warrant can be issued for a police officer to enter premises in order to identify a dog thought to be responsible for worrying livestock. Identification of the dog is an essential element of a successful prosecution, so it is important that farmers, landowners, etc, note the errant dog's breed, size, colour, coat and sex.

COMPENSATION

Where there is an injury or loss, the magistrates court may award compensation; but regardless of whether there is a conviction or not, a claim can be made through the civil courts.[1]

---

[1] See page 224, Animals Act 1971.

ANIMALS ACT 1971[1]

The Dogs (Protection of Livestock) Act 1953 is somewhat restrictive in that the criminal offence can only be committed on agricultural land, is limited to certain types of livestock and does not include game. The Animals Act 1971 is a civil law which enables claims for damages to be made, extends the definition of livestock[2] and is not restricted by the location.

DAMAGE

Animals Act 1971 Death, lacerations, fractures and abortion are obvious
Section 3 examples of damage, but there can also be an indirect loss:
& 6 (3) (4) for example, where a dog barks at cattle and they run into barbed wire, or hens go off lay due to the disturbance caused by the dog.

KEEPER'S LIABILITY

As a general rule, if a dog kills or injures livestock, then the keeper of the dog is liable for damages to the livestock owner. The keeper of a dog is usually the owner or person who has it in his possession, but if that person is under sixteen or no one within a household is prepared to admit ownership there can
Section 3 be problems in establishing the keeper. In a family, the husband will often be regarded, legally, as the head of the household and consequently the keeper of the dog. Disowning
Section 5 (1) the dog does not affect liability because a person remains the dog's keeper until another person becomes its keeper.

A person does not become a keeper if he takes possession of the dog to prevent further damage or to return it to the owner.

Under Section 3, the keeper's liability is almost absolute in that, regardless of his involvement, he is responsible for the dog's actions. There are two exceptions:

1 Where damage to the livestock is due wholly to the fault of the person suffering the damage.

---

[1] The Animals Act 1971 does not apply to Scotland, but similar provisions are contained in the Civic Government (Scotland) Act 1982.

[2] *Livestock* includes cattle, horses, asses, mules, hinnies, sheep, pigs, goats, deer not in a wild state, domestic varieties of fowls, turkeys, ducks, geese, guineafowls, pigeons, peacocks, quail and, while in captivity only, pheasants, partridges and grouse.

2 Where the damage took place on land on to which the *Section 5 (4)*
  livestock had strayed and either the dog belonged to the
  occupier or the presence of that dog on the land was
  authorised by him (e.g. shepherd's dog, gun dog).

Where two dogs act together to cause injury, each dog is
regarded, in law, as causing the whole of the damage. If the
dogs have different keepers, one of the keepers may be held
responsible for compensation in full.

SHOOTING OF DOGS

The Dogs (Protection of Livestock) Act 1953 does not
provide any power for a farmer to shoot a dog worrying
sheep: it merely creates a criminal offence committed by the
owner or person in charge of the dog.

A summary execution, without trial, must be carefully
considered: a dog is someone's property; it may also be of
great value owing to its pedigree or expertise and consequently
the owner may take out a civil action to claim damages for the *Animals Act 1971*
loss of his dog. Section 9 (1) of the Animals Act 1971, *Section 9 (1)*
however, provides a defence in any civil proceedings to the
killing or injuring of a dog worrying livestock, if the court is
satisfied that the defendant acted for the protection of any
livestock and was a person entitled to do so; and that the
police were notified of the killing within forty-eight hours.

Under Section 9 (2), a person is entitled to protect *Section 9 (2)*
livestock if, and only if, the livestock or the land on which it
is belongs to him or to anyone acting on his authority.
However, this entitlement does not extend to the killing of a
dog worrying livestock which has strayed on to land and the
dog belongs to the occupier or is on the land with the
occupier's permission.

Under Section 9 (3) (4), a person may only act for the *Section 9 (3) (4)*
protection of any livestock if, and only if, he has reasonable
grounds to believe that either:

1 The dog is worrying or is about to worry the livestock and
  there are no other reasonable means of ending or preventing
  the worrying, or

2 The dog has been worrying livestock, has not left the
  vicinity and is not under the control of any person and
  there are no practicable means of ascertaining to whom it
  belongs.

DOGS ATTACKING WILD ANIMALS AND GAME

The Animals Act 1971 provides a defence to a civil claim for killing or injuring dogs which attack or worry livestock, but it is doubtful whether any similar defence exists for the protection of wild animals.

There has been controversy over the right to kill dogs or cats[1] attacking game; this has revolved around whether game is classed as *property* which has an owner or whether the right to take game is a *right or interest in or over land*.

Dogs and cats are property and capable of being stolen, damaged through injury or destroyed by killing. Theft is covered by the Theft Act 1968 in England and Wales and the Common Law in Scotland. There is also a Common Law offence of damage in Scotland and an offence of vandalism under Section 78 of the Criminal Justice (Scotland) Act 1980; these are virtually identical to offences of damage and destruction contained in English law.

Criminal Damage   Section 1 of the Criminal Damage Act 1971, states:
Act 1971 Section 1

A person who without lawful excuse destroys or damages any property belonging to another intending to destroy or damage such property or being reckless as to whether any such property would be destroyed or damaged shall be guilty of an offence.

So, unless there is a lawful excuse for killing or injuring a dog or cat, the offence of causing criminal damage will be committed.

The definition of property is substantially the same as for the Theft Act;[2] consequently, wild animals can only be damaged if tamed or in captivity. For this reason, a person killing game can only be prosecuted for poaching and not criminal damage, unless the damage or destruction takes place in a breeding pen, for example, where the birds are captive.

LAWFUL EXCUSE

Section 5 (2) The law recognises that a person cannot stand idly by and watch his property being destroyed and therefore creates

---

[1] The domestic cat enjoys a unique legal position in that the owner is not liable for the damage caused by the cat. There are no provisions for destroying cats worrying livestock or wild animals and to do so may lead to a civil claim for damages by the cat's owner.

[2] See page 19.

provision for the protection of property. A person will have a lawful excuse to damage or destroy property belonging to another:

1 If at the time of the act, he believed that the person whom he believed to be entitled to consent to the destruction of, or damage to the property had so consented, or would have consented to it, if he had known of the destruction or damage and its circumstances; or

2 If he destroyed or damaged property in order to protect property belonging to himself or another, or a right or interest in property which was or he believed to be vested in himself or another, and at the time of the act believed:
(a) that the property, right or interest was in immediate need of protection and
(b) that the means of protection adopted or proposed to be adopted were or would be reasonable having regard to all the circumstances.

Basically, lawful excuse may amount to a genuine belief that the owner of the dog or cat had consented to its destruction or would have so consented if he had known of the circumstances. It is doubtful whether any such owner would consent to its destruction for chasing wild animals or game, but if the person killing the animal can convince a court that he genuinely believed this to be the case he will be found not guilty.

The second part of lawful excuse is more relevant in that a person may destroy the dog or cat to protect his own property, provided that his property was in immediate need of protection and the means used were reasonable. It would have to be shown that what was protected was classed as property. For example, birds in an enclosed pheasant breeding pen or pigeon loft would be classed as property; should a cat enter the pen and attack the birds, the court would have to be satisfied that killing the cat was a reasonable means of protecting them.

As wild animals and game are not normally classified as *Section 5 (4)* property, the killing of dogs or cats to protect them is not a lawful excuse; but for the purposes of section 5 (2), a right or interest in property includes any right or privilege in or over land, whether created by grant, licence or otherwise. It has been argued that the killing of dogs or cats taking or dis-

turbing game on a managed shoot amounts to the protection
of a right or interest in the land (i.e. the sporting or game
rights). In fact, the killing of dogs or cats attacking game is
an attempt to protect wild creatures which the holder of the
sporting rights has a right to take; it cannot be said that if a
dog attacks game, it thereby threatens a person's right to take
game, as the sporting rights remain intact. Consequently, it
is the game which is being protected, not the individual's
right or interest in or over the land and it is doubtful whether
a court would look favourably on a keeper who kills a dog
attacking game. Even if the court did accept the argument, it
may not then be satisfied that killing the animal concerned
was a reasonable means of protection.

KILLING DOGS IN SELF-DEFENCE

Where a dog attacks a human being, the victim in self-
defence may kill or injure it; the dog may also be killed or
injured by a witness to the attack. The victim or witness
must fear that a life is endangered or that serious injury may
result from the attack. The dog must also be capable of
causing death or serious injury. It is no good pleading self-
defence after shooting the neighbour's miniature poodle!
The killing of the dog would have to be a reasonable action
taken as a last resort with no other means being available.
The situation where the dog is killed as it runs away after an
attack is unclear: in the same situation between human
beings there is no legal justification in injuring or killing a
fleeing attacker.

THE SPORTING TERRIER

Regardless of moral arguments on the use of dogs underground, the courage of the terrier in entering a hostile,
subterranean world has to be admired. In recent years,
however, this admiration has been tempered; for the
reputation of the sporting terrier has been tarnished by its
association with badger baiting and dog fighting. The
proponents of these unlawful pursuits have discredited the
terrier and the terrierman to such an extent that the National
Working Terrier Federation and the British Field Sports
Society have had publicly to condemn illegal activities and

Digging at a sett.

issue a code of conduct, in an attempt to improve the situation:

Five Rules for the Terrierman
1 Learn signs of badger and avoid them.
2 Obtain permission of farmer, landowner or occupier of land.
3 Do not run away if challenged.
4 Join a recognised terrier club.
5 Observe club codes of conduct.

Advice on the law, how to avoid risks, badger tracks and signs are also included in the booklet. The code of conduct gives good advice as far as it goes and emphasises that the best way to avoid being accused of digging for badgers is to leave well alone anything which might be a badger sett.

The law in relation to digging for badgers is dealt with in detail on pages 249–54 and dog fighting on page 233.

CHAPTER 15

Cruelty to Animals

Some wild animals and birds are protected to various degrees by a number of Acts, in particular by the Wildlife and Countryside Act 1981, in so far as legislation provides for their preservation and restricts the methods that may be used to kill or take them.

Wild animals, however, are not protected by legislation from acts of cruelty unless they are captive. For example, the hedgehog is protected to the extent that certain methods may not be used to kill or take it, but it is not illegal to attack and beat one to death with a stick, as a youth did recently. In another horrifying example, a vixen was found nailed to a tree; but because the fox is not protected under any legislation,[1] it is not illegal to kill one in this repulsive manner.

In field sports, the responsibility rests with the individual to ensure that he has the appropriate gun, ammunition or other equipment, is able to identify his quarry, has the capability to take it and consequently despatch it quickly, efficiently and humanely.

---

[1] See page 237 for the special circumstances in which a hunted fox might become 'captive'.

The Protection of Animals Act 1911 and the Protection of *Protection of*
Animals (Scotland) Act 1912 cover various forms of cruelty, *Animals Act 1911*
but the list of animals protected by the Act is strictly
confined to those defined as being domestic or captive:

Domestic
Farm animals, fowls, dogs, cats or any other species which is
tame or which has been or is being sufficiently tamed to serve
some purpose for man.

Captive
Any species of animal, bird, fish or reptile which is in
captivity or confinement or maimed, pinioned or subject to
any contrivance for the purpose of hindering or preventing
its escape. Generally, wild animals are not included unless
tamed or in a state of captivity.

CRUELTY TO DOMESTIC ANIMALS

Section 1 (1) is divided into five groups – (a) to (e) – of
cruelty offences:

ILL-TREATMENT

It is an offence: *Protection of*
    to cruelly beat, kick, ill-treat, over-ride, over-drive, *Animals Act 1911*
torture, infuriate or terrify any animal, or *Section 1 (1) (a)*

    to cause the animal any unnecessary suffering by wantonly
or unreasonably doing or omitting to do any act (e.g.
failing to treat injuries).

The first part is mostly concerned with physical abuse and
the infliction of pain or injuries; the second part deals with
acts carried out by a negligent or uncaring owner (e.g.
unsanitary conditions, lack of food, neglecting health).

The courts have decided that causing unnecessary suffering
may amount to a cruel act and if the action was not
reasonably necessary nor justified, a conviction could follow.
The infliction of pain for a necessary purpose (e.g. proper
treatment of the animal concerned) is not a cruel act, but the
unnecessary and unreasonable abuse of the animal may
amount to cruelty. Specific examples are not quoted within

the Act and a court would have to decide whether the actions were necessary or reasonable.

If this interpretation is applied to terriers, it can be argued that sending a dog to earth in pursuit of badger or fox is likely to result in injuries. It is well known that terriers receive injuries to the face, jaw, neck and chest in underground conflict, a fact confirmed by the many accounts in magazines and books on terrier work. In foxing articles dogs are described, with a sense of pride and achievement, as having puncture wounds on the nose and around the eyes. In 1984 a trophy was offered for the 'Best Battle Scarred Veteran Terrier' and such veterans can be seen regularly at shows and country fairs. If a terrierman knows that there is a high possibility of injuries resulting from putting the dog to ground, and such injuries result, then this could amount to causing unnecessary suffering to the dog.

Neglecting wounds or failing to provide treatment could also amount to a cruelty offence by the owner or keeper of the dog.

Cruelty under this section may also arise if a saboteur kicks or beats a hound or horse or sprays noxious substances in its eyes.

Abandonment

There have been several examples of owners abandoning their dogs underground if the animal has become trapped, refuses to come out or, where an illegal act was being committed, left the dog to make good their escape. Sett entrances have also been filled in to prevent a dog escaping.

Protection of Animals Act 1911 (amended) Section 1 of the Protection of Animals Act was amended by the Abandonment of Animals Act 1960 to include the following offence:

Section 1 Abandonment of Animals Act 1960 If a person having charge or control of any animal abandons it, permanently or not, without reasonable cause or excuse, in circumstances likely to cause the animal any unnecessary suffering, he is guilty of a cruelty offence within the terms of Section 1 of the Protection of Animals Act.

This is most relevant to the terrierman working his dogs or anyone walking his dog through a wood when the dog goes to ground; but it can also be applied to other circumstances: for example, a goat tethered on a small island in a river in flood and rising; or to other animals, e.g. a ferret left in a warren.

TRANSPORTATION

It is an offence to cause unnecessary suffering through the *Protection of* manner in which an animal is conveyed. Carrying dogs or *Animals Act 1911* foxes in the boot of a car may amount to such an offence. It is *Section 1 (1) (b)* essential that animals are properly and humanely contained. In addition, an offence may be committed under the Transport of Animals (General) Order 1973.

FIGHTING AND BAITING

It is an offence: to cause, procure or assist at the fighting or *Section 1 (1) (c)* baiting of any animal or to keep or use premises for the purpose.[1]

Causing a dog to fight any animal is illegal.

Sending dogs to earth
It can be argued that sending a dog to earth will result in its fighting with a fox or badger and amount to an offence. In 1911 this may not have been the intention of the legislators, but since then society has changed and there is greater public concern about animal welfare generally.

Quail fighting
Quail fighting is now a regular event within certain communities, particularly in city areas. Quail are a Schedule 4 bird under the Wildlife and Countryside Act and as such must be registered with the D.O.E.

---

[1] See chapters on dogs, badgers and cockfighting

POISON AND DRUGS

Protection of It is an offence to administer any poisonous or injurious drug
Animals Act 1911 or substance to any animal.
Section 1 (1) (d)   This does not prevent the use of poison in pest control, but
there are some restrictions laid down by Section 8 of the
Protection of Animals Act 1911.[1]

OPERATIONS

Section 1 (1) (e) It is an offence to subject any animal to an operation which is
performed without due care and humanity.
     This could include the stitching of wounds by an
unqualified person, docking tails, removing dew claws, and
dubbing game cocks. Some operations can be carried out by
unqualified persons in certain circumstances. Advice on such
operations may be obtained from M.A.F.F. Divisional
Veterinary Officers.
     The Animals (Scientific Procedures) Act 1986 provides for
a system of licensing control of experimental and other
scientific work carried out on living animals.

LIABILITY OF THE OWNER

Anyone can commit cruelty offences, but the owner shall be
deemed to have permitted cruelty, if he failed to exercise
reasonable care and supervision in protecting his animals
from cruelty.

INJURED ANIMALS

Section 11 Where a police officer finds an animal[2] in such a condition
that it cannot be removed without cruelty he may, if the
owner refuses or is not present, call a veterinary surgeon. If
the vet certifies that the animal is mortally injured, severely
injured or so diseased or in such poor physical condition that
it is cruel to keep the animal alive then the police officer may,
without the owner's consent, cause the animal to be
·slaughtered. If the animal is on a public highway, the police

[1] See predator control pages 150–4; Sections 5 and 11 of the Wildlife and
Countryside Act 1981 pages 114 and 126; and the Deer Act 1963 page 166.
[2] For the purposes of Section 11 only, *animal* means any horse, mule, ass, bull,
sheep, goat or pig. In practice, the same procedure is also applied to dogs and cats.

officer may also arrange for its removal. The costs involved may be recovered as a civil debt from the owner.

ARREST

A police officer may arrest anyone he believes is guilty of a *Section 12 (1)* Section 1 cruelty offence, whether upon his own view of the situation or on the complaint and information of a member of the public. The complainant must give his name and address to the officer.

SEIZURE OF ANIMALS AND VEHICLES

When a person in charge of a vehicle or animal is arrested, *Section 12 (2)* the police may take charge of the vehicle or animal and keep them in safe custody until the termination of the proceedings, or until the court directs that they are returned to the person or the owner. The costs of detention and veterinary treatment, where required, shall in the event of conviction for an offence in respect of the animal be recovered from the owner of the dog as a civil debt; or, if the owner is convicted, shall be part of the costs of the case.

The Canine Defence League is willing to take into its care, re-train and re-home dogs forfeited by a court.

PRODUCTION OF ANIMALS

A court may issue a summons to the owner of an animal *Section 13* requiring him to produce it for inspection by the court either before or at the hearing. Failure to comply is an offence.

POWER OF ENTRY

There is no power of entry under the Protection of Animals Act or facility for a search warrant to be obtained. Where there is evidence of illegal betting taking place at dog fighting, badger baiting, cock fighting and similar events, a warrant may be obtained under Section 51 Betting, Gaming and Lotteries Act 1963.

In addition, in England and Wales, Section 36 of the Town *Town Police* Police Clauses Act 1847 creates an offence committed by *Clauses Act 1847* a person who keeps, uses or acts in the management of a *Section 36* house, room, pit or other place for the purpose of fighting, baiting or worrying any animals. Police officers have the power to enter such places and arrest anyone inside, on the authority of the Chief Constable. A formal search warrant is not required.[1]

---

[1] See also page 255 and page 257.

CHAPTER 16

Hunting and Coursing

The use of hounds, lurchers, terriers, etc. in pursuit of fox, deer, hare, mink or coypu is not an offence of cruelty under Section 1 (1) (c) of the Protection of Animals Act 1911[1], if the quarry is *wild*, a principle which is embodied in hunting's code of conduct.

Hunting mink and coypu in rivers populated by otters, however, may amount to an offence of disturbing a Schedule 5 animal, since the otter and its holt (shelter) are protected under the Wildlife and Countryside Act 1981.[2]

HUNTING OF CAPTIVE ANIMALS

Captive wild animals are protected by Section 1 of the *Protection of* Protection of Animals Act 1911. However, Section 1 (3) (b) *Animals Act 1911* makes an exception for hunting and coursing: in this Section *Section 1* the term *captive wild animal* does not have its normal everyday meaning.

Section 1 (3) (b) states that nothing in Section 1 shall apply *Section 1 (3) (b)* to the coursing or hunting of any *captive* animal, unless it is

[1] In Scotland, the Protection of Animals (Scotland) Act 1912
[2] See page 124.

liberated in an injured, mutilated or exhausted condition; *but* a *captive* animal shall not be deemed to be coursed or hunted before it is liberated for the purpose of being coursed or hunted; *or* after it has been recaptured; *or* if it is under control. A captive animal shall not be deemed to be coursed or hunted if the coursing or hunting takes place in an enclosed space from which it has no reasonable chance of escape.

The exceptions are confusing, but they may be simplified as follows:

1 In general, the hunting or coursing of captive animals is permitted.

2 Acts done in such hunting or coursing may amount to offences of cruelty if:

(*a*) The animal is a domestic animal.

(*b*) The animal to be hunted or coursed is a captive animal i.e. one that has been captured by man and retained in captivity for a period of time and then:

(*i*) liberated from the receptacle in which it is confined in an injured, mutilated or exhausted condition *or*

(*ii*) subjected to a cruel act before being liberated (i.e. before it is set free from the receptacle in which it is confined) *or*

(*iii*) subjected to a cruel act after it is recaptured *or*

(*iv*) subjected to a cruel act when the animal is under control (e.g. held on a line) *or*

(*v*) hunted or coursed in an enclosed space from which it has no reasonable chance of escape.

Over the years, the courts have been called on to give interpretations on two main questions relating to Section 1 (3) (b):

1 Was the action taken within the normal meaning of coursing or hunting?

2 Was the animal in a state of captivity?

There are several cases which have examined these points. In two important cases the Chief Justices presiding both commented on the difficulty of interpretation, but their deliberations have provided the means to answer these questions.

ENCLOSED AREA

In Waters v Meakin (1912), rabbits were released into a field of about three acres to be coursed by whippets. The area was enclosed by a fence with small escapes at various places on the perimeter. A rabbit was taken from a crate and placed sixty yards from the dogs which were slipped when the referee fired his pistol. None of the fifty-five rabbits released that day reached an escape, although some ran to the fence and bounced off. It was decided that there had been cruelty and unnecessary suffering caused, but there was no offence as the actions formed part of coursing under the exception, Section 1 (3) (b).

At the time of passing the Act in 1911, it was a common practice to course captive rabbits in an enclosed area or to hunt deer kept and released for the purpose, and the law probably sought to allow these and similar activities to continue. In 1921, however, coursing or hunting captive animals in an enclosed area from which there was no reasonable chance of escape was made illegal by an amendment Act.

LIBERATED

The case of Waters v Meakin (1912) also considered the term *liberated*, and it was decided that liberation meant release from the crate or pen in which the animal was confined and not on to open ground.

RELEASING IN AN EXHAUSTED OR MUTILATED CONDITION

Coursing and liberation in an exhausted condition were examined in another rabbit coursing case, Jenkins v Ash (1929). Two men dangled a rabbit by its hind legs in front of two greyhounds. The rabbit was then thrown on the ground where it remained, only hopping a couple of yards when flicked with a hat. The dogs were slipped and the rabbit killed. When prosecuted, the men relied on the coursing exception, but the court stated that when the rabbit was dangled in front of the dogs, it was captive and subjected to unnecessary suffering. It was also the court's view that when it was released on to the ground, the rabbit was exhausted and the coursing exception did not apply.

The League Against Cruel Sports has documented cases of bag foxes being held in reserve and released if the hounds do not pick up a scent. The practice is generally denied by hunts, but it is not illegal, provided that the fox is wild, e.g. not a domestic animal through being reared as a pet *and* that, when liberated, it is not in an injured, mutilated or exhausted condition. It is also reported that opponents to hunting have been known to release a bag fox and then blame the hunt. The animal must be completely free and not restricted by ropes, chains or other devices to prevent its escape. Neither should the animal be injured or mutilated, by slashing its pads or breaking limbs.

CRUEL ACTS IN CAPTIVITY

Whilst in captivity, on recapture or under control, the exception under Section 1 (3) (b) does not apply and cruelty offences can be committed. It would therefore be unlawful to train young terriers by setting them on a wild or tame fox contained in a shed or box or to transport a hare in circumstances which caused unnecessary suffering.

Opponents of fox hunting often ask why hunt terriermen are not prosecuted for putting dogs to fox underground, on the basis that it is an illegal pursuit if the fox has no chance of escape.

Hunting with hounds in the normal manner is not illegal; but what is the situation when the fox goes to earth or the deer seeks refuge in a garden or building? Is it then a captive animal or still in the course of being hunted? In most cases of causing a fox to bolt from an earth, it is probably not a captive animal.

Rowley v Murphy (1963)

A decision on the term *captive or in confinement* was made in Rowley v Murphy (1963), where a hunted stag jumped a fence on to a road, slipped on the tarmac surface and fell under a parked lorry from where it was pulled out by two or three men and then dragged and carried into a nearby enclosure and killed with a knife.

It was argued that in the period from being pulled from under the lorry to its death, the stag was in captivity or confinement and the manner in which it was killed amounted to a cruelty offence. The Chief Justice felt, at first, that the simple plain meaning of the term captivity should apply, but on reviewing the 1911 Act and previous Acts from which it was derived, concluded that 'a mere temporary inability to get away was not a state of captivity'. Consequently, the stag was not a *captive animal* and not covered by the Act.

ACTS OF DOMINION

It was also the court's opinion, in Rowley v Murphy, that Section 1 (3) (b) only applied to animals which have been subjected to but subsequently released from a state of captivity. The court expressed an opinion that where an animal was captured and then subjected to further *acts of dominion* it could then be in a state of captivity. Some courts have since been persuaded to broaden this concept of captivity. One such example was where a fox entered or was placed in a land drain, netted at one end. Two dogs were entered and fought with the fox for over an hour. This concept could be applied to foxes gone to earth where all entrances but one are subsequently blocked (i.e. acts of dominion over the fox) and dogs entered. If, however, the entrances are netted to catch a bolting fox to be taken or killed humanely there is probably no offence.

END OF THE HUNT

Rodgers v Pickersgill (1910) considered whether certain acts of cruelty at the end of a hunt came under the exception which allows the infliction of pain or suffering through coursing or hunting: for if it could be shown that the hunt had finished, the exception would not apply. In this case, during a deer hunt, a hind took refuge in a yard and backed into a shed. The hind was poked and whipped to make it run and the dogs were set on again. The hind returned to the shed where it was poked and whipped again until it ran out along the road and into a garden. Driven out by the pack, it injured its chest on a barbed wire fence and returned to the yard. The hind was then dragged manually along the road where it died of exhaustion.

The court noted that 'in the early stages making a sulky animal run may be said to be part of the hunt'. So the whipping and poking to make the hind leave the shed were part of hunting and not cruelty offences. The court condemned the actions as 'very cruel, very foolish and very wrong', but stated that the Act was not concerned with sportsmanlike hunting. In the latter stages, from the point where the hind returned to the yard for the second time, the court felt that the dragging of the animal into a road and the events leading to its death could not be said to be in the course of hunting. The view was also expressed that the exception applied to pain and injury caused by the pack pulling down and pursuing the quarry to its death. To go beyond this, hunting could be used as an excuse 'to perpetrate any form of torture or cruelty'.

HUNT CODES OF CONDUCT

The governing body of foxhunting is the Master of Foxhounds Association; the Masters of the 193 recognised hunts have to be members and abide by the Association's rules and instructions. Failure to do so could result in expulsion, in which case the name of the hunt would be erased from the recognised list.

Rules of the Association
Rule 1

Foxhunting as a sport is the hunting of the fox in his wild and natural state with a pack of hounds. No pack of hounds, of which the Master or Representative is a member of this Association, shall be allowed to hunt a fox in any way that is inconsistent with this precept.

Concerning this rule please note that:
(*a*) when a fox is run to ground, the Master must decide what is to be done. If the decision is that the fox be killed, it must be humanely destroyed before being given to the hounds.

If, through the hunt's acts of dominion at the earth, a fox can be said to be in captivity, the throwing of a live fox to the hounds could amount to a cruelty offence.

(*b*) Every effort must be made to prevent hounds hunting a fox into a built-up area.

(*c*) Should a fox enter an inhabited dwelling, or building adjacent thereto, every effort must be made to stop hounds. They must be taken away and the fox not hunted again. At the same time the owner or occupier, or his representative, shall, if possible, be consulted as to how he or she would like the fox dealt with.

The phrase 'if possible' should not imply that, if the occupier is not present to state his wishes, the hunt may then continue on his property and deal with the fox as the hunt wishes. To do so would be a trespass.[1] Where occupiers give permission to hunt their land arrangements to cover these circumstances ought be completed in advance of the situation.

(*d*) Hounds by law are not allowed on a motorway. Therefore they must be stopped when there is any possibility of their getting on to a motorway.

To permit dogs, horses or pedestrians on a motorway is an offence which would lead to a prosecution, but the fine could be minimal compared with resulting civil claims for damage to vehicles, injury and even death of drivers and passengers. Railways hold a similar status in that it is a criminal offence to trespass on a railway line or to obstruct an engine or carriage.

(*e*) Badgers are currently protected by law and the Masters of Hounds must be conversant with this legislation.

Conservation groups are not necessarily anti-hunting, but the response from some hunts to their complaints on the manner in which setts are stopped and the failure to re-open them leaves much to be desired.

Earth stopping
The Master of Foxhounds Association has no official procedure for earth stopping; but as the Association gives advice to members on a strictly confidential basis, it is possible that such a code exists. The Forestry Commission's *Authority to Hunt* stipulates how setts are to be stopped and should be standard practice for all stopping:

1 All stopping shall be undertaken in the morning of the hunting day.

2 Stopping shall normally be accomplished by the minimal use of loose soil and, if required, bracken, grass or leaf litter. The soil shall not be packed hard, nor shall the tops or sides of the holes be cut or interfered with. Alternatively, paper sacks may be used, either empty or filled with loose soil, bracken, grass or leaf litter.

[1] See page 9 for trespass by hunts.

3 No other material shall be used.

4 All materials must be removed not later than sunset of the day of the hunt.

COURSING

There have been numerous Bills put before Parliament in recent years in unsuccessful attempts to ban coursing. Although many people believe that hares are captured, boxed and released into enclosed areas to be pursued and killed, coursing of this nature has not taken place in this country, in official contests at least, since 1900.

Coursing is a test of the speed and agility of the greyhound, a dog which hunts by sight or gaze. The winning dog is the one which scores the most points behind the hare before it escapes or is killed. A dog killing a hare may not score any points at all as points are awarded for the dog's ability to turn the hare.

Competitions under the rules of the National Coursing Club are strictly controlled. Wild hares are driven by a converging line of beaters on to an open field which may only be bordered by ordinary farm hedges or fences which allow the hare through. On some estates special escape soughs may also be constructed or cover crops planted for the purpose. The dogs, being gazehounds, will not follow the hare when out of sight.

The Slipper judges whether the hare is fit enough to be coursed, taking account of its condition and age and slips the dogs when at least 80–100 yards away.

Many hares escape to cover, but steps are taken to ensure the speedy despatch of those caught by the dogs. Two dog catchers must be on the course together with four pickers-up for this purpose.

Organised coursing events are generally for the true greyhound or saluki, but there are also lurcher events – some of them held in secret.

Unofficial coursing events often take place at two days' notice, with a rendezvous at cross-roads and the event taking place on nearby fields. Coursing land is often abundant with hares and consequently advertised events attract unofficial events before and after the official meeting. On occasions the landowner is unaware of the event until he sees as many as a hundred people, dogs and bookmakers on his land.

Lurchermen have gained a reputation as poachers, but there are genuine followers of the sport.

There are lurchermen who work their dogs legally on land where they have obtained permission, but there are many instances where this is not the case, with farmers and keepers being threatened with personal violence for interfering with the sport.

CODE OF CONDUCT

The British Field Sports Society has distributed a seven point code for lurcher owners:

1 The hare coursing season is from 15 September to 11 March.
2 It is illegal, in England, to take a hare by any means on a Sunday.
3 Never take dogs onto anyone's land without permission.
4 Never loose more than two dogs on a hare and always give enough law (distance between hare and dogs).
5 If a hare is brought down, make certain as quickly as possible that it is dead.
6 Never use dogs with the intention of coursing deer (illegal in Scotland).
7 Above all, respect all livestock.

Unofficial events or the lone man with his lurcher are not bound by any controls – only by the law. Provided that no poaching laws are broken, it is lawful to course hares and rabbits by day or night or deer by day, although such methods may not meet with the approval of field sports organisations, especially in respect of deer, which cannot be legally hunted or coursed with dogs in Scotland.

CHAPTER 17

Badgers

When midnight comes a host of dogs and men,
Go out and track the badger to his den,
And put a sack within the hole, and lie
Till the old grunting badger passes by.

They get a forked stick to bear him down
And clap the dogs and take him into town,
And bait him all the day with many dogs,
And laugh and shout and fright the scampering hogs.

The dogs are clapped and urged to join the fray;
The badger turns and drives them all away.
Though scarcely half as big, demure and small,
He fights with the dogs for hours and beats them all.

The heavy mastiff, savage in the fray,
Lies down and licks his feet and turns away,
The bulldog knows his match and waxes cold,
The badger grins and never leaves his hold.

He falls as dead and kicked by boys and men,
Then starts and grins and draws the crowd again,
Till kicked and torn and beaten out he lies
And leaves his hold and cackles, groans and dies

from *Badger* by John Clare

This eighteenth-century poem describes a practice still much in evidence today, although the 'sport' of badger baiting is now a clandestine affair in a backyard or secluded wood. Modern fights are even more cruel with the odds so weighted against the badger that he never wins.

In a free encounter, the badger with its powerful jaw and clawed limbs is a match for any terrier, and to overcome their fear young dogs are put to cubs. A proven dog will maintain an attack on a badger and hold it at bay until it can be dug out; such a dog could command a price of several hundred pounds.

If the badger cannot be taken to the dogs, then the dogs are taken to the badger. Somewhere in Wales there is a terrierman who offers a week's holiday where a man can stay with his dogs and put them to badger. The package is not available from a regular travel agent, but like most other information regarding sett locations, dog fighting, etc., details are passed on wherever unscrupulous terriermen meet.

The ultimate test of a good dog is to face brock in the sett. Initially the badger has a home advantage, as tunnels of the sett often turn upwards at the end forcing the dog to attack uphill. An experienced dog will stand at bay marking its position by barking until it can be dug out with the badger, but very often dog and badger may be locked jaw-to-jaw causing severe injuries to both animals. This can be the start of a long, slow, painful death.

When the badger is exposed in the sett, it is drawn out by the dogs until it can be 'tailed' by the diggers and dropped into a sack.

The badger can now be taken away and prepared for the impending sport. To give the dogs a chance, the badger is sometimes injured by breaking the lower jaw or rear legs, fracturing the skull and extracting teeth, eyes or claws. Once prepared, it may be set upon by dog after dog or a number of dogs at the same time. Baiting takes place in an opened-out blind tunnel in the sett, or a pit or trench at or away from the sett, in enclosed yards or buildings. Artificial setts have been created from oil drums and pipes where badgers can be kept before being channelled into a baiting pit.

'Drawing the Badger' by H. Alken. Historically, a dog was used to draw the badger from a box open at one end.

Pictorial evidence of baiting events is rare, but a home video acquired from a group of baiters during an investigation by the *Sunday People* shows up to six dogs, including an alsatian and a mastiff, engaged in a series of frenzied attacks for over an hour. When the weakened badger was no longer able to defend itself, it was rested, then goaded into action by prodding with a stick and by dropping bricks on it. Finally, the animal was hacked to death with a spade.

PROTECTION OF BADGERS

The badger is protected by the Badgers Act 1973, as amended by the Wildlife and Countryside Act 1981 and Wildlife and Countryside (Amendment) Act 1985. The Police and Criminal Evidence Act 1984 also gave the police increased powers of arrest, search and seizure.

UNLAWFUL KILLING AND TAKING

Under Section 1 (1) of the Badgers Act 1973, it is an offence *Badgers Act 1973* to wilfully kill, injure or take any badger or attempt to do so; *Section 1 (1)* but a person will not be guilty if he can show to a court that his action was necessary to prevent *serious* damage to land, crops, poultry or other property.

Unscrupulous terriermen have been known to offer to remove badgers from a sett on these grounds. However, this defence only covers the unforeseen emergency. Where it is apparent that action will have to be taken against badgers (for example where sett tunnels are preventing the use of agricultural equipment on land, or damaging race-horse gallops, or badgers are rolling in corn, grubbing up greens on golf courses, or raiding nearby gardens) a licence[1] for trapping or relocation must be applied for. Effective preventive measures can usually be taken and local naturalist trusts or badger groups willingly give advice and assistance.[2]

If it can be reasonably concluded that a person was attempting to kill or take a badger, the onus is on that person to prove to the court that he was not,[3] or that his actions were permitted under the terms of a licence, or he had a defence under the Badgers Act.

PROHIBITED METHODS OF KILLING

Wildlife and Countryside Act 1981 Section 11 The badger comes under Section 11 and Schedule 6 of the Wildlife and Countryside Act 1981, which prohibit certain methods of killing: for example, self-lock snares, traps, poison, nets, lights, gas or smoke, bows and crossbows.

DEAD BADGERS: POSSESSION AND SALE

Badgers 1973 Section 1 (2) It is an offence under Section 1 (2) of the Badgers Act 1973 to possess or control a dead badger, part of one or even something derived from it, unless it can be shown that the badger has been killed in circumstances which were not in contravention of the Act (e.g. following a road accident) or it had been sold and the person buying it had no reason to believe it had been killed illegally.

There is a considerable trade in skins and mounted specimens.

Anyone found committing a Section 1 offence may be asked for his name and address and ordered to leave the land by the occupier, owner or their servants or a police officer. If

---

[1] Licences are issued by the Nature Conservancy Council or the Ministry of Agriculture Fisheries and Food.
[2] See page 141 for badger control orders.
[3] Wildlife and Countryside (Amendment) Act 1985.

the person does not leave or give his name and address, he commits a further offence under Section 5. There is no *Section 5* power to remove him from the land, but the owner or occupier could forcibly remove him as a trespasser.[1]

LIVE BADGERS: POSSESSION AND SALE

It is an offence under Section 3 of the Badgers Act 1973 to *Section 3* sell, offer for sale, possess or control a live badger.

The Badgers Act recognised the existence of the trade in live badgers and sought to prevent it. The demand for baiting is still strong and one can surmise that high prices are often paid. Badgers are also bought by the baiters to restock areas decimated by their own actions. However, large fines are now being imposed by some courts in an attempt to make the trade less attractive.

Possession of a live badger is permitted for a contractor employed to transport animals; but this would only be for animals obtained under a licence or where it was necessary to take the animal for treatment following action taken under a licence.

CRUELTY AND DIGGING

The Wildlife and Countryside (Amendment) Act 1985 strengthened the enforcement of the law in digging cases. However, it is still not an offence to dig in a badger sett, occupied or otherwise, or to disturb the badger.[2]

Under section 2 of the Badgers Act 1973 it is an offence to: *Section 2*

1 Cruelly ill-treat any badger. It is generally assumed that this refers to baiting and inflicting harm or injury, but it could also cover keeping the animal in a sack, cage, car boot, etc. Considering the badger's instinct to fight and defend its territory and family group, putting dogs to ground in an occupied sett may also be considered to be an offence or at least an attempt.

2 Use badger tongs to kill or take a badger.

---

[1] See page 7.
[2] The offence is to dig *for* badgers.

Bagging a badger with the aid of tongs.

3 Dig for a badger, unless permitted by this Act. The Wildlife and Countryside (Amendment) Act 1985 puts the onus on the accused to show he was not digging for badgers.

4 Use certain firearms to kill or take a badger. A shotgun, of not less than 20 bore, or a rifle using ammunition having a muzzle energy of not less than 160ft/lb and a bullet not less than 38 grains are permitted where there is lawful justification to shoot a badger.

When found digging in a sett, the digger may claim that it is not a registered or occupied sett or that he is digging for foxes, rabbits, rats or mink.[1]

In digging cases, the prosecution has to show that the sett, registered or otherwise, was occupied and consequently that

[1] Registered sett is the term used by mammal society recorders and naturalists' trusts for a sett that has been recorded. Badgers do move from sett to sett and consequently setts are not always occupied. However, evidence of registration can show that holes in the ground at the time of the survey or subsequent surveys were occupied by badger.

it was possible to dig for badgers. Following the Wildlife and Countryside (Amendment) Act 1985, the accused has to show that he was not digging for badger and in doing so may claim the sett was not a sett or was not occupied. Most police officers are not qualified in such matters and so the sett is often examined by an expert to look for signs of badger. Some of these signs are listed in the *Five Rules For The Terrierman*[1] and may be backed up by sightings of badger before and after the incident.

DIGGING FOR FOXES

Digging for foxes is a common defence in digging cases, but often the consent of the landowner or occupier has not been obtained or has been gained in a dubious or underhand fashion; for example, by telling the occupier that the landowner has given his permission. It is sometimes stated that any occupier would want to be rid of foxes, so why get his permission in the first place?

No one should knowingly commit acts of trespass and when permission has not been gained, it leaves the obvious assumption that the digger has something to hide. There are, quite apart from unlawful trespass, many reasons why occupiers do not want strangers with dogs on their land: game and livestock may be disturbed or they may just wish to preserve the fox. When digging for foxes, written permission is advisable and the person giving it should be asked if there are any areas not to be touched and whether there are setts on the land. The occupier should be satisfied as to the terrierman's intentions, as he may be accused of assisting or abetting an illegal act.

The presence of foxes in setts is often the cause of arguments in court. The badger is a permanent subterranean dweller, unlike the fox which only goes underground for emergency cover,[2] in prolonged periods of wet, cold weather and to rear its young between March and June. As a general rule, the badger will not normally tolerate the fox in its sett. Whether a fox is allowed to remain in residence will depend upon the size of the sett and its badger population; but to

---

[1] See page 229.
[2] Hunts stop sett entrances for this reason. See pages 243–4 for methods of earth stopping.

avoid being accused of badger digging the best advice is not to enter dogs in any hole that looks like a sett or may contain badgers.

DAMAGE TO LAND

There have been some notable cases where large numbers of firemen have spent several days digging out dogs trapped in setts. Sometimes the land requires extensive repair at a considerable cost and landowners may consider a civil action to recover those costs from the dog owner. Digging out a sett in itself may also cause damage to the land, since the excavation can be seven or eight feet deep; where this is done without the authority or consent of the occupier, it could be an offence of criminal damage which is triable in a magistrates court. Criminal damage is a far easier offence to prove than badger digging, but it would require the occupier's co-operation and the ability to place a value on the damage caused – possibly the labour and material costs incurred in restoring the land.

GENERAL EXCEPTIONS UNDER THE BADGERS ACT 1973

Section 8 Section 8 of the Badgers Act 1973 provides the following defences for any offence under the Act:

1 A disabled animal was taken for the purpose of tending it.

2 A seriously injured or diseased animal was killed as an act of mercy.

3 The killing or injuring was unavoidable and the incidental result of a lawful action (e.g. a road accident, provided the car was not involved in an unlawful action such as speeding or driving without a licence). Road or building construction and quarrying often destroy setts, but where this is done unknowingly there is no offence.

POWERS OF THE POLICE

If a police officer suspects that offences under the Badgers Act are or have been committed and that evidence is to be found on the suspect, his vehicle or any article he may have with him, then the officer may:

1 Stop and search that person, vehicle or article.

2 Arrest the person, using his general power of arrest under the Police and Criminal Evidence Act 1984. In Scotland the police may only arrest if the man does not give his full name and address to the officer's satisfaction.

3 Seize and detain anything which may be evidence (e.g. nets, tongs, lamps, spades, bleepers, cameras, dogs,[1] sacks, cages and vehicles) or liable to be forfeited (badgers, skins, weapons or articles).

The Protection of Animals Act 1911, Protection of Animals (Scotland) Act 1912 and the Town Police Clauses Act provide for additional powers of arrest and entry in respect of cruelty[2] and baiting. See further on pages 235 and 257. Where betting is involved in baiting cases a warrant may be obtained under Section 51 Betting, Gaming and Lotteries Act 1963.

---

[1] The Canine Defence League is prepared to take into care, re-train and re-home any dog which a court has ordered to be forfeited.
[2] For cruelty to and abandonment of dogs see further on pages 231–2.

CHAPTER 18

Cockfighting

Cockfighting, like the baiting of dogs and badgers, is an illegal and secretive practice which legislation has failed to eliminate. It has an ancient history, probably originating in Greece about 500 B.C. In Britain, it was the sport of all classes and its general acceptance made it difficult to ban. Edward III prohibited it as early as 1365, as did subsequently Henry VIII, Elizabeth I and Cromwell, but all with little success.

In England and Wales, a further attempt to stop cockfighting was made in the Cruelty to Animals Act 1835, which was followed with tougher penalties in 1849. However, the sport continued quite openly throughout the country, most fights being too well organised for the police and R.S.P.C.A. to obtain evidence to sustain a conviction.

As late as 1930, a cockpit where the Chief Constable and magistrates were spectators was guarded by local police. Today, cockfighting does not have such powerful defenders, but the clandestine nature of the sport makes it difficult to enforce the law against it.

LEGISLATION AGAINST COCKFIGHTING

Cockfighting is prohibited by three Acts of Parliament.

Section 1 of the Cockfighting Act 1952 makes it unlawful *Cockfighting Act* to possess any instrument or appliance designed or adapted *1952 Section 1* for use in connection with the fighting of any domestic fowl.

Two-inch steel spurs clamped to the legs of a fighting bird.

The actual fighting of the birds and use of premises for the *Protection of* purpose is prohibited under section 1 (1) (c) of the Protection *Animals Act 1911* of Animals Act 1911 (see page 233). *Section 1 (1) (c)*

Section 36 of the Town Police Clauses Act 1847 (England *Town Police* and Wales only) makes it an offence to keep or use a house, *Clauses Act 1847* room, pit or other place for the purpose of fighting, baiting *Section 36* or worrying animals. (Most of the offences in this Act are offences only if committed in a street or public place, but there is no such restriction on Section 36.) See pages 235 and 255 for police powers of entry.

SELECT BIBLIOGRAPHY

British Association for Shooting and Conservation: *Handbook of Shooting*, Pelham Books.

British Field Sports Society: *Predatory Birds of Game and Fish*.

Chevenix-Trench, C.: *Poacher and the Squire*, Longmans.

Coles, Charles: *Shooting and Stalking*, Stanley Paul.

Countryside Commission: *Out in the Country*.

Forestry Commission: *Wildlife Rangers Handbook*.

Game Conservancy: *Predator and Squirrel Control*.

Gregory, Michael: *Angling and the Law*, Charles Knight.

Humphreys, John: *The Shooting Handbook*, Beacon.

Metcalfe, J. C.: *Taxidermy*, Duckworth.

Neal, Ernest: *Badgers*, A. & C. Black.

Parkes, C.: *Law of the Countryside*, Association of Countryside Rangers.

Prior, R.: *Modern Roe Stalking*, Tideline Books.

Richman, J. and Draycott, A. T. (eds.): *Stone's Justice Manual*, Butterworths.

Sandys-Winsch, G.: *Animal Law*, Shaw and Sons.

Sandys-Winsch, G.: *Gun Law*, Shaw and Sons.

Scottish Rights of Way Society: *Right of Way*.

Sedgwick, N. M., Whitaker, P. and Harrison, J.: *The New Wildfowler in the 1970s*, Barrie and Jenkins.

Smith, J. C. and Hogan, B.: *Criminal Law*, Butterworths.

Williamson, R. B.: *Powers of Water Bailiffs and Wardens to Enforce The Salmon and Freshwater Fisheries Acts*, Department of Agriculture for Scotland.

INDEX